The Writer
as Shaman

The Writer as Shaman

The Pilgrimages of Conrad Aiken and Walker Percy

Ted R. Spivey

MERCER

ISBN 0-86554-199-X

The paper used in this publication meets the minimum requirements
of American National Standard for Information Sciences—
Permanence of Paper for Printed Library Materials, ANSI Z39.48-1984.

Library of Congress Cataloging-in-Publication Data
Spivey, Ted Ray, 1927–
The writer as shaman.

Includes index.
1. American fiction—20th century—History and
criticism. 2. Shamanism in literature. 3. Pilgrims
and pilgrimages in literature. 4. Aiken, Conrad,
1889-1973—Religion. 5. Percy, Walker, 1916—
—Religion. 6. Quests in literature. 7. Religion in
literature. I. Title.
PS374.S48S65   1986   813'.5'09   86-12433
ISBN 0-86554-199-X (alk. paper)

Contents

To Deene and Paula

Preface

When a book with the ponderous title of *The Message in the Bottle: How Queer Man Is, How Queer Language Is, and What One Has to Do with the Other* appeared in 1975, its author, Walker Percy, was beginning to receive the kind of attention a major spokesman in the humanities deserves. The book was twenty years in the writing and consisted of essays that, except for one, had been published in a variety of journals. It was an important philosophical statement made by a man who had already become a major American novelist, one who had achieved both a popular and a critical success. This book, along with his fourth and fifth novels in 1977 and 1980, had made Walker Percy, by the decade of the eighties, one of the few major American men of letters.

During this century when serious writers often play the role of journalist or sportsman or farmer, an authentic man of letters like Walker Percy is relatively rare. Percy is in the European mold of the creative writer; he has a philosophical mind and does not hesitate to make general statements about moral and cultural problems. Above all, he has the background and education as well as the philosophical insight gained through long study and contemplation to play a role for which Americans are seldom equipped. But what makes Percy almost unique among American writers is that he is well versed in both the humanities and the natural sciences. His great subject is the split that has taken place between these two areas and a resulting failure of language and communication in the modern world. T. S. Eliot's term "dissociation of sensibility" has for several decades been used to conjure with the split in modern consciousness due to the dissociation of science and the arts. But in his most significant single nonfictional work, *The Message in the Bottle,* Percy goes more deeply than Eliot into the problem of dissociation by referring to what he calls "this monstrous bifurcation of man into angelic bestial components."[1]

As one who turned to religion to seek the part that transcendence plays in unifying the objective and subjective aspects of humanity, Percy came to the conclusion that the "proper question is not whether God has died" but "whether it is possible that man is undergoing a tempestuous restructuring of his consciousness which does not presently allow him to take account of the Good News."[2]

That Percy has struck deep chords by raising certain questions in both his fiction and his essays can be seen in what amounts to a cult following. As Panthea R. Broughton has said, his "style is winningly lucid; his art is sharp but never vitriolic" and "by tempting readers to identify with his people and to recognize his ideas, he creates a large and enthusiastic public following."[3] Although his ability to reach a large audience has not kept away serious readers—his books are regularly studied in college literature courses—his brilliant achievement in speaking directly to large numbers has obscured for many the depth of his thinking and the relevance of his imaginative work to the need for cultural renewal now present in all societies, a renewal that must bring with it some form of rapprochement between humanistic studies and the natural and social sciences if civilization is to continue. One of the reasons I have chosen to study Percy in connection with a slightly older writer, Conrad Aiken, who was also deeply immersed in the arts and the sciences and was also an authentic man of letters, is that I hope to pinpoint some of the significant contributions of Percy to the necessary dialogue between the two "cultures," as C. P. Snow has called the advocates of science and the humanities. Yet Aiken in his own right deserves a serious consideration and in fact is receiving close attention from a growing number of scholars. As a man of letters, he is more

---

[1]Walker Percy, *The Message in the Bottle: How Queer Man Is, How Queer Language Is, and What One Has to Do with the Other* (New York: Farrar, Straus and Giroux, 1979) 113.

[2]Ibid.

[3]Panthea R. Broughton, ed., *The Art of Walker Percy* (Baton Rouge: Louisiana State University Press, 1979) xiv-xv.

widely read in Europe than Percy, his poetry having been translated by, among others, the Italian Nobel Prize winner Salvatore Quasimodo.

Aiken also has a dimension in his philosophy that carries us out of Western civilization altogether, possibly to the very goal of our striving for cultural rebirth. Aiken was deeply influenced by the *I Ching* and by Chinese philosophy generally, and in his later work we see him playing an active role in what F. S. C. Northrop considered the most important fact of modern times: the meeting of East and West. If anything, Percy is too bound up in Western philosophy, but like Aiken he is deeply aware of the modern chaos that is dissolving all of the old cultures and threatening to dissolve humanity itself. The problems they both deal with in their work are so great and so similar that no other two writers better sum up philosophical, religious, and literary attempts to bring together two basic elements of the human make-up: the imaginative, intuitive, visionary aspects of life and the analytical, empirical, objective aspects.

Although Percy goes into existential philosophy to find some of his deepest insights and Aiken gathers from Santayana as well as from Pythagorean and Chinese philosophy many useful concepts, it is finally as extenders of the tradition of American liberal thought that they should be most highly prized. Jay Telotte has demonstrated that Percy's work "draws heavily upon an established American intellectual tradition, such as that represented by Peirce."[4] He goes on to show at what point the pragmatism of C. S. Peirce is basically similar to modern existential thought, that is, in "its elevating the act of being over and above any fixed and timeless nature or essence."[5] The most famous American liberal philosopher, William James, both developed and popularized Peirce's pragmatism. James's greatness as a philosopher lies partly in his ability to deal with broad human issues in a way that takes into full account scientific, philosophical, and even political issues. As I will later suggest, James's ability to be pragmatic about large issues is similar to the abilities of Aiken and Percy to deal with science, art, and transcendence. To illustrate the basic views of all three—James, Aiken, and Percy—concerning the relationship of science and art, I would cite a quotation of James made by Lewis Mumford concerning science and the individual: "There is nothing in the spirit and

---

[4]J. P. Telotte, "Walker Percy: A Pragmatic Approach," *Southern Studies* 18:2 (Summer 1979): 224.

[5]Ibid., 223.

principles of science that hinders science from dealing successfully with a world in which personal forces are the starting point of new effects.'' James himself speaks of science's belief ''that in its own essential and innermost nature our world is a strictly impersonal world.''[6] Like James, Aiken and Percy wrote about the need to see science in terms of a personalized existence, but unlike James their learning was deeper and more imaginatively perceived. Aiken and Percy both began with liberal viewpoints that were laid down by William James and similar thinkers, but they continued to go back into the past to establish a firm connection with a wisdom that allowed them to see both science and the arts as part of a living continuum necessary for civilized life. Thus their thought and their imaginative works provide an antidote to the fanaticism of those who believe that the world can be saved only by ''religion'' or those who cling to science as saviour or even to humanists who believe all answers are to be found in their disciplines.

Both Aiken and Percy then are among that small group of people who in the second half of the twentieth century have maintained a living connection with those earlier masters of the Renaissance, the Middle Ages, and the ancient world who took into full account both man's science as well as his experiences in the arts and in religion. Aiken, through his early association with George Santayana as teacher and later as friend, maintained a deep connection with this tradition. Walker Percy, through his association with W. A. Percy and through his own years of serious study, is not far behind Aiken in this respect. What Percy offers people of the late twentieth century is a closer connection than Aiken ever knew with the ordinary life of contemporary Americans. In fact, he maintains a balanced view of both the virtues and vices of modern man. This vision of modern man and his own view of the role of the novelist were both well stated in a speech made at the University of Tennessee at Chattanooga in the spring of 1981.

In his Chattanooga speech, which is similar in some ways to Faulkner's Nobel Prize speech in that it is addressed to young novelists and is a statement about art and the spirit, Percy reveals attitudes that are basic to the philosophical viewpoint that runs through both his novels and his essays. He begins by suggesting that the novelist cannot be expected to have ready answers for what people should do and what, for instance, the nature

---

[6]Lewis Mumford, *The Pentagon of Power* (New York: Harcourt Brace Jovanovich, 1964) 434.

of evil is. Hiding his wisdom behind his humor, Percy suggests that those accepted as "wise" in our time try to tell us far more than they can possibly know. He goes on to state that he is not the enemy of science or religion or art or any other basic human activity. Rather, he sees reductionism as the great human enemy, that tendency to reduce all wisdom and finally all existence to one set of principles or one system of knowledge. Reductionism is in fact central to the theme of Percy's most recent book, *Lost in the Cosmos* (1983), a work that makes explicit most of the ideas in the Chattanooga speech.

In *Lost in the Cosmos* Percy links the religious vision to the problem of how properly to view the Cosmos: "The wonder to the scientist is not that God made the world but that the works of God can be understood in terms of a mechanism without giving God a second thought." Then Percy, in possibly his most telling point in the book in terms of his own philosophy, writes, "The real wonder is not that the Cosmos is now seen as wonderful but that it is not."[7] These statements sum up the mature wisdom of both Aiken and Percy, men who most of their lives viewed the universe through the eyes of both the arts and the sciences. The mature wisdom of both men grew out of their continual relating of the arts and sciences to the insights of religion, chiefly in the form of Catholicism for Percy and Unitarianism and New England transcendentalism for Aiken. In achieving this wisdom they gained religious insights that correspond to certain basic visions of all the higher religions, particularly visions that see the cosmos as a unified whole interpenetrated by the grace and love of one God. Similarly, from this religious viewpoint it is possible to see interpersonal human relationships as being based on the encompassing power of love. With this view in mind it is also necessary to see the failure of human relationships as well as the failure of all types of relationships with the cosmos, extending from environmental relationships to relationships to outer space, as being caused by a failure to be aware of the enveloping and unifying grace that sustains all that exists.

The mature wisdom of Percy and Aiken did not suddenly descend upon them. Instead, it emerged slowly as a result of what both men called their pilgrimages. These pilgrimages did not begin with a desire to unite the arts and the sciences with a theological vision. Instead, they began for both men

---

[7]Walker Percy, *Lost in the Cosmos: The Last Self-Help Book* (New York: Farrar, Straus and Giroux, 1983) 89.

with the early trauma of parental suicide and the resulting alienation. For both, there would be the memory of parental love and its sudden loss, followed by their quests for love between two individuals and a larger quest for the love that underlies group relationships as well as the cosmos itself. In their approach to concepts concerning love, neither author is essentially theological; rather, as I have suggested, both are pragmatic in their attitudes toward the problem of essence. For them essence, or being, is either manifest or is not to individuals; the proof of this manifestation is the awareness by individuals of a power that draws them creatively both to others and to their environment so that a sense of well being is experienced, if only for brief periods of time. One metaphor for this sense of harmony and well being for both authors is music, and when they perceive the pragmatic power of being at work in individuals' lives, they write as if they were experiencing a harmony and a joy associated with music. Thus Aiken ends possibly his greatest work, his autobiography *Ushant,* with these words: ''we rise, ourselves now like notes of music arranging themselves in a divine harmony, a divine unison, which, as it had no beginning, can have no end—.''[8]

Yet what is central to the work of Aiken and Percy is not so much their visionary moments but rather their own and their characters' difficult pilgrimages, journeys on which appear those visionary insights that James Joyce called epiphanies. To understand the pilgrimages recorded in their works one must also know something about the lives of the two men. To approach their lives seriously is to discover an underlying unity between their lives and works. This unity is perhaps best expressed in their recovery in their later years of the almost lost world, for Americans, of the ''man of letters.''

As men of letters in an old-fashioned sense of this term, they served as guides and helpers to many who sought to make sense of the role of both literature and the humanities in a world in which science and technology seemed to most people to represent the peak of human achievement. The understanding that Aiken and Percy brought to the split between the humanities and the sciences constituted a view almost unique among modern American writers. It was based on an acceptance of and a relationship with both the arts and the sciences and was closely tied to an ability to see these two essentially human activities in terms of divinity.

---

[8]Conrad Aiken, *Ushant* (Cleveland: The World Publishing Company, 1962) 365.

I have suggested that the two men were both pragmatic rather than theological concerning divinity and human activities. Yet there is an implied theology in their work, one that could well be summed up in the words of John Polkinghorne:

> If science is the pale reflection of the rationality which is in God, so our experience of beauty is a pale reflection of his joy, our moral insights the pale reflection of his purposes of love. Nor, I believe, is it mistaken to see that same Word at work, under different cultural constraints, in the religious experience of all mankind.[9]

Polkinghorne, a Cambridge University physicist and an Anglican priest, writes thus about the connections between religion, the arts, the sciences, and morality. Yet the theological approach is not the best approach, I believe, in understanding the four themes I have chosen to discuss in connection with Aiken and Percy: the unity of science, art, and God; the unity of life and work; the overcoming of alienation; and the recovery of the role of man of letters. Instead I will seek to show how as writers who put the concept of pilgrimage at the center of their lives and works Aiken and Percy achieved in time the status of modern shamans.

Mircea Eliade, the greatest living authority on shamanism, tells us that the shaman "can be healer and guide as well as mystic and visionary."[10] Obviously, Aiken and Percy were not shamanic in the same way as those early shamans that Eliade describes in his many works. Yet they served in various shamanic functions, chief among them being the apprehension of a realm of love and beauty existing behind and within human relationships and in the cosmos generally. Thus their view of the arts and sciences was that these activities, properly engaged in, could open up a sense of both love and wonder.

To understand the shamanic functions of Aiken and Percy, it is also necessary to see their work in terms of the relationships of myth and modern literature as described, for example, by the leading myth critic of our time, Northrop Frye. What Aiken and Percy both call pilgrimage is for Frye the quest myth, which he identifies as the "central myth of literature in its

---

[9]John Polkinghorne, *The Way the World Is* (Grand Rapids MI: William B. Eerdmans Publishing Company, 1983) 109.

[10]Mircea Eliade, "The Yearning for Paradise in Primitive Tradition," *The Making of Myth,* ed. Richard M. Ohmann (New York: G. P. Putnam's Sons, 1962) 86.

narrative aspect."[11] The patterns of imagery found in the quest myth represent the oracular or visionary insights granted to questers on a journey that for many individuals in different traditions has been called a life pilgrimage. Thus Aiken, in this older tradition, did not hesitate to call himself a "divine pilgrim." Like James Joyce, who used the term epiphany to describe the visionary moment, Aiken and Percy both wrote of individuals seeking love who achieve brief visions of a realm of wonder, joy, and love. Thus Frye describes "the epiphanic moment" as "the flash of instantaneous comprehension with no direct reference to time."[12] Seen as quest myths, or pilgrimages, the lives of Aiken and Percy, along with some of their best works, reflect the achievement of a comic vision of the unified community and the joyous cosmos. As Frye tells us, the comic vision sees the world of humanity as a community, and this vision includes "images of symposium, communion, order, friendship, and love."[13]

The early shamans went on their own pilgrimages, discovering through their visions a cosmic order containing love and joy, and then they returned to their own communities to restore the society's shattered rites so that this vision could be ritualistically presented to everyone in the community. Thus the shaman, Eliade tells us, recalls a lost paradise and presents visions of that paradise in terms of epiphanies of love and cosmic order and joy: "It was the yearning for Paradise, which haunted the minds of Isaiah and of Virgil, sustained the sainthood of the Fathers of the Church and came to glorious flower in the life of Saint Francis of Assisi."[14] In their own ways Aiken and Percy, like earlier shamans, began their pilgrimages with a sense of personal and social alienation; in time with the help of the arts, sciences, and religion they discovered for themselves and others a unity of life and work and a role as men of letters whereby they could guide others.

Understanding the essential unity between the lives and works of Aiken and Percy is not the least of the chief themes with which I will deal. I am, of course, aware that it is impossible in a comparative work of this type to assess fully the unity of life and work of each author. Others have done this and will continue to do it. I myself for some years have been at

---

[11]Northrop Frye, "The Archetypes of Literature," *Myth and Method,* ed. James E. Miller, Jr. (Lincoln: University of Nebraska Press, 1960) 158-59.

[12]Ibid., 155.

[13]Ibid., 160.

[14]Eliade, "Yearning for Paradise," 97.

work on an interpretation of Aiken's life and work. What I seek to do in this study is to highlight the similarities and differences in the approaches of the two authors to several of the most significant problems of modern civilization. That two writers who hardly were aware of each other's work should arrive at similar solutions to problems concerning early alienation and the persistent need of authors, and others, to find a continuing significance in life as they grow older is a matter of great interest to many. An analysis of the similarities and differences in the handling of personal problems as well as the use of these problems and their solutions of them in the evolution of works of literary art reveals the possibility of an artistic affirmation that has not often been found in modern writers. This affirmation is expressed in terms of the possibility of discovering love in alien surroundings. Commenting, for instance, on a statement by a character in Percy's *The Second Coming,* Jac Tharpe says it "has considerable importance for the (semireligious) matter of interpersonal subjectivity (loving another) that Percy studies here."[15] The possibility of loving another is for both Aiken and Percy the great hope, fulfilled in important moments in their lives and works, for overcoming alienation and its accompanying phobias, manias, and depressions. Percy began his own pilgrimage, which led to renewed moments of love and expanded consciousness in his own life, with a study of the Protestant theologian Kierkegaard and continued it with the Catholic philosopher Marcel. Aiken began his pilgrimage as a youth with Shakespeare, continued it with the help of George Santayana, his Harvard teacher, and brought it to fulfillment in his mature poems with a deepening awareness of Jesus, Li Po, and the Buddha. Both men discovered in their pilgrimages the shaman's vision of a remembered world of joy and love and, through this continuing vision, found an acceptance of and love for others.

Finally, I cannot write about two authentic men of letters of our time without mentioning their human presence. To have known both of them personally is one of the happy events of my life. To report them as they appeared in the flesh is something anyone who loves literature and who has personally encountered them always feels moved to do. What follows is mainly a critical study of their works and an attempt to understand and appreciate their contributions as men of letters who, because of their pilgrimages, could open the doors of shamanic perception. It is also an attempt to

---

[15]Jac Tharpe, *Walker Percy* (Boston: Twayne Publishers, 1983) 108.

discover something of the meaning of their lives. In this respect, I would agree with W. H. Auden in his assessment of Charles Williams as one who must be written about as both a man and an author. And I would agree, in discussing Aiken and Percy, with the statement by T. S. Eliot about Charles Williams that Auden approvingly quotes: ''To have known the man would have been enough; to know his works is enough; but no one who has known both the man and his works would willingly have foregone either experience.''[16]

---

[16]W. H. Auden, Introduction to Charles Williams's *The Descent of the Dove* (New York: Meridian Books, 1956) v.

Abbreviations

The following abbreviations occur in the text.

Conrad Aiken:
        CP *Collected Poems*
       3 N *3 Novels*
        U *Ushant*

Walker Percy:
       LR *Love in the Ruins*
      SC *The Second Coming*

The Split
between Science and Art

Chapter I

Probably the greatest single split in modern thought is that between science and ethical and aesthetic values. This split has existed at least since the time of Descartes. It has expressed itself in twentieth-century philosophy in the inability of the two chief international schools of thought—analytic philosophy and existentialism—to find any basis of reconciliation. Alfred North Whitehead in *Science and the Modern World* tells us that the great task of the philosophical schools of the century should be "to bring together the two streams into an expression of the world picture derived from science, and thereby end the divorce of science from the affirmations of our aesthetic and ethical experiences."[1] In ordinary civilized life today,

---

[1]Alfred North Whitehead, *Science and the Modern World* (New York: The New American Library, 1949) 157.

the split between philosophy and values is seen in the difficulty that representatives of the social and natural sciences have in interacting fruitfully with those who work in the arts and humanities. In the intellectual life of the West from the late seventeenth century to the present, there has been the sometimes sharp dichotomy between those who take a "rational" or "scientific" view of life and those who consider themselves to be "artistic." T. S. Eliot with his term "dissociation of sensibility" popularized in intellectual circles the concept of a split between head and heart that he thought began in the seventeenth century, and though his concept has often been challenged, it remains as a sign to many of a problem still inherent in modern civilization.

By the 1970s scientific studies of the two hemisperes of the brain were presenting to the public a mass of data indicating that the human mind does in fact have two sides, one dealing with "rationalistic" and "empirical" aspects of life that are often associated with what we call science and the other devoted to the "imaginative and intuitive" realm of existence. These studies reveal that certain people rely more on one side than the other but that there still remains the need to see exactly how the two sides of the brain interact. Yet practical observation in the twentieth century is that many people develop one part of the brain so much that other functions of the mind seem to atrophy. Because of the Cartesian and scientific nature of most modern educational systems, the general tendency is for individuals to develop that part of the mind which is "rational." There are others who deny their "rationalistic" faculties and devote themselves entirely to a realm they believe to be "creative," with the result that those necessary aspects of modern life that come under the heading of science are ignored almost totally. Then there is a third group who deny both the scientific and creative sides altogether and try to bury themselves in primordial instincts. Clearly, the aberrant behavior of many people in this century is related to a one-sided approach to the mental and emotional energies that make up human existence.

Awareness of the one-sidedness that modern people are prone to can be seen in the great interest taken in interdisciplinary studies and activities. Anyone in our time who resembles what was called in the nineteenth century a renaissance man draws attention because that person seems to have escaped the trap of one-sidedness. Scientists and mathematicians like J. Bronowski and Alfred North Whitehead who have shown a genuine concern for creativity in all its forms have made a mark on the times, but the man of letters who surveys his times and seeks to gain an overarching vision of his world is sadly lacking in the twentieth century, particularly in English-speaking countries. Many novelists and poets often pose as specialists playing a very limited role in their society whereas others hide themselves from the civilized world altogether or even renounce both the scientific and creative values of civilization in the name of blind instinct.

Any writer in America who sets out to cultivate an overarching vision that sees all the human faculties working together is apt to be either misunderstood or neglected or even both. Conrad Aiken possibly more than any other modern American writer aptly deserves to be called a man of letters in the European tradition, and beginning in the seventies with the publication of the first volume of his letters, his role as man of letters has been increasingly recognized. Yet his basic imaginative vision is still generally misunderstood for the reason that an artist who also cultivates science is a very unusual person in the English-speaking world. In fact, to understand better the importance of Aiken's vision, it is essential to look at it in relationship to that of a more recent author who is also a man of letters but whose chief works are more accessible to contemporary readers. That author is Walker Percy.

The creative careers of Conrad Aiken and Walker Percy span the period from 1914 to the present. They represent two generations of modern writers and two periods of modern literature—the first that creative outburst of modern art beginning shortly before World War I and ending with the onset of World War II and the second beginning after World War II and continuing to the present. What makes the two writers most alike is that they early absorbed the viewpoint of modern science and yet worked from early manhood onward in the realms of philosophy and literature. Aiken was the son and brother of doctors, and all his life he closely associated himself with members of the medical profession, particularly psychiatrists. Percy is an M. D. who never practiced but who has maintained his interest in medicine throughout his life. Both could and did think in medical and scientific terms throughout their literary careers, yet both found it possible to work creatively in literature and philosophy at the same time. What made this fact possible was that they achieved an overarching vision whereby they were able to conceive of an underlying unity within both the mind and the universe. The cultivation of this unity was related to their own search for and finding of a relationship with transcendence.

One may well ask what makes these two authors so unusual in our time and also what makes them so much alike. For various reasons, which I will later discuss, both men were willing to engage in a long apprenticeship to literature, philosophy, and psychology to prepare themselves for what would be their most important work at a time of life when most writers have sunk into repetition or silence. This long apprenticeship, which is partially responsible for keeping them out of the public eye a large part of their lives, also enabled them to establish themselves in the chief tradition of Western art and thought so that they became, in the Emersonian sense, representative men of civilization in a century when most artists were in partial or total revolt against the past and most philosophers and scientists were becoming narrow specialists.

What their precise links with the mainstream of Western culture were will be dealt with at length later, but one aspect of their relationship with the past can be seen by examining their place in the American liberal tradition. Both were attached in many ways to the mainstream of a tradition whose center was first Boston and later New York. Aiken was always destined by family association for Harvard. When he finally got there in the first decade of the century, he found himself drawn to the philosophy of the professor of that university who more than anyone else is probably the chief nineteenth-century inspirer of modern liberalism in all its diverse ramifications. That man is William James. In the thirties, Percy would attend the University of North Carolina, the most liberal university in the South, and then go on to medical school at Columbia University, which— inspired by John Dewey and others who followed in the steps of James— took over from Harvard after World War I a large part of the leadership of the philosophical tradition of American liberalism. Yet neither man swallowed whole the tradition of James and his diverse followers. Important events in their lives, as I will suggest in succeeding chapters, made it impossible for them to become typical liberals of the twentieth century. However, their continuing concern with the roles of social and political man, their belief in the values of the sciences (both social and natural) for the development of civilization, and their belief that change in American life from a rural to a predominantly urban environment must be fully accepted made them both, in a sense, modern liberals throughout their lives.

Possibly the leading writer and critic in the American liberal tradition of this century is Lionel Trilling. His book *The Liberal Imagination* discusses, at times brilliantly, the relationship between the movement of liberalism and modern creative writing. Aiken is not mentioned, and one of his best critics, Reuel Denney, rightly says that there are "grounds for considering the best of Aiken's work as having provided some of what Trilling said he could not usually find."[2] But Aiken no doubt seemed to Trilling at the time he wrote *The Liberal Imagination* to be one of America's exiles, like T. S. Eliot, who chose to reside in Europe rather than in America. Yet in spite of his role in London and England in the twenties, Aiken also played a part in the literary scene of New York during the period between the wars, being personally close to writers like William Carlos Williams and Maxwell Bodenheim. And until nearly the end of his life Aiken maintained a small apartment in New York, where he liked to spend a part of every year.

Aiken and Percy in their early years were greatly influenced by the new burst of intellectual life in New York, and this influence never left them. In one of his last essays, "Some Notes for an Autobiographical Lecture," Lionel Trilling speaks of "the great burst of national self-consciousness in the 1920s," of which New York was the intellectual center.[3] Trilling goes on to define the intellectual class then developing in New York and says that essential to this class was "the idea of *society* and the idea of *culture,* both of which are believed to be susceptible to a conscious intention to change and correct them."[4] Trilling also tells where these ideas came from as well as how they were kept vital at Columbia University. He traces their beginnings back to the nineteenth century and beyond when he describes the influence of his Columbia teacher, John Erskine. Erskine's views were based on Sir Philip Sidney's *Defence of Poesie;* but more precisely Erskine drew inspiration from his own teacher, George E. Woodberry, himself the pupil at Harvard of Charles Eliot Norton, who was a friend of Carlyle, Ruskin, and Arnold. The humanistic liberalism of Arnold and Norton lies back of much of the thinking of the new intellectual elite of New York, to which Trilling belonged. What this elite stood for Trilling states as the idea that was basic to the General Honors Course at Columbia: "Great works of art and thought have a decisive part in shaping the life of the polity."[5] For Trilling liberal humanism as he knew it faced two chief problems: the

---

[2]Reuel Denney, *Conrad Aiken* (Minneapolis: University of Minnesota Press, 1964) 5.
[3]Lionel Trilling, *The Last Decade,* ed. Diana Trilling (New York: Harcourt Brace Jovanovich, 1979) 229.
[4]Ibid., 230.
[5]Ibid., 233.

slide into Marxism by some of its members and the tendency that Santa-yana describes of the liberal arts to become "genteel." Becoming "gen-teel," Trilling says, happens in this way: "The conception of the 'good life,' of the 'examined life,' of life illuminated by *reason* and shaped by *art,* can be inert and passionless, or encapsulated."[6] Trilling tells us that he and his Columbia and New York associates escaped this fate "by the nature of the time as we in New York experienced it." He goes on to say that by responding to the demands of his urban environment he and others escaped the loss of vitality experienced by those who could not accept the turbulence of modern life.

In one sense everything that Trilling says of himself can also be said of Aiken and Percy. Both of them experienced in the lives of their parents and families as well as in their education the beliefs that society and culture could be connected and changed and that "great works of art and thought," to use Trilling's words, could play a decisive role in changing society. These inherited beliefs never left them, but their lives and work became after many years statements that the tradition of liberal humanism was not enough to maintain, let alone improve, the polity. They devoted their lives, like Trilling and so many others, to the study and practice of both the arts and philosophy. But unlike Trilling they maintained a deep interest in the nat-ural sciences and managed to integrate concepts from these sciences into their thinking. Both Aiken and Percy then always felt at home in both the arts and sciences and also on college campuses. Aiken taught for a year at Harvard and often spent time on and near the Harvard campus. Percy taught for a year at Louisiana State University and always felt drawn to certain aspects of university life. Still, a new set of beliefs painfully arrived at over years of study and personal struggle made them outsiders to the main-stream of the liberal tradition, particularly as it has expressed itself in An-glo-American education during much of this century.

In brief, what set them apart from the mainstream was their own strug-gle with a strong awareness of individual and family chaos. Both sprang from upper middle-class parents who had the advantages of superior ed-ucation and who maintained a lively interest in the arts and sciences. Ai-ken's father, in fact, was an M.D. who was also an inventor and a poet, something even of a "Renaissance man." Yet the brilliance of these par-ents did not prevent family dissolution, that most painful of events for chil-

---

[6]Ibid., 235.

dren under any circumstances but doubly painful because it was precipitated by parental suicide. Aiken was eleven when his father killed his mother and then turned his gun on himself. Percy was thirteen when his father committed suicide; his mother would die two years later in an automobile crash. Both boys would grow up in their teens with relatives, and both would inevitably know alienation. Both as youths would outwardly cope with life's problems, and yet in their literary works one can easily see how early alienation was the essential spur to the quests of both men for the good life not only for themselves but for others. Also, both would know further alienation after maturing. Aiken would find himself unsettled much of his life by a continuing illness he called a *petit mal* as well as by suicidal impulses. After completing medical school at Columbia, Percy would contract tuberculosis and because of his illness would suffer an enforced idleness for several years, during which time he would immerse himself in literature and philosophy.

Both writers would deal with their continuing awareness of personal and social dissolution in much the same way. Aiken's friend Henry A. Murray, the eminent Harvard psychiatrist, would write in his article on the subject that Aiken had in effect made "creative uses" of his own sometimes overpowering sense of dissolution.[7] Both authors in their own artistic work show their plunge into psychic dissolution and their emergence out of it to a life beyond personal and social alienation. This new life does not, however, begin to emerge until the two men approach old age. A sense of artistic and personal strength is manifested in both the lives and works of the two in their fifties. There is, in fact, an amazing parallel between their lives and works, though there are also some important differences because, for one thing, they belong to two different generations. The most important single parallel is that both wrote first novels (*Blue Voyage* and *The Moviegoer*) that describe the struggles of young men much like themselves against personal dissolution. Then both would publish at approximately the same age (Aiken at 63 and Percy at 64) works that portray the progress of protagonists very much like those of their first novels. In Aiken's *Ushant* (1952) and Percy's *The Second Coming* (1980), we can see the completion of a continuing creative use of personal and social dissolution that has led slowly to a new unification of personality in which

---

[7]Henry A. Murray, "Conrad Aiken: Poet of Creative Dissolution," *Wake* 11 (1952): 95-106.

seemingly disparate elements like the scientific mind and the artistic imagination are working together harmoniously. Aiken and Percy all along their routes of personal and artistic development were aware they were taking a path that was essentially mythic. But they do not seem aware that this path is also shamanistic. The researches of Mircea Eliade, which increasingly became known after World War II, show that the shamanistic process is often at work in lives that one would call mythic and that this process takes place in modern civilization as well as in primitive tribes. In her biography of C. G. Jung, Barbara Hannah quotes Eliade in her detailed description of how this process went on in Jung's life:

> "The primitive magician, the medicine man or shaman is not only a sick man, he is above all, a sick man who has been cured, *who has succeeded in curing himself.*" The idea always is that the body is put together better than it had been before.[8]

The achievement then of Aiken and Percy is that they gained a renewal of creative power and a unity of personality at an age when many modern artists and thinkers become burned out. This unification is expressed in *Ushant* and *The Second Coming* as a growing awareness of love; for them the transcendent principle, or God, is expressed in terms of both the ability to love others and the growing unification of all one's faculties, particularly of those aspects of the mind that are devoted to a rational and empirical view of life as well as those values connected with imagination, emotion, and artistic creativity. Neither author shows in his work a single breakthrough into some great illumination, but rather each reveals a growing process yielding small illuminations concerning a transcendent principle of unification along with an awareness of a developing spiritual maturity. Also, each is aware of a continual facing in himself and in the world of the principle of dissolution that threatens extinction but that if faced with a continuing belief in the transcendent principle yields greater creative life. This process essentially is what I take Murray's seminal article to be about—the creative use of dissolution; and yet Murray himself shows a lack of understanding of the mythic and shamanistic qualities of Aiken in that he does not reveal in his article the positive results of shamanistic renewal.

---

[8]Barbara Hannah, *Jung: His Life and Work* (New York: G. P. Putnam's Sons, 1981) 283.

The shaman, as Eliade, Jung, and others have shown, plunges into the midst of his own psychic and physical dissolution and discovers the transcendent power in the form of a center of creativity. By the continuing invocation of this center, the shaman-to-be gradually achieves a unification of his various faculties, and from this achievement flows the power of love that makes possible the creative unity of social groups. The events that launched Aiken and Percy on the path are those of childhood and youth, and the process itself that began their creative use of dissolution is what I call their long philosophical and artistic apprenticeship.

Percy is well known as a novelist who was first a publisher of articles in professional philosophical journals. He has in many ways remained a philosopher who writes novels, though his skill as a literary artist is considerable. Aiken's philosophical activities are less well known. They emerge early in his literary criticism and continue both in his mature poetry and in *Ushant,* his autobiography written in the form of a novel. Aiken's philosophical literary criticism, particularly *Scepticisms: Notes on Contemporary Poetry* (1919), has been gaining in reputation since the sixties. Yet I. A. Richards, probably the most philosophical critic writing in English in this century, recognized early in the twenties the profundity of Aiken's critical views. Like Richards, Aiken was seeking to understand poetry in its relationship both to society and to the universe. Aiken, in fact, is the only American critic mentioned in Richards's early work.

Throughout their philosophical speculation Aiken and Percy are seeking to unify disparate elements in the human makeup. Percy's enforced idleness during the time it took to recover from tuberculosis saw him turn from his inherited liberalism and his scientific studies, which had dominated his life from the period when he was an undergraduate at the University of North Carolina, to a study of Kierkegaard, Dostoyevski, and other existentialist writers. Kierkegaard taught him that the individual human being could not entirely be accounted for in the categories of science. Taking Kierkegaard and Dostoyevski quite seriously, Percy embraced the necessity of the religious life for the full development of one's humanity and at age thirty became a Roman Catholic convert. But his search continued for a balance between the radical existentialism of a Kierkegaard with his emphasis on the "leap of faith" as the one essential for the good life and the need of humans to develop a culture that included both a ritualized, communal religion and the sciences. This search led Percy to the work of Gabriel Marcel, the French Catholic existentialist who himself was influenced by William James. Thus in time James, the chief father of American liberalism, began to play an important part in Percy's thinking.

Aiken, on the other hand, began his college career at Harvard under the influence of James and liberalism generally but soon followed his teacher George Santayana, himself earlier a disciple of James, to a rejection of some of James's most important concepts. What Santayana and Aiken, following him, did not find in James was a governing metaphysical principle. James in his outlook was scientific, in fact was the chief founder of psychology as a science, and he was also concerned with moral problems as well as with what he called the "will to believe." Yet he never had much idea that there was any essence beyond the physical universe to believe in. His attitude toward religion as reflected in his influential *Varieties of Religious Experience* was that religion consisted mainly of various aberrant experiences. As Santayana noted, James had no awareness of the life of religion as a normal and necessary element of human culture.

Aiken, like Percy, would in time firmly establish himself in a religious tradition, choosing as he grew older to become a disciple of his grandfather Potter, one of the leading New England Unitarian ministers of the last century. Potter believed that religion and modern science could work together because at their deepest they both spring from an awareness of a central unifying power working for good in man and the universe. Ironically, Percy's real turning to religion began with a radical Protestant like Kierkegaard and progressed to full acceptance of the ritualism and community of Catholicism whereas Aiken discovered himself as a religious being through Santayana, a man in some ways deeply Catholic, but later turned increasingly to the teaching of his highly individualistic Protestant grandfather. Yet to know the religious views of the two men, we must study their creative works, and there we find a shamanistic struggle to achieve deeper unified being in the midst of chaos. This struggle leads in many directions. We find Percy, the Catholic who often emphasizes ritual, sounding at times like the Protestant Kierkegaard, particularly in *The Second Coming*. And we find Aiken, who was always partially under the influence of both Santayana and Spanish culture, sometimes sounding like a Catholic in his emphasis on ritual.

What really unites the two men is their great emphasis on modern psychology as a means of linking both the scientific and religious sides of humanity. Both are often empirical, as was James. In fact, Percy follows closely in both his philosophical essays and his novels the general viewpoint of Marcel, which F. H. Heinemann describes as that of a mysterious empiricism. Heinemann calls Marcel a "mysterious empiricist" who "starts with an analysis of his own concrete experience."[9] Here in Marcel the influence of James is great; the French philosopher prized James because he rejected the abstractions of metaphysical systems to look closely at the strange experience of man himself. Out of this close scrutiny came his deepest philosophical speculation. Both Percy and Aiken, partially and sometimes unconsciously Jamesian liberals, turn always to the mysterious growth and development of the human as their chief subject of scrutiny. Yet it is not to James's psychological speculation as such that they turn but rather it is to the new school of depth psychology first developed by Freud and continued along various lines by disciples like Jung, Adler, and Rank. As religious writers and thinkers Percy and Aiken are both modern and liberal in their general refusal to be influenced by abstract theological and metaphysical speculation and in their embracing of the mysterious qualities of humanity as we see them studied by psychologists.

Freud was the great psychologist always for Aiken because he used scientific methods and because he proclaimed what became for Aiken the two great concepts: love and self-knowledge. Freud first opened Aiken's eyes to these concepts, the poet tells us, but in *Ushant* and in his philosophical poetry he gives greatest credit to Jesus and Socrates as the progenitors of our present-day visions of love and self-knowledge. Percy, on the other hand, often seems to be satirizing Freud in his novels, but he is really attacking the abstractions of a contemporary Freudianism that sees the human only as a sick animal. Like Aiken, Percy always upholds the primary fact of love as the basic metaphysical principle. Aiken and Percy both are saying in effect that though abstract theology has been discarded by most modern people, still we are able to experience the mysterious nature of God through human love. In the best work of both we seem to hear Tolstoy's affirmation that where love is, there is God.

What keeps Aiken and Percy from the easy and even sentimental affirmation of love is that they also reveal in their work a strong sense of what Jung called the shadow archetype—the dark side of humanity that seeks dissolution. But also they are aware of Jung's ideas concerning the Self, or the creative center represented by the archetype of the mandala,

---

[9]F. H. Heinemann, *Existentialism and the Modern Predicament* (New York: Harper Torchbooks, 1958) 134.

and much of their best work is mythic in the sense Jung means when he says each human must discover his own living story, or myth, in order to achieve full individuality.

The work of Aiken and Percy, however, cannot be seen as an artistic illustration of modern psychology. Their visions lie somewhere beyond the insights of the great depth psychologists. The knowledge of psychology provides statements of basic human understanding that man must have on his journey, which is based on a series of conscious choices leading toward ever greater unification of the personality, of the achievement of that hero within that Otto Rank thought was what all humans instinctively felt the need to encounter. But neither is content with a view of man seeking a power within while at the same time being unaware of the mysterious universe governed by a loving God. We see Aiken in his last book-length work, *Thee* (1967), addressing and even struggling with God. Also we are often aware in Percy's novels of the breaking through of the grace of God when it is least expected. Yet the religious views of neither writer are ever separated from both the problems of the lonely, anxious modern individual drawn to self-destruction and the problems of modern culture dying and being reborn in the creative choices of individuals. Both men, for instance, are closely connected in their lives and their writing with two cities—Aiken with Savannah and Percy with New Orleans. Both men are involved with the concreteness of urban life, facing the inner and outer violence and the drift of many urbanites into the personal dissolution offered by even such ordinary drugs of the spirit as certain types of motion pictures or casual sexual experiences.

Yet Aiken and Percy both saw the problems of modern humanity not primarily in terms of dissolution but in terms of a split condition that leads to an absolutizing of only one aspect of existence, an absolutizing that is also a withdrawal from the pain of creative choices necessary to achieve wholeness. They were all too painfully aware of what Erich Fromm has termed the escape from freedom, carrying with it the loss of individuality. William Barrett states in *The Illusion of Technique* (1979) that it is the fear of mystery that causes humans to choose to accept a single part of existence as an absolute.

> The examples could be multiplied: in each case we take a partial truth and make it total. We become totalitarians of the mind; but we ourselves are our own victims, for we have imprisoned ourselves in a total ideology be-

yond which we cannot see. We are no longer free to let things be what they are, but must twist them into the framework we impose.[10]

William Barrett was himself one of the New York liberals, having served for a time as an editor of *The Partisan Review,* but as he became more philosophical in the seventies we find him taking a path similar to that of Aiken and Percy. Having rightly been called an existentialist, Barrett reveals in *The Illusion of Technique* the nature of his own quest for a metaphysical ground of existence. In nature he seems to find meanings and experiences that can never be fully summed up in human abstractions. Yet he is unlike Emerson or, for that matter, Aiken and Percy because his psychology does not go very far beyond that of William James. Barrett lacks what Aiken and Percy were continually discovering in their own inner lives—a sense of unity that, when it is experienced, lends grace to ordinary life.

Barrett, in spite of his quest for metaphysical certainty, still is caught up in the problem of the opposites, which if not solved leads either to a continuing tension difficult to live with or to a falling into the prison of the absolutes. Lionel Trilling finally tells us that his own great task as a liberal intellectual was to combat the slide into Marxism that became a strong movement in liberalism when the form of scientism developed by Marx came to seem more important than the old liberal quest for freedom and development of the individual. Basic to Trilling's liberal program was the belief that "reason and art" can be used to improve both individual and society. But Marxism meant an absolutizing of one part of experience, and when it was translated into action, Trilling found, reason and art disappeared and the individual was reduced to a cipher in a giant system. Yet Trilling never got beyond the opposites of reason and art, and all around him he found, as the old liberal tradition passed into decline after World War II, individuals absolutizing some aspect of rational thought or imaginative art. But then even in a sunnier period of history when Matthew Arnold, one of Trilling's chief masters, was recommending his own brand of liberal humanism, the absolutizing tendency was well under way. Reason was put to the service of creating systems like Marx's in which large scale violence was welcomed, and art was used in various systems of Aestheticism to recommend the life of the ivory tower above the hated masses. By

---

[10]William Barrett, *The Illusion of Technique* (Garden City NY: Anchor Press/ Doubleday, 1979) 166.

1900 the modern mind was being dragged irresistibly into various systems of thought, and ideology was becoming for modern man what God was in a religious age. The result was a diminishing of individual life. What Gladstone said of Bismarck could be applied in the twentieth century to many civilized people: he made Germany great and Germans small. The antiheroic man of the twentieth century would finally look out on a world governed by systems developed by scientism and would vaguely hope for renewal through art. But he would see no way of healing the split between science and art.

Aiken and Percy began their struggle against the absolutizing tendencies of modernity long before they were aware of them as such. They grew up in an Arnoldian atmosphere, but it did not save them from the shock of childhood catastrophe. Arnold recommended reason, thought, intelligence, art, and even religion; and the two men had those in their lives from the beginning. But they were not enough. Realizing that something was missing in their own lives caused them to search not simply for an intellectual "meaning" or explanation of the problems of modern life but for a series of experiences that would give them what Arnold would call a "joy whose grounds are true." They found these experiences in a growing relationship to an inner and outer unity that they believed to be implicit in the universe. The result was that they would be able to think in terms of both science and art, doing justice to both without excluding either in order to exalt the other. At the same time, they explored in their works their growing awareness of underlying unity in themselves and in the cosmos. The increasing attention paid to the work of Aiken and Percy since 1970 has still not led to a thorough investigation of the two authors' awareness of unity in human affairs.

In the early eighties an authorized biography of Conrad Aiken was being written by Joseph Killorin, who was also at work editing a second edition of the poet's letters; and critical studies of Walker Percy by Panthea R. Broughton and Jac Tharpe that delved more deeply into that author's work than any previous studies were published. With the expected publication of Percy's sixth novel in the second half of the eighties, more critical studies will doubtless appear. Yet basic human problems associated with the psyche that intensely concerned both Aiken and Percy still call for new exploration by commentators. The growth of Jungian criticism since 1970 has led to new approaches to these problems. Both Aiken and Percy seriously studied Jung and used some of his insights, with a critical perception, in their works; yet both of them expressed to me personally certain reservations about Jung. For instance, Jung for Aiken was "too mythopoeic." With their keen interest in the natural sciences, both authors were interested in empirical approaches to problems that I think can be called matters that should be placed under the heading of shamanism.

Mircea Eliade, as I have suggested, helps to provide, with his own empirical and theoretical studies of the shaman in many cultures, more of a factual approach to essential problems than Jung does. Recent studies of the two hemispheres of the brain might come even closer to what Aiken and Percy seemed in much of their work to be searching for. Interestingly enough, a book on this general subject by a medical doctor, David Loye, appeared the same year as Percy's *Lost in the Cosmos* (1983). In *Lost in the Cosmos* Percy challenged a widespread contemporary philosophical assumption, popularized by Carl Sagan, that reality is nothing more than what the everyday conscious mind can apprehend. Loye, using the work of David Bohm, discusses the differences between "our explicate-order consciousness" and a hypothetical area (called implicate-order consciousness) that must be affirmed if we are to experience certain modes of being necessary for life itself. Bohm, Loye explains, says that human beings have the ability to apprehend these modes of being "because our consciousness is embedded within and part of the implicate order." Thus, he goes on, "we may on occasion range beyond our limited explicate-order consciousness, which captures the major portion of all our lives, to apprehend the abiding truth 'out there' beyond the illusion."[11] For Aiken and Percy the way to one aspect of this implicate order, an aspect commonly called love, was through the process of pilgrimage. It is the same process that Eliade shows to be the method whereby shamans of many societies, primitive and sophisticated, break through to an apprehension of a realm of love and joy. Like earlier shamans, Aiken and Percy penetrated into this implicate-order consciousness and experienced the life-giving force of love, which they long believed they had, for the most part, lost because of childhood tragedy.

---

[11]David Loye, *The Sphinx and the Rainbow* (Boulder CO: New Science Library, 1983) 152-53.

Urban Settings
and Early Violence

Chapter II

I

The search by Conrad Aiken and Walker Percy for unity both of the mind
and of the arts would be accomplished through lifelong pilgrimages that
would begin with family violence experienced at early ages in their respective Southern cities, Savannah and Birmingham. The pilgrimages
would begin slowly, leading to long apprenticeships in science, art, and
philosophy, and would serve the purpose of freeing them from the psychic
wounds of childhood tragedy. But also both men would use the facts of
parental suicide and all that followed it in their lives as raw material for
some of their profoundest imaginative work; thus they would in time exorcise the pain of early trauma, though the careful reader of both authors

will note that the exorcism is a continuing process throughout their literary careers. Aiken, whose early psychic devastation from the immediate loss of both parents was the greater of the two, would imaginatively ponder all of his life the facts of the death of his parents. Percy, more hesitantly, would seem to place his father's suicide and his mother's subsequent death behind him in his creative work, except in *The Last Gentleman,* until with the publication in 1980 of *The Second Coming* we see a searching fictional examination of the problem of parental suicide. Both authors thus made the most important single facts of their early lives central events in some of their best imaginative creations. Yet their treatment of these events should not be viewed strictly as autobiography because through the imaginative employment of metaphor both Aiken and Percy have lifted their personal agony to a universal level so that their early suffering from violence becomes in part the suffering of everyone from family violence and disruption in the modern city.

When Aiken and Percy were growing up, the idea that the American city could regularly be a dangerous and violent place was not common. Both authors sprang from brilliant families. Their parents, though young, were considered by all who knew them to be well on their way to social and intellectual leadership in their respective cities. During Aiken's childhood in the eighteen-nineties, the small coastal city of Savannah was coming into its own again after the disasters of the Civil War, although there was still bitterness underneath the surface as the young Aiken regularly experienced when he was taunted for having Yankee parents. But his father was a successful doctor who dabbled in a variety of fields, including literature, and his mother was a beautiful woman who had found in spite of her Northern upbringing a welcome place in the sparkling society of one of the oldest cities on the Eastern seaboard. As Aiken's mother's brother said of Conrad's parents, and as the poet himself recorded in *Ushant,* his autobiography: "They were brilliant creatures, both of them . . . they were social, they were gay, they lived richly." And he continued, "They *lived*— even if it ended tragically; they lived!"[1]

In *Ushant,* we see the poet still mulling over the paradoxes of his early family life. This book, first published when Aiken was sixty-three, reveals his continuing interest in all the details of his early life. When I first met Aiken, he was seventy-five, and I was amazed by how in our first lengthy

---

[1]Conrad Aiken, *Ushant* (Cleveland: The World Publishing Company, 1962) 123.

conversation he talked freely but unobtrusively about his family. On a later occasion he showed me a picture of the black nurse who had cared for him and his two brothers, and he told me that even as an old woman she had kept this same picture always near her. There was a "Southern" side of Aiken that I immediately noticed, a readiness to talk about details of family life in the distant past. What I was not prepared for was the obvious emotion he showed in discussing his childhood nurse, although in *Blue Voyage* the Negro nurse is an important figure in the protagonist's life. But what most amazed me was that Aiken even at our first meeting could refer comfortably to the central trauma of his life. Whenever I talked to him, he would be sitting in the house on Oglethorpe Avenue where he spent his winters in Savannah, next to the fatal house where his childhood in effect ended. He had since 1961 returned to live part of every year in Savannah after the poet Hy Sobiloff had bought the whole block on Oglethorpe Avenue and offered to let him live in any house he chose. Those who visited Aiken and his wife Mary would find him conversing easily in the second-floor sitting room with only one wall separating him from the place where the event had occurred. Once, I said something very general about all he had suffered in his life, and he smiled deeply and said, pointing to the wall, "Yes, it all began right over there."[2]

Aiken was always a confessional poet, one far more devoted to the actual events of his own life—both in fiction and reality—than better known confessional poets of modernism, Robert Lowell, for instance. Yet confession was not from the first an easy thing for Aiken—he went for years unable to talk about his parents' death—and one might just as well see the poet as a man of many masks and disguises. The fact is that Aiken was always shy. And much the same could be said about Walker Percy except that he talks hardly at all to interviewers about the traumas of his childhood. Interviewing Percy, I found him to be, like Aiken, a ready and easy talker—Southern in this sense even more than Aiken—yet people I interviewed who had conversed extensively with Percy found him to be reticent, as in fact most novelists are, about discussing personal traumas. Nevertheless, the track of traumatic agony can be followed everywhere in Percy's fiction. He does not discuss his parents' tragic deaths, as Aiken did in time, but his handling of a father's suicide in *The Last Gentleman* is one

---

[2]For more information about Aiken in Savannah after 1961, see my article "Conrad Aiken: Resident of Savannah," *The Southern Review* 8 (Autumn 1972): 791-804.

of the most moving scenes in contemporary literature. Interestingly enough, Aiken was sixty-three when he published his autobiography; Percy published *The Second Coming* in his sixty-fourth year. Both *Ushant* and *The Second Coming* deal with an essential problem in the early lives of their authors: the problem of how people of financial and social well-being—people often brilliant by the standards of a pre-World War II period when many lived poorly, particularly in the South, and a few by contrast lived beautifully—could exist for years on the edge of tragedy without being aware of what was happening to them. In other words, what went wrong in the lives of people who had achieved the best that the nation seemed to offer at that, or any other, time?

Yet it was not possible for Aiken and Percy to record—as F. Scott Fitzgerald did—the lives of affluence lived out to a disenchanted and even violent conclusion. Both suffered too much to be simply recorders or confessors of personal agony. What both as artists felt called to accomplish was the universalizing of personal tragedy. Their artistic and personal pilgrimages caused them to search into the particularities of their own experience to find values and visions that could allow them and their readers to live with and profit from all human trauma. But before the essential philosophical similarities are examined, it is necessary to point out in detail how the two men came to terms artistically with violence in the urban setting.

II

For many years after he left Savannah at age eleven to live with relatives following the death of his parents on the morning of 27 February 1901, Conrad Aiken saw his native city largely in terms not only of the violent moment of parental death but also of the suffering that had preceded that death due to the growing madness of his father. In fact, in *Blue Voyage* Aiken speaks of Savannah as the city where ''my pride and will were broken before I had come to my seventh year.''[3] He speaks in *Blue Voyage* of being in continual terror, and in *Ushant* he says frankly that his childhood was destroyed. In *Ushant,* besides actually describing his entrance to his parents' room after first hearing two shots and then finding their bodies,

---

[3]Conrad Aiken, *Blue Voyage,* in *The Collected Novels of Conrad Aiken* (New York: Holt, Rinehart and Winston, 1964) 54.

he speaks of the "family *petit mal*," a strain of mental unbalance in his family that hounded Conrad himself for years, driving him to attempt suicide in 1932. The family mad streak was a monkey on the back of several generations, and Aiken makes no secret of it. By the same token, we are told by the Greenville, Mississippi novelist Ellen Douglas that suicide went back many generations in the Percy family. And Will Barrett in *The Last Gentleman,* a figure much like Percy in some ways, has a *petit mal* that takes the form of a kind of amnesia.

Many of the details of the events leading up to the Aikens' death as well as the poet's own reactions are set down by Alexander A. Lawrence in an article in *The Georgia Review* in 1968. As a fellow Savannahian who was a distinguished judge for many years in the city, Lawrence rightly shows the original Aiken residence and its occupants to be central to Aiken's thought about his native city. "Aiken has made 228 Oglethorpe more famous in literature than any Savannah dwelling is or probably ever will be."[4] In fact, as Lawrence points out by numerous quotations from *Blue Voyage* and *Ushant,* Savannah was on Aiken's mind throughout his life.

Although Savannah was the city where his youth was destroyed, in which even the number of his parents' house "held his life in its poisonous coils," it was for Aiken always the "miraculous" city. Thus a study of Aiken's relationship to Savannah is a study of the gradual repossession of the love of his parents, which was often present those early years. As a young man in New England, where he went to live with relatives after losing his parents, Aiken felt alienated from those around him, though while attending Middlesex School in Concord, Massachusetts, he was, as Killorin reminds us, "an enthusiastic athlete and . . . formed fast friendships."[5] But Killorin goes on to note his loneliness and shyness (a trait he never lost) and says that he "felt marked by the whisperings around him about his family tragedy."[6] Aiken himself put it succinctly in *Ushant* as "the staining sense of guilt and shame."[7] But when he went to Harvard, he began to read his father's writing, and gradually he found himself re-

---

[4]Alexander A. Lawrence, "228 Habersham Street," *Georgia Review* 22 (Fall 1968): 319. Lawrence was a friend of Aiken's; he several times told acquaintances that Aiken had told him that he wept when he read the article, admitting the truth of it all.

[5]Joseph Killorin, ed., *Selected Letters of Conrad Aiken* (New Haven: Yale University Press, 1978) 5.

[6]Ibid.

[7]Aiken, *Ushant,* 103.

possessing his past. Yet it was not until 1936 that he could return to Savannah. And when he stepped out of the DeSoto Hotel to begin the walk to the house on Oglethorpe Avenue, a current of emotion began to flow. Aiken in *Ushant* would look back on this pivotal walk and its emotional overflow with a sense of awe: "in the midst of this all-healing recapitulation, this triumph of repossession, flooding his veins and arteries with recollected beauty and power."[8] From what was in effect a vision of personal renewal, Aiken can be said to have begun that personal and literary mastery of a city that was, in Killorin's words, the lodestone of his life.

Savannah, as well as Charleston, the city most like it in the nation, is not what most non-natives imagine. Though it is a city that has been one of the centers of Southern culture since the early eighteenth century, it is not and never was the closed center of Anglo-Saxon Protestant Southernism some imagine it to be, though elements of this nature can be found there. But if one looks carefully at the skyline of Charleston or Savannah, he will see a variety of churches and public buildings indicating that various faiths and ethnic groups have prospered there. One who studies the forces of people and the nature of the architecture in the metro-areas of the two cities will sense a polyglot and even cosmopolitan urban character that is found in many of the port cities of the world and particularly on the east coast of America.

Aiken, who was much traveled and was at home in New England, New York, Great Britain, and even Spain, always found Savannah a variegated and cosmopolitan city and enjoyed living near its center in the late years of his life. In every conversation I had with him in the sixties, he spoke of his delight in walking nearly every day in the city and observing the details of its architecture. Incidentally, like a true native, he preferred Savannah to Charleston because, as he said to me once, its inner city had possessed more of the life of the people from its earliest times; for him it had less of the museum quality than modern Charleston. But Aiken loved both cities as cosmopolitan urban areas of the eastern seaboard because finally he was more a writer of the American east coast than anything else and for this reason felt that Edgar Allan Poe was in many ways his chief literary forebear.

Aiken was deeply aware of another aspect of Savannah—its connections with the lushness of the tropics to the south, with the exotic mystery,

---

[8]Ibid., 339.

when he was growing up, that emanated from Florida and the West Indies. In another sense, he saw Savannah as unique because of its beautiful and extensive cemetery called Bonaventure, where his parents were buried and where he today is buried next to them. This cemetery, along with the Revolutionary War cemetery across the street from where he lived, plays a big role in Aiken's prose and poetry, evoking as it does not only early memories of pain and violence but the very subject of death itself, which is central to much of his best work. Bonaventure Cemetery is on the road leading to Tybee Beach, which was always for him one of the key places of his life. As he said in *Ushant,* other places were beautiful, but "they could never become part of one's own language in the way that Tybee Beach would always mysteriously be, or Tuckerman's Ravine."[9] Savannah then would be always seen not only in terms of its inner city where he lived and played as a child but also as a city of the living connected with a beautiful city of the dead stretching on out to Tybee Island, which in itself evoked the other Southern islands and finally the tropical world of buccaneers and Spanish galleons. Fittingly, a landmark in Savannah since the eighteenth century has been that venerable restaurant, with all its literary associations, called the Pirate's House.

But how did Aiken relate his parents' death to his own life so that he was not finally driven mad by the psychic wounds he bore so long? He did it in three ways: first, by evoking nature with its beauty and its seeming everlastingness; second, by the use of psychological understanding; and, third and most important, by religious vision based on his Unitarian beliefs.

Aiken as he grew older realized how much he had over the years absorbed of his grandfather Potter's Unitarian philosophy. In his seventies he was regularly reading Potter's sermons and, under their inspiration, writing in Savannah his last book-length poem, *Thee,* based on the religious meditations of his last full decade of life. But early in his literary career, he came to see that his abiding concern with nature and with the new depth psychology pioneered by Sigmund Freud was harmonious with his inherited Unitarian concern with nature and science.

In two of his best stories and in what is probably his best known poem, "Tetélestai," Aiken has dealt with both his parents' death and the events leading up to it. In the story "Strange Moonlight," he captures the sense

---

[9]Ibid., 335.

of violence in the air, the strange atmosphere that his house and the city of Savannah have in that time of growing apprehension before the death of his parents. The story begins with a young boy reading Poe and having "a delirious night in inferno," continues with the sudden death of a young friend, Caroline Lee, and thoughts of Bonaventure Cemetery, and then moves on to its climax with his father covering himself with sand and with the boy clairvoyantly seeing him as dead: "How exactly like a new grave he looked!"[10] Yet though the boy has suffered the death of his friend and has had an eerie vision of his own father's grave, he still sees all that is happening through the beauty and strangeness of natural surroundings. The story affirms life through the boy's will to identify with the forces of nature: "and his strong arms flashed slowly over and over in the sunlight as he swam far out. How magnificent! . . . He would like to be able to do that, to swim out and out and out, with a sea-gull flying close beside him, talking."[11] By the end of the story when the boy and his family have returned to the house in Savannah from their outing at the beach, the boy realizes that everything was now "changed and ghostly," but somehow the beauty of nature extending even into the heart of the city undergirds the boy's strange sensations: "The long street, in the moonlight, was like a deep river, at the bottom of which they walked, making scattered, thin sounds on the stones, and listening intently to the whispering of elms and palmettos"[12] No better statement about the poetic achievement of this rich story with its encompassing of human tragedy with the ultimate serenity of the macrocosm, symbolized by natural beauty, has been made than the one by Aiken himself to Jay Martin: "Invention and synthesis coming to the rescue of disorder and early sorrow."[13] This is the same method of writing the author would use many times in his best fiction and poetry.

The single work that deals most profoundly with the author's childhood is his best known story, "Silent Snow, Secret Snow." It goes so deeply to the heart of Aiken's early agony that the author could never speak of its obvious autobiographical elements. When I questioned him about it, he smiled and said, "Everyone asks me about that one." To Jay Martin he wrote concerning the story, "As I said before, invention, imagination going

---

[10]*The Collected Short Stories of Conrad Aiken* (Cleveland: The World Publishing Company, 1965) 393.

[11]Ibid.

[12]Ibid., 294.

[13]Killorin, *Selected Letters of Conrad Aiken,* 313.

far afield from a small premise."[14] But, one may ask, far afield from what? Certainly the story seems so deeply felt, so painful even for the teller and the reader, that it must be personal agony that is being unfolded by the author. What that agony is, of course, is clear from *Ushant* and from the highly autobiographical novel *Blue Voyage*. It is a boy's fear of a father's cruelty and of his own schizophrenic withdrawal into a world of his own. But the story contains something else so frightening that Aiken and most other people have not been able to confront it clearly. That frightening element is psychic incest.

Aiken was early drawn to Freud's work, and Freud in turn was drawn to Aiken's work, keeping one of his novels on the waiting room table for patients to read while awaiting their turn on the master's couch. Freud, as I will show later, gave Aiken an intellectual framework to deal with his own oedipal problems, and thus helped Aiken to write a kind of psychological fiction that even today is taken seriously by many psychiatrists and psychologists. Aiken was well aware of the value of what he wrote for modern depth psychology, but he was also aware of the imaginative aspects of the art. Thus he rightly speaks in his letter to Martin of "invention and imagination," and we will probably never know just how much of the story is based on the actual facts of his life. But we do know that Aiken faced the two psychological problems that Freud defined as the Oedipus complex and the fear of castration. Aiken dramatizes both of these problems in "Silent Snow, Secret Snow" and relates them dramatically to the plight of a boy going insane. Thus he has in part exorcised the agony of a psychological suffering so intense that the sufferer can deal with it only at second or third hand. If one should forget the fear with which the world received Freud's pronouncements on these matters, let him remember that after the pioneer depth psychologist began to write seriously about incest, old friends in Vienna would cross the street to keep from speaking to him.

From what we know of the facts about Aiken's early life, as recorded in Alexander A. Lawrence's article, for instance, or in *Ushant,* the father of the poet had a destructive and castrating influence on the children of the family, and the mother pathetically clung to the young Aiken, so much so as to amount to something like an incestuous relationship. In "Strange Moonlight," a story Aiken admits is autobiographical, we see the child seeking to escape forever by swimming into the ocean. Yet the overall ef-

---

[14]Ibid., 312.

fect of the story is to show nature containing the fear of death and repressed violence in a larger creative framework. But in "Silent Snow," the love of an element of nature—snow, which is particularly powerful among children of the Deep South where it is so seldom seen, becomes linked with a sinister psychic force. The child is throughout the story being drawn by a "seamless hiss" into a world that is "a vast moving scene of snow" that seemed to speak to the boy as it seemed to engulf him by the end of the story: "but even now it said peace, it said remoteness, it said cold, it said sleep."[15] However, the climax of the story is not the child's final engulfment by the vision of snow. It is instead the confrontation with his two parents who are seeking to discover what is wrong with the child—a confrontation that causes him to turn at last to a complete acceptance of the destructive vision of snow.

The confrontation with the parents, along with a doctor they have called to the house, illustrates the Freudian concepts of castration and incest. The father is the chief agent of castration, described as he is in terms of punishment and cruelty: "This was the Father's voice. The brown slippers again came a step nearer, the voice was the well-known 'punishment' voice, resonant and cruel."[16] But then the father, the mother, and the doctor turn on the child: "And without precisely facing them, nevertheless he was aware that all three of them were watching him . . . as if he had done something monstrous, or was himself some kind of monster."[17] Immediately there began a new sound that in time he knew would become the roar of a storm of snow that he would at last fully accept. But a psychic force even more horrible than his castrating father appears: "This thing rushed at him, clutched at him, shook him—and he was not merely horrified, he was filled with such a loathing as he had never known."[18] What he feels is the incestuous power of the mother seeking to possess him, and he cries out the "exorcising words": "Mother! Mother! Go away! I hate you." And, the narrator immediately tells us, "everything was solved, everything became all right." By verbalizing his hatred of the incestuous mother, he at last can accept the sinister vision of snow as the one ultimate reality of his life, a reality that will become a timeless sleep.

---

[15]*The Collected Short Stories of Conrad Aiken,* 235.
[16]Ibid., 233.
[17]Ibid.
[18]Ibid., 234.

In his best fictional moments Aiken creates imaginative visions based partly on his own early experiences, but he does so by the magic of art. In a story like "Silent Snow, Secret Snow," he writes not so much about himself as an individual but instead about the crushing burdens of the psychically molested child. Like all imaginative artists, he moves from the particulars of individual suffering to the universalization of childhood agony. Yet, at the same time, Aiken was fulfilling the injunctions of his master Freud to bring up to consciousness the hidden and destructive contents of the unconscious mind so that he might be freed from hidden anger and despair. Aiken provided the artistic means for others to do the same, and he did it so well that it is no wonder Freud admired his work. But facing destructive unconscious contents is only one way Aiken dealt with his childhood traumas. Another and more important way was his continuing efforts to come to terms with his dead parents, to forgive them and to understand them, and finally to love them.

Probably no author in modern literature has done more throughout his entire life, both personally and artistically, to come to grips with the meaning of his parents' lives. Fittingly, his most anthologized poem, "Tetélestai," deals directly with the problems of the growing madness and violent death of his father. Yet Aiken has in this poem lifted his father's agony to an archetypal level so that the protagonist of the poem becomes the modern faceless man of the crowd who is frustrated in his efforts to find his true individuality. The "I" of the poem speaks from the grave in a willow-shaded cemetery near a river that is clearly Bonaventure Cemetery. It was to his parents' graves there in sight of the Wilmington River that during his late Savannah years Aiken came to pour a libation of wine on the single stone marking them. The voice of the "I" speaks of himself as "The struggler with shadows. / The one who went down under shoutings of chaos," but his essential message is that he too was heroic and not, as he announces himself at the beginning of the poem, "only one of millions, mostly silent."[19] The poem is essentially about a man who feels that the "fates of time and space obscured me" but one who nevertheless announces his own inner heroism. He sums up his own tragic flaw by describing himself as one "who could not capture / The secret of self."

The resolving of the paradoxes of this poem concerning one who is at once one of the silent millions and yet is also heroic in stature must be found

---

[19]Conrad Aiken, *Collected Poems* (New York: Oxford University Press, 1953) 299, 296.

in Aiken's religious vision, which was from young manhood onward essentially that of his Unitarian grandfather, William James Potter. The very title of the poem is Christ's statement on the cross that the process of crucifixion is finished, and the "I" in the poem compares himself with Christ, though he is also modern man who cries out, being "vanquished / By terror of life," and is "answered by silence." Aiken in effect is admitting that he has seen the vision of his father's life as a continuing crucifixion, and yet he is also saying that the life of modern anti-heroic man is also the life of continuing suffering due to a kind of psychic castration in which the "fates . . . like great spiders / Dispatched me at their leisure."

I will return to the place of this highly imaginative poem in Aiken's work when I analyze the development of his religious vision because anthologists have rightly seen that it is one of his most powerful works. Yet he was to write greater poems on the subject. In a sense, "Tetélestai," published in 1917, corresponds to T. S. Eliot's "The Love Song of J. Alfred Prufrock." The two friends would both state in memorable early poems their struggles with their elders and with their own feelings of psychic castration. But these poems would mark the beginnings of a lifelong pilgrimage, both personal and artistic, for the two poets, both of whom would solve many of the problems first stated so memorably in "Tetélestai" and "Prufrock" by an expanding of their personal visions of man's relationship to the universe.

III

Walker Percy also searches deeply into his own wounded past and thereby encounters the figure of his violent father. Like Aiken, Percy extends his own religious vision over many years of creative activity so that he can achieve both understanding and forgiveness, not only for members of his own family but also for a way of life in the aristocratic Old South that helped to shape him and his family but left him with an unconscious load of violence almost too heavy to bear.

Hemingway is the most famous modern author to write about his father's suicide. When he was once asked who his psychiatrist was, Hemingway is supposed to have replied, "my typewriter." Although he made full use of personal experience, Hemingway is possibly America's best known consciously fictional artist. He was a man devoted to his fictional art both as craft and high visionary calling. Even so, the autobiographical elements are often recognizable in his work. Possibly all literary artists since Goethe have found it necessary to be, at least in part, confessional poets. If, as Harold Bloom says, "any true biography is the story of how anyone suffered his own family,"[20] then the agony of family relationships must find its way into literature; and the good literary artist helps his readers even more than himself exorcise the inherited destructive vibrations of every generation growing more inwardly and even outwardly violent as time takes us to the end of the century. Thus Walker Percy even more than Aiken spells out much of the meaning of our violent past. Yet, though sometimes autobiographical, he always seeks in his art to raise his vision of family violence to an impersonal level so that it becomes the inherited violence of everyone in the twentieth century. What ties Aiken and Percy together is not direct literary influence but the fact that they belonged to a school of modern literary figures headed by T. S. Eliot and James Joyce who, faced with extreme early suffering, exorcised personal ghosts not only with the Freudian methods (which have always been used, Freud only naming them for us) but with what Eliot, in discussing Joyce, called the "mythical method." It is this method, more than any artistic device, that enables the writers of this school to rise above the biographical and the personal levels. Through this method the modern writer could, like earlier shamans, turn sickness into new psychic health.

Like Aiken, Percy was drawn to Freud early in his intellectual life, but also like Aiken it is through the extension of mythic and religious vision that he achieves his reconciliation with the violence of early memory. Thus both men, through an imaginative use of mythic and religious vision, go beyond the biographical analysis of Freud while still using many of his concepts in their fictional and nonfictional works. In one sense, their writing cannot be separated from a Freudian view of life because so much of their best work grew out of the traumas of childhood and because Freud inspired them both to bring forth out of their unconscious minds dangerous psychic contents so that this explosive material could be defused before serious personality disorder set in. Thus the act of writing was for both an encounter with repressed psychic contents, and for this reason some of their best work can be read on one level as an illustration of Freudian psychology. In fact, Aiken's novel *King Coffin* was at one time required reading

---

[20]Harold Bloom, *The Anxiety of Influence: Theory of Poetry* (London: Oxford University Press, 1973) 94.

in psychology courses at Harvard, and Robert Coles, professor of psychiatry and medical humanities at Harvard Medical School, uses Percy's novels to make psychological statements. But the error of reading Aiken's *King Coffin* on this level alone is pointed out by one of his best critics, Jay Martin, in his statement that a psychological reading concentrates only on the novel's protagonist "and ignores the structure of the book."[21] It is precisely in the examination of the structure of both authors' works that we see the mythic element combined with psychological elements. Thus we must take into full account some of the insights of C. G. Jung and archetypal criticism as well as the visions of some of the continental existentialists and writers of the "mythical method," like Eliot and Joyce, to appreciate fully both the complexity and depth of the two writers' most significant literary accomplishments. Of course, as I will show later, Aiken and Percy were conversant with the best of Jung and the existentialists and were, in fact, working in a tradition in which Joyce and Eliot were the acknowledged masters.

There is indeed a remarkable similarity in the way Aiken and Percy use childhood memories of parental suicide, and Percy's most recent novel, *The Second Coming,* makes it clear what he was working on in his earlier book, *The Last Gentleman.* Published in 1980, *The Second Coming* takes up the story of Will Barrett, the protagonist of *The Last Gentleman,* published in 1967. The central event described in these two books is the suicide of the protagonist's father. This literary fact is paralleled in Aiken's life by two books, *Blue Voyage* (1927) and *Ushant* (1952). The latter is rightly called Aiken's autobiography, but it is written in the form of a stream-of-consciousness novel and has as its protagonist the character Demarest, who is also the protagonist of *Blue Voyage.* Parental suicide does not stand out as necessarily the central theme in either book, but it is nevertheless the central psychological fact in both, having propelled the protagonist on his journey to seek expanded consciousness. The suicide of the father is also not the chief theme of *The Last Gentleman* and *The Second Coming,* but it is undoubtedly the central psychological fact in them, and it provides the impetus for some of the author's best writing. It is clear that both authors took up the theme early in their careers and then put it down, only to take it up later and deal with it in terms that structurally must be

---

[21]Jay Martin, *Conrad Aiken: A Life of His Art* (Princeton: Princeton University Press, 1962) 148.

called both mythic and archetypal. The most amazing similarity here is that Aiken published his second book of this series in his sixty-third year while Percy published his at age sixty-four. Both Aiken and Percy were the eldest of three sons. It took therefore almost the same amount of time for both writers to come to full literary terms with parental suicide, and it is thus clear that both used their art to liberate themselves from early trauma.

In *The Last Gentleman* Percy delves deeply into his and his family's past, but in this his second novel he has perfected his art so that he deals not with autobiographical material but with the search of a psychically wounded American into the violence of the Southern and the American past. Williston Barrett, the central figure of *The Last Gentleman,* sets out from New York on an archetypal journey into a South he thought he had left forever. Like Percy, finding his way back to the Deep South after his medical education at Columbia and his bout with tuberculosis in a Northern sanitorium, Barrett must go back, suffering with recurrent bouts of amnesia, to experience again a South he had thought he could escape in the scientifically oriented culture of the North. Barrett has even, absurdly, taken unto himself the title of ''engineer'' in order to associate himself with the dominant scientific and technological viewpoint of the North.

But, like a Hemingway hero, he can never escape his parental past; yet, unlike Hemingway and his best protagonists, Barrett knows he cannot keep running forever. He must go back, and the main fact he must face is his father's life and death. Probably the most powerful passage in the book is the one describing his own reliving of his father's death. Indeed, it is possibly the most powerful passage in the whole of Percy. Louis D. Rubin, Jr. undoubtedly thought so because he selected it for his recent (1979) anthology, *The Literary South.* However, Rubin is wrong to say that ''It is not too difficult to see Percy's spiritually disturbed protagonists as the latest exemplars of a long line of estranged Southern fictional wayfarers, including Quentin Compson, Wolfe's Eugene Gant, . . . Warren's Jack Burden, Tate's Lacy Buchan, Styron's Cass Kinsolving, and Katherine Anne Porter's Miranda.''[22] The fact that he is indeed *not* like this long line of protagonists in flight is seen in Percy's depiction of Barrett's returning to the scene of the suicide in order to overcome that fear within him that has caused the flight. By this act of the will in overcoming his partially repressed fear and despair due to early suffering, Barrett can play a cre-

---

[22]Louis D. Rubin, Jr., *The Literary South* (New York: John Wiley and Sons, 1979) 664.

ative role in the life of at least three other people. By the end of the novel, his newfound creativity has enabled him to talk a suicidal friend into accepting the burden of life, a life that can be lived only if one does not model himself on the worn-out ideals of the past. The proof that Percy is not writing about fleeing and suicidal characters like Faulkner's Quentin Compson is seen in his next novel, *Love in the Ruins,* when another of the fleeing heroes turns and faces his suicidal impulses. Finally, the renewal of Barrett's story in *The Second Coming* lays out the whole problem of a father's suicide, and Barrett faces this event at an even deeper level than in *The Last Gentleman.* The fact that Percy at sixty-four could publish this novel of the triumph of a protagonist over his traumatic childhood should be a sign that he has moved into the post-modern world of fiction, leaving behind him much of the modernism of Faulkner, Hemingway, Wolfe, and Warren.

The key moment in *The Last Gentleman* that reveals the movement of Percy beyond the fleeing protagonist of modernism comes in chapter five when Barrett relives his father's death and suddenly sees that the whole earlier generation had gone wrong: "*Wait.* I think he was wrong and that he was looking in the wrong place. No, not he but the times. The times were wrong and one looked in the wrong place."[23] From that moment on, Barrett is no longer the last of a long line of dying Southern gentlemen but is a searcher in a new sense. Before this time he had been blindly looking for the source of his despair, but when he sees that he has been living in the old death pattern of his ancestors, a new way can begin for him.

Percy is not ready in *The Last Gentleman* to state exactly what it is Barrett has found that makes the new life possible. He cannot name the element he has touched, but his choosing to touch it permits a spring of creativity to flow. The proof of this flow is that he is able to play a role in the salvation of both Jamie and Sutter. But, though Barrett suddenly sees in a kind of Joycean epiphany that the whole way was wrong and that there is a possibility of a new way, Percy wisely does not state at this stage of his protagonist's journey what it is he apprehends.

Wait. He had missed it! It was not in the Brahms that one looked and not in solitariness and not in the old sad poetry but—he wrung out his ear—

---

[23]Walker Percy, *The Last Gentleman* (New York: The American Library, 1968) 260.

but here, under your nose, here in the curiousness and drollness and ex-
traness of the iron and the bark that—he shook his head—that—[24]

Percy is here nearer to Flannery O'Connor than most readers might realize. Both writers were influenced by James Joyce, and both extended this
master's concept of the epiphany to include a subtle flow of what O'Connor called grace, which is a creative and supernatural energy of healing
and unifying proportions. Percy greatly admired O'Connor as a person and
an artist but wisely used different literary methods and techniques while at
the same time employing viewpoints and methods basic to Joyce.

The problem of suicide and childhood trauma still haunts the Percy
novels after *The Last Gentleman* as if the author had not exorcised himself
of this all-important fact of his life. In the next novel, *Love in the Ruins*,
Tom Moore, the protagonist, attempts suicide. In the following novel,
Lancelot, there is a remarkable parallel to Aiken's *King Coffin*, whose protagonist, the author tells us, has "self-destruction" as "his unconscious
aim from the outset."[25] But in *The Second Coming*, the novel that follows
Lancelot, Percy devotes his deepest artistic attention to the full effects of
suicide on a child and on the man that child becomes.

The Second Coming, of all Percy's novels, is the profoundest statement of the meaning of pilgrimage, the central theme they all share. It is
not as poetic as *The Moviegoer*, nor as deeply touching and funny as *The
Last Gentleman*, nor as philosophical as *Love in the Ruins*, and it lacks the
sheer imaginative and psychic power of *Lancelot;* yet it is a kind of summing up of all of Percy's most important themes and ideas. It is the kind
of novel only an author who had slowly matured both artistically and intellectually could have written. It is, in short, the work of an authentic man
of letters. Because it states so well the fulfillment of Percy's search for renewal, I will examine it in detail in a later chapter as an example of a culmination point in the author's work. Yet it is necessary here to mention
two points the book makes about urban life and early violence.

The Second Coming continues the story of Will Barrett begun in *The
Last Gentleman* but shifts the locale. Percy's own early life was lived out
in an affluent suburb of Birmingham until he went to live in his mother's
hometown of Athens, Georgia, after his father's suicide. The suburbs or
exurbs of a Southern city are often the scene of Percy's best work. After

---

[24]Ibid.
[25]Conrad Aiken, "Author's Preface," *3 Novels* (New York: McGraw-Hill, 1965) 12.

World War II the concept of the exurban community was developed in order to take into account the growth of large residential areas that are beyond the reach of the ordinary suburbs but that still, like the suburbs, are attached to a city. Such locales figure largely in Percy's later novels. Thus in *The Last Gentleman* he writes about affluent suburbs of Birmingham, but in *The Second Coming* he moves on to an affluent area of western North Carolina and presents it in essence as an exurb of Atlanta. Interestingly enough, *Lancelot* is set in an exurb of New Orleans whereas his first book, *The Moviegoer,* has a suburb of New Orleans as its setting. His only other novel, *Love in the Ruins,* is set in an affluent exurb that could be attached to any large Southern city of the near future.

But whether Percy is writing about the affluent extensions of New Orleans, Birmingham, or Atlanta, he has one important point to make about what he sometimes satirically suggests is an American dream of paradise realized: that the suburban-exurban Edenic world has been invaded by a violence as deep as any in the inner cities of America. It is a violence often hidden but one that in time breaks forth in murder and suicide. Conrad Aiken was to make this point about the old colonial center of nineteenth-century Savannah. In 1980 we see Percy still dealing with it in *The Second Coming,* which looks into the next century when cities like Atlanta will in effect extend for hundreds of miles beyond their old boundaries by spawning the kinds of almost endless exurbs seen in the Los Angeles-San Diego area of California. In some of his best poems and fiction, Aiken makes a similar point about violence among the affluent in two ways. He shows first the nature of violence itself in the form of murder and suicide as well as in many lesser acts. He also depicts, as in his great story "Silent Snow, Secret Snow," the nature of the castrating forces exuded unknowingly by certain people, forces that drive children in particular into a schizophrenic isolation.

In *The Second Coming* Percy takes up the very same problems Aiken dealt so well with in "Tetélestai" and "Silent Snow, Secret Snow." In "Tetélestai" Aiken shows us the inner workings of a mind haunted by chaos until it finally breaks down, and in "Silent Snow, Secret Snow" he shows us a child being driven mad by his chaos-haunted parents. Percy's *The Second Coming* shows in a series of flashbacks a child under the constant psychic battering of a father so chaos-haunted that he is driven at last to kill himself. That child is Will Barrett, the protagonist of his most sensitively wrought novel of psychic quest, *The Last Gentleman,* and the central figure of *The Second Coming,* which shows the final struggle that releases him from a chaos-ridden past. In another character in *The Second Coming,* the young girl Allison, Percy outlines in detail the destructive effects that the manipulative parent can have on a child and goes on to show how a person under constant manipulation will often attempt to commit psychic suicide by withdrawal into isolation. However, *The Second Coming* is not a case study of schizophrenia. Instead it is an artistic rendering of the mythic quest that shows two people, Allison and Will, overcoming the chaos of their past in order to live fruitful lives together. But that basic theme of the book is part of the larger motif of pilgrimage in Percy that I will examine later, and therefore it is necessary here only to point out that in *The Second Coming* Percy has dealt more fully with the themes of suicide and schizophrenia than he has anywhere else in his fiction. Yet—and this is all-important for both Percy and Aiken—it is not enough to see the work of the writer dealing with psychological themes purely in terms of links with his biographical background. What should be central to any literary concern with such writers is an examination of their art because as literary figures they will stand or fall on that basis.

IV

Conrad Aiken is quite clearly, particularly in much of his best work, a confessional poet. The same cannot be said of Percy because he is always careful in his novels to disguise the facts of his own life. Yet the facts of his psychological ups-and-downs, as far as they are known (and Percy is often reticent in these matters, as Aiken was not), parallel in essential ways the inner development of the main characters of all five novels. But both Aiken and Percy, whether confessional or not in their art (and Aiken is not always confessional), have lifted problems that can be called psychological and sociological to a plane that must be called imaginative and artistic. As I have suggested, and as Aiken and Percy knew, material from their works can be seen as valuable for both psychological and sociological insights. Yet it is chiefly through his imagination and reason that the man of letters comes to grips with his environment, and it is through the exercise of imagination and reason that he gives meaning to both nature and the city. In establishing his artistic vision, the true man of letters should be able to master imaginatively the environment in which he resides. In performing this creative function, he lends his meaning and his artistic aura to the world around him. Cities where men of letters have played prominent roles—London or Paris, for instance—have gained an aura that only the creative artist can provide, and in spite of the urban blight they might contain, these cities draw the people of the world to them because of some mythic quality they possess. Raw cities that have not known the healing work of the creative artist lack some finer tone that combats the mental and emotional emptiness that inspires flight. What the man of letters—or any creative artist—gives to the city where he resides is something from the depths of his inner life. The artist in order to create must develop an inner life, often at great pains to himself and against the deepest wishes of his neighbors. If he continues this development, then eventually his art will bear fruit and enrich those around him and their descendants, sometimes for centuries after his death.

The inner life of the artist is the place where we must locate the germination of the art work, and great artists in the past prepared themselves carefully for their life's tasks. Conrad Aiken and Walker Percy are like artists of the Renaissance in that both underwent long and careful apprenticeships for their work. Unlike earlier artists they found a very weakened tradition to work within. Nevertheless, by diligent application to science and philosophy as well as to the art of letters, they achieved an inner development that continued to fructify even into old age, enabling them to create some of their best work after sixty—a time when most modern writers suffer a diminution or even death of creative energy. Of course, one of the reasons both authors took so long in their apprenticeship was the difficulty of dealing with early psychological traumas. Both would return over and over in their work to their early sufferings, and it is always necessary to take certain biographical facts into account in order to understand the two authors. But what I hope to do in the chapters that follow is to rise above the biographical level in order to show the inner meaning of the art of both men and to examine the fruit of that art in terms of their achievements as mature men of letters.

The New Criticism, which Aiken himself helped to bring to birth, did its best to eliminate biographical criticism as an important factor in the study of literature. Biography is a valuable element in the study of certain writers, but if the writer's art is of value it must be considered in terms of its function as art rather than as a convenient illustration of someone's activities. Yet even Percy himself acknowledged the importance of suicide in the career of the contemporary novelist when he said in a well-known "self-interview" in *Esquire* that "a novelist these days has to be an ex-suicide."[26] It is necessary in the deepest sense to ask what Percy means by this statement and how it illuminates both the meaning and the value of his art. The trouble so far in much of the criticism of both Aiken and Percy is that there is no serious effort to rise above the facts of either biography or philosophical influence to search for an understanding of artistic meaning and literary value. Two books about Aiken by Jay Martin and Frederick J. Hoffman miss, as Aiken himself sometimes pointed out to friends, the essential vision within the poet's works. Both Martin and Hoffman perform a valuable service by giving biographical details, discussing influence, and cataloging themes, but they seldom glimpse the full vision of the poet. Percy has been even more unfortunate in two books devoted entirely to his work. In *The Sovereign Wayfarer* Martin Luschei goes into pertinent facts about the author's life, discusses the philosophical influences, and then catalogs the themes of the novels. Robert Coles's book on Percy at times brings us close to the man, but his analysis of Percy's work is vitiated by an all-inclusive concern with psychology and sociology.

Literature is always being reduced to something else, as Harold Bloom reminds us: "The issue is reduction and how best to avoid it."[27] Most of the people who have written about Aiken and Percy have reduced their work to psychology, philosophy, biography, thematic conceptualization, patterns of imagery, arrangements of symbols, or what have you—but of course this is what most people who write about literature tend to do. Some do it in a very subtle manner; others do it quite blatantly. The reason reduction is inevitable for most critics is that there is no clear idea anymore of what art is nor is there a very clear picture in many minds about the value of art in society. One of the chief reasons for studying Aiken and Percy together is that in their long apprenticeship they evolved for themselves both theories of art and certain ideas about the role of art in relationship to science in modern society. The success of these early and long endeavors enabled them to become at last not only valuable literary artists but that great rarity of the times, men of letters.

---

[26]Walker Percy, "Questions They Never Asked Me: A Self-Interview," *Esquire* 88 (December 1977): 184.

[27]Bloom, *Anxiety of Influence*, 94.

The Long Apprenticeship

Chapter III*

I

The man (or woman) of letters traditionally views literature as part of the forward movement of world civilization, a movement that has helped to lift humanity out of a savage past. Thus, the man of letters feels called, in his prime, to make large statements in terms of both art and philosophy about the growth and development of civilization. These telling statements are often made in essay form or even in oral communication, and sometimes—as in the case of Samuel Johnson's verbal wit—they form the chief basis of the person's literary reputation.

The need has always been great in twentieth-century America for a generalist like the person of letters, one who is able to make large state-

*The author gratefully acknowledges permission to use material from his article "Conrad Aiken and the Life of Reason," *Southern Quarterly* 21 (Fall 1982): 148-58.

ments about the transformations of modern civilization; an attempt to fill this need is seen in the efforts of the American press to turn William Faulkner into a man of letters by dubbing him the sage of Yoknatawpha. Faulkner and Hemingway, in spite of their lack of higher education, had acquired far more learning on their own than most people realized, but they seldom ever spoke as participators in the process of civilization. This is because Faulkner and Hemingway are solidly a part of that branch of serious American letters from Whitman and Mark Twain down to the present that has denied the systematic use of knowledge and concepts as a part of the tools of the conscious literary artist. From Whitman and Twain through Frost, Faulkner, Hemingway, and Dos Passos, it has been assumed that the literary artist must fail if he accepts knowledge and ideas as important ingredients of his art. In fact, in the twentieth century this movement, which is now worldwide, proclaims the necessity of the artist's turning only to man and nature for material without reference to the main current of civilization. It is believed that civilization itself is dead and that the artist must "express" himself or even, like D. H. Lawrence or G. B. Shaw, become a prophet who will create a new civilization.

Western civilization—the only one still alive, Toynbee tells us—is undergoing enormous transformation, but civilization itself has not been abolished, no matter how loudly the barbarians cry that they stand on its corpse. The need to renew culture and civilization through a reviving of basic concepts is, as much as anything, the reason that there has been since the later sixties a renewal of interest in the life and work of Conrad Aiken. Certain other modern artists have more imaginative power, and Aiken himself was always the first to admit this when speaking and writing about his early friends T. S. Eliot and Ezra Pound or about men like Dylan Thomas and William Faulkner, whom he promoted with his criticism and personal support. But Aiken always had a deeper view of letters as a profession than these and other literary figures. When Eliot plunged into the medieval past and gave new life to his early prejudices and Ezra Pound became a crackpot prophet against usury, Jews, Roosevelt, and democracy, Aiken continued to work as poet, fiction writer, and essayist in the ongoing literary tradition that he had inherited from Emerson and the English Romantics. But—and this is one of the chief reasons Aiken was rediscovered in the sixties and seventies—he could without giving up any of his heritage become a full participator with Eliot, Pound, Joyce, and Faulkner in the movement of modern letters, which is often deeply iconoclastic. Aiken too could be iconoclastic but not to the point of surrendering civilization and its traditions. Aiken held on to, all of his life, that part of the literary tradition he claimed as his own mainly because for many years he prepared himself for playing a role in the intellectual tradition of Western civilization. This preparation is what I call the long apprenticeship, and in a sense it continued all of his life. Early in his years at Harvard and possibly even before, Aiken realized that to be a poet he would have to immerse himself in the literature of the past and present. However, as he studied with George Santayana and other professors in what has been called the greatest period in Harvard's history, he came to see clearly that he could not allow science and philosophy to slip beyond his grasp while he was preparing himself for the profession of letters. Instead, he began to build a viewpoint based in the main on certain nineteenth and twentieth-century concepts. Growing up and writing poems as early as the late eighteen nineties, the young Aiken was aware of the growing movement of Aestheticism with its emphasis on the artist's withdrawing into art as a kind of refuge. After all, the twentieth century was to be a time of intense specialization. Why should not the artist limit himself strictly to his art? For Aiken to become a generalist in a world of specialists, including even most literary people, would indeed mean a long apprenticeship. Perhaps, he sometimes thought, the new barbarians were right when they maintained that the intellect cripples the imagination. But Aiken knew that Emerson and those of the mainstream of English and Continental literature had indeed created imaginatively while still holding to both knowledge and concepts. Aiken, always a poet of the American liberal tradition, was also deeply conservative, refusing to surrender his portion of the intellectual heritage of the West.

Only two important American literary figures of the contemporary scene have been as determined as Aiken in maintaining his role as artist while still affirming the intellectual traditions of the West. These two are Walker Percy and Saul Bellow. In *Humboldt's Gift* and *The Dean's December*, Bellow revealed his deep awareness of the continuing tradition of the sciences and the humanities in Western civilization. Percy, like Bellow, has continued to maintain in his art a worldview that takes into account knowledge and concepts found in science and the humanities. In order to be able to do this, Percy, like Aiken, underwent a long apprenticeship that enabled him not only to perfect the artistic form of the kind of novel he felt called to write but also to develop, slowly and over many years, a view of life that took into account both the violence and pain of the disintegrating aspects of American culture as well as the existence of the intellectual foundations that still undergirded American life. Percy, like Aiken, had a tenacity that caused him to hold onto certain knowledge and concepts that most serious American writers in their drive to become literary "successes" simply never had time for—and probably never very much believed in.

Most American writers, even when they are learned, are shy about it and hesitate to formulate concepts based on their learning. But Percy, like Aiken before him, is secure in his definition of his profession as literary artist. He has stated in interviews that he feels closer to modern continental novelists than to his American counterparts, pointing out, as he does in one interview in 1974, that "European novels are more philosophical, more novels of ideas."[1] In 1980 in an interview in the *New York Times,* which appeared shortly after publication of *The Second Coming,* Percy again stated his belief in the importance of ideas in writing his kind of novel. He went on in the same interview to describe the influence of Sartre and Camus on his fiction: "The American novelist tends to distinguish between reflections on our universal predicament and what can be told in fiction, whereas the French see nothing wrong with writing novels that address what they consider the deepest philosophical issues."[2] Like Sartre, in particular, Percy began his career with a major interest in philosophy and moved on out to larger considerations of man through imaginative literature. Like other intellectuals before him who believe no basic separation between art and intellect should be observed—like, for instance, Dostoyevski, whose work helped launch Percy's philosophical career—the Louisiana author has for years now believed that it is possible through combining literature, philosophy, and science to arrive at a holistic understanding that will bring man closer to his own reality than will any of the abstractions of social science, which have come to represent the height of man's knowledge about himself for most people.

Percy began his intellectual course as a man of scientific abstractions by preparing for a career in medicine. He had an obvious literary bent, writing sonnets for sale to fellow students in Greenville (MS) High School, but the strong effect of his foster father, W. A. Percy, in urging him to

---

[1]Barbara King, "Walker Percy Prevails," *Southern Voices* (May/June 1974): 6.

[2]James Atlas, "A Portrait of Mr. Percy," *New York Times Book Review,* 29 June 80, 30.

choose a profession led him into the specialization of premedical training when he entered the University of North Carolina. When Percy, because of tuberculosis, was forced to give up active work in medicine not long after receiving his M.D. from Columbia, he turned to reading writers like Dostoyevski, who convinced him that man cannot be summed up in scientific abstractions. But at the same time he in no way sacrificed his knowledge of science on the altar of literature. He was not suddenly "converted" to either the literary or the philosophical view. The basic similarity with Aiken's development is striking. There are many outward differences, some of them due to the times and some to individual upbringing, but both men, one might say, began life with a strong respect for the learned professions and even for higher education in the Ivy league. Despite all the suffering he endured at the hands of his father, Aiken never lost his respect and admiration for medicine and numbered among his close friends many doctors and psychiatrists. Charmenz S. Lenhart, who knew Aiken well when he was Poet in Residence at the Library of Congress and afterwards, describes the pride the poet sometimes displayed as being both the son of a doctor and a graduate (and the son of a graduate) of Harvard University.[3] Aiken was also proud of his father's poems and other literary efforts, and in later years read them with great satisfaction.

Percy too was deeply influenced by his foster father, Will Percy—a lawyer, poet, and author. Yet he felt the need to break with this poetic heritage in order to take up the profession of medicine. No doubt at the time he made this decision in the thirties, the gap—always widening—between literature and the sciences made him feel it was necessary to choose science as a way of life. Certainly his later criticism in his fiction of those who settle on science as the only true knowledge about man indicates his grasp of an important modern problem: the failure of scientific abstractions to provide an adequate understanding of man. The problem for Aiken was somewhat different. Because of the example of his father and his maternal grandfather Potter and later of George Santayana, the strongest influence on him at Harvard, Aiken never suffered that split between the literary intelligence and the scientific mind that Percy and many others in our times inevitably had or have to undergo. Yet his refusal to go along with the prevailing notion of art as a realm unto itself made Aiken always something of a loner in modern literature and helped to keep him from receiving the

---

[3]Unpublished letter to author.

kind of attention that T. S. Eliot, say, found awaiting him once modernism was fully accepted as a literary movement. By the same token, Percy's insistence on adapting scientific and philosophical views to fiction made him for a time a literary loner until in the seventies he began to receive widespread recognition.

For reasons going back in part to childhood trauma, both writers were destined to be loners—not personally because both have had a wide circle of friends but rather professionally. Yet this role of loner, or intellectual outsider, was always significant in their development and helped to make them the unusual and important literary figures that they have become in the late twentieth century. It well may be a key factor in making their work an important influence in the postmodern literature that should come into its own in the twenty-first century. It was the life of the outsider that made it possible for them to undergo the long apprenticeship that finally resulted in an imaginative and philosophical solution to certain human problems neglected by more prominent thinkers and artists. Above all, that apprenticeship helped to give them the stature they have today as American men of letters.

II

The long apprenticeship to science, philosophy, and literary art that can be discerned in the lives of Conrad Aiken and Walker Percy—an apprenticeship continuing, in a sense, into the old age of both—was necessary because of the difficulty of the times in which they worked and the problems with which they dealt. These problems can be defined in different ways: the separation between the sciences and the humanities, the loss of humanity through the modern emphasis on specialization, the split between the mind and heart of man, the modern soul that is disowning its humanity in order to destroy itself in increasing cycles of violence, the death of language and the failure of communication. As a young man, even while at Harvard studying with Santayana and closely associated with T. S. Eliot, Aiken pursued an apprenticeship on all three fronts: science, philosophy, and poetry. When tuberculosis ended his full-time devotion to medicine, Percy became a philosophical apprentice without giving up his studies in science. Unlike Aiken, whose publications as a young man are important, Percy remained silent until 1954, when he published his first philosophical essay in *Thought Quarterly*. Then in the late fifties he turned to the novel, writing two apprentice works before submitting for publication his match-less *The Moviegoer,* which appeared in 1962.

In spite of the outward differences in their careers, there is a basic sim-ilarity in their approach to modern man's most important problems. Both made their first major efforts through a philosophical approach to language and communication. Both went on to define the problem of failed com-munications in terms of the split between reason and the emotions (head and heart) and the desire of millions of people on the side of reason to ig-nore and repress the emotions and the equally strong desire of other mil-lions to deny reason a place in human affairs. In his first essay, "Symbol as Need," Percy stated the modern problem in terms of "the disastrous effects of the mind-body split."[4] Here also he enunciated the most impor-tant discovery of his long apprenticeship: the concept of the true symbol as being in essence a means of bridging the gap between what are often perceived as basically different realities. For Aiken too, language was the means of reconciling man's warring opposites. Jay Martin, in fact, sums up Aiken's conclusions concerning language, which were reached in his early criticism, as the poet's "insistence that language is the means by which man is perfected and saved."[5] For Aiken poetry was the highest form of communication, and in his greatest collection of poems—those poems he called the Preludes—the poet continues searching for the meaning and use of the true symbol. The result of this poetic exploration was that Aiken developed a clear vision of a fact he had glimpsed in his earlier essays: that man cannot center his life on language alone, as some literary artists have tried to do, if he is to use it effectively. Instead he must come to understand the world before he can use language to bring good to man and to the world by creating order out of chaos—an order, a harmony, that establishes a right interaction between the different levels of human reality.

But what roads did Aiken and Percy take to reach their conclusions about language as being the key to solving the problem of the dissociation of the modern sensibility? Aiken had a direct link to nineteenth-century transcendentalism through his maternal grandfather, William James Pot-ter, the New England rebel minister who was Emerson's close friend; and

---

[4]Walker Percy, *The Message in the Bottle: How Queer Man Is, How Queer Language Is, and What One Has to Do with the Other* (New York: Farrar, Straus & Giroux, 1979) 292.

[5]Jay Martin, *Conrad Aiken: A Life of His Art* (Princeton: Princeton University Press, 1962) 137.

he studied with one of the important twentieth-century philosophers, George Santayana. Percy worked in the area of academic philosophy, publishing in scholarly American journals, but he also was influenced by existentialists like Søren Kierkegaard and Gabriel Marcel. In fact, his novels can even be called existential fiction much in the manner of the fiction of Camus and Sartre. But there are important differences. Percy's fiction does not simply explicate a philosophical position, as some of his critics have suggested. For both Aiken and Percy, imaginative literature is the major tool of philosophical investigation. It does not merely reflect the ''rational'' thought of certain philosophers but instead points toward a particular solution to human problems—a solution that may be defined as the unification through symbols of the split within the soul, the split between humans themselves, and the split between man and nature as well as between man and God. But, as Aiken and Percy have suggested, people cannot live in a world of words. Effective language must grow out of a worldview based on lived experience. Therefore a brief description of how the two authors arrived at their world visions is necessary.

III

Conrad Aiken always considered his Unitarian grandfather a central influence on his life and work. In *Ushant* and in certain key poems, he sees William James Potter as representative of the influence of all of his ancestors. In fact, Potter becomes, in Jungian terms, an archetype of the wise old man: that initiatory figure without whose help the pilgrim of the soul can never make his journey toward expanded consciousness. Thus, as Martin has said, Potter is to Aiken ''present both as past and future, dead and living.''[6] But besides serving as an archetype that activates certain latent powers in the unconscious mind, which the true archetype always does, Grandfather Potter was at once a living remembered presence and a direct influence as well as a literary and philosophical conduit through which Aiken received his New England heritage of Emersonian transcendentalism. Martin rightly says that Aiken ''inherited this philosophy [transcendental-

---

[6]Ibid., 240.

ism] more directly than almost any other modern poet.''[7] Aiken, of course, profoundly modified nineteenth-century transcendentalism to suit the purposes of modernism, but at heart he always saw himself as one continuing what he believed to be a central tradition of Western civilization that in both his and his forebears' eyes always pointed toward a rebirth into a higher form of Western culture, which by the end of the century had become the dominant culture of the entire world. The one thing Potter, Emerson, and the others had missed—Aiken believed—was the power of chaos, a power that Melville had understood and had effectively dramatized in his best fiction. Aiken, one of the first modern critics to plumb the depths of Melville, knew that everything in Melville's vision of chaos had to be faced. But he also believed, most of the time anyway, that the optimistic vision of transcendentalism could still be affirmed in our century while taking into full account the forces of chaos and the negatives inevitably accompanying an awareness of these forces.

The problem with calling Aiken a transcendentalist and a Unitarian is that those words have lost much of the meaning they had for earlier generations and for Aiken himself. Today we see transcendentalism as an aspect of the Romantic movement and therefore a kind of emotional and mystical revolt against the rationalism of the eighteenth century. Unitarianism today connotes a rational viewpoint that is mainly liberal and nonstructural in its religious aspects. But transcendentalism for Emerson and his friend William James Potter was not so much a revolt against anything as it was a statement concerning the need for a new synthesis of knowledge, reason, and the powers of heart and soul: one that proclaimed the need for a creative man seen as the remolder of cultural values and not as a recluse or a rebel separated from culture and society. For Potter, Unitarianism should have been the religious expansion of the transcendental

---

[7]Ibid., 209. Martin goes into detail concerning the similarities between Emerson and Aiken. Martin knew Aiken the man and the writer very well and no doubt wrote with the poet's full approval these words: ''A comparison of Aiken to Emerson's description of Goethe is apt; for it seems to me that Aiken has consistently developed toward the image of the Poet and Writer as Emerson characterized them in *Representative Men*. And he has attempted to fuse both roles in his career. I do not mean to imply that Aiken has deliberately or consciously imitated Emerson's sense of Goethe and Shakespeare, but by temperament and education he naturally followed in the tradition of the nineteenth-century sage, epitomized in Emerson's books, and recently discussed in John Holloway's *The Victorian Sage*. Sometimes Aiken's work so closely parallels Emerson's descriptions that his poetic activity seems to be a comment on them'' (208).

movement, but, like Emerson, he found the Unitarianism of his day already too narrow to encompass his own kind of transcendentalism, whose chief tenet was that man would eventually become godlike in nature. Potter left the main body of Unitarianism and carried his New Bedford parish with him, becoming minister of the First Congregational Society in New Bedford. He rebelled against the religious mainstream of his day, but he found a place in society (in his own eyes) as a leader in the reshaping of a culture grown stale. As one who took his role of cultural leader seriously—one, as Martin suggests, who became a kind of Victorian sage in the tradition so well described by John Holloway—Potter not only accepted the visionary aspects of transcendentalism, but he also cultivated those aspects related to the conscious reasoning process. Potter studied at Berlin, Tübingen, and Heidelberg and even visited Baron Alexander von Humboldt. He fully accepted Darwinism and believed that any religion that would undergird modern culture must withstand the most searching rational criticism. Potter no doubt saw himself as one of the sages called to lead man into a new era in which reason would be joined with spiritual vision to form the religious and other cultural institutions that would renew the life of humanity.

Aiken knew only too well that the twentieth century did not open out to the new vistas that the transcendentalists foresaw. Or was there a necessary delay for man to fight the mythic chaos monster before the new age could dawn? *Ushant,* Aiken's deepest book, says as much. Aiken never gave up his grandfather's vision of the unity of religion, science, philosophy, and the arts. In the *Paris Review* interview of 1968, Aiken still proudly speaks of his grandfather as one who had learned "a determined acceptance of Darwinism and all the rest of the scientific fireworks of the nineteenth century."[8] In my own discussion with Aiken in the late sixties, the poet gave every indication he was continuing his apprenticeship to the published sermons of William James Potter. He reiterated what he had already said in the 1968 *Paris Review* interview: "I regard myself simply as a continuance of my grandfather, and primarily, therefore, as a teacher and a preacher."[9]

Aiken spoke to me several times with deep feeling about the influence of George Santayana on his thought and work, even stating that the philosopher

---

[8]"Conrad Aiken: An Introduction," *Paris Review* (Winter/Spring 1968): 117.

[9]Ted R. Spivey, "Conrad Aiken: Resident of Savannah," *The Southern Review* 8 (October 1972): 802.

had at the same time had an influence on T. S. Eliot which, Aiken said, Eliot was careful to cover up. It was Santayana, nearly as much as grandfather Potter, who provided intellectual and visionary aid as part of the poet's long apprenticeship. Martin is excellent in showing Aiken's roots in nineteeth-century transcendentalism, but his book contains only one brief reference to Santayana.[10] Martin makes too easy an interpretation concerning the growth of Aiken's mind and art out of nineteenth-century transcendentalism. It was Santayana who more than anyone else helped the young Aiken to link some of the best insights of an earlier New England culture with the unusual demands made on the artist by the chilling winds of the twentieth century. Santayana had faced the cultural rootlessness of modern man, the isolation the modern poet and thinker was forced to endure even in cultural hubs like Boston. And yet he could affirm what he called the life of reason, a term that provided the title for a major philosophical work published in 1905 and 1906 just before Aiken began his career at Harvard in 1907. Few budding men of letters could have been more fortunate than Aiken was when he entered the foremost university in America in the early twentieth century. Always in need of new philosophical insight and already devoted to the calling of letters, the young poet in time found himself sitting in the class of a man whose lectures were to find their way into the book *Three Philosophical Poets,* a work that would always be central in Aiken's apprenticeship as man of letters.

The lectures that were to be turned eventually into *Three Philosophical Poets* helped to give the young Aiken insights into the philosophical poet as one whose imaginative vision encompassed the prevailing vision as well as the general thought of his age. In writing about Lucretius, Dante, and Goethe as poets who were also philosophers, Santayana helped to reinforce the inherited view of Potter's transcendentalism that the great poets always show man a way of life on which all human faculties—reason, emotion, intuition, and will—could be harmoniously blended in the same person. But what Santayana no doubt most deeply imparted in the lectures Aiken heard was what he had most profoundly stated in possibly his greatest philosophical book, *The Life of Reason.* In this work, published when its author was forty-two, San-

---

[10]Martin's book is generally quite good, but it neglects the role of Santayana in developing the poet's thought. Aiken was aware of this and other limitations of the book, which was written with the close cooperation of the poet, Martin being a longtime disciple of his. Aiken told me that he believed Martin would have liked to rewrite the book after its publication. Another book, *Conrad Aiken* by Frederick J. Hoffman, appeared the same year as Martin's book, 1962. Aiken disliked this book.

tayana laid down the basic premise of his philosophical speculation: the highest goal of humanity is to attain the life of reason.

Santayana has always been considered a maverick among modern philosophers, though his importance has not been totally denied by the prevailing school of analytical thinkers in Anglo-American philosophy. A poet and a novelist as well as a brilliant essayist, Santayana was also a technical philosopher who played a specialized philosophical role in the realm of aesthetics in particular and in the analysis of myth as a means of understanding the religious life of earlier times. Yet his deepest philosophical thrust could not be accepted by most modern philosophers, who mainly believe that philosophy can exist only in a specialized category presided over by certain high priests whose qualifications are supposed to be a disciplined reason. In *Scepticism and Animal Faith,* Santayana demolishes in one sentence the pretensions of much of modern philosophy: "Philosophy fell into the same snare when in modern times it ceased to be the art of thinking and tried to become that impossible thing, the science of thought."[11] The snare Santayana has earlier referred to in the text is that of modern historians who read their own subjective impressions into philosophers and poets. Santayana's key statement follows: "Thought can be found only by being enacted."

Thus Santayana shows his relationship to Emerson and that New England transcendentalist's dictum that the scholar is man thinking. Born in Spain but brought to Boston at an early age, Santayana was never able to find a meaningful life upon return to the land of his birth. Boston with its transcendental associations provided a certain cultural food for him. But, like one who followed Emerson's basic rule of "Trust thyself," Santayana was not content to elucidate various aspects of Bostonian or even modern European culture. He was a man thinking and not primarily a student of other people's philosophies. Therefore, he went back to the course of what he came to call the life of reason: the classic Greeks. Santayana's preference for the Greeks tells us something about his own philosophical background. As a thinker and a literary artist, he sought to embrace a concept of harmonious living. In doing so he reminds us that we are victims of a subjectivist rebellion against rationalism. Instead of modern subjectivism, Santayana emphasized the possibility of human life based on an idea of reason, not defined as we do today in terms of conscious thought but in earlier terms of the deepest principle within man.

---

[11]*The Philosophy of Santayana,* ed. Irwin Edman (New York: The Modern Library, 1936) 436.

Most modern thinkers see reason as a tool that can be used to accomplish aims related to the objective world, and, because they are still under the spell of the Cartesian split, they assume that the subjective life out of which art springs must be governed by some principle of its own separate from reason. Santayana, following the classic Greeks, said in effect that all men's activities, when rightly performed, spring from the life of reason. And thus concerning art, he could write, "Of all reason's embodiments art is therefore the most splendid and complete."[12] Thus Santayana could divide his multivolumed work on reason into such categories as "Reason in Society," "Reason in Art," and "Reason in Science." As a student of aesthetics and a literary artist himself, Santayana believed art to be the highest achievement of reason. He also believed that science, religion, and even that ordinary thought we know as common sense spring from the same center of power and understanding within humanity that the Greeks thought of as reason.

The maverick quality of Santayana, which Aiken loved because he too was a maverick, caused him to view the life of reason not as some remote, intellectualized life above human feeling, as the title of his book might suggest to the modern mind. Instead, for Santayana, reason is based on a category that has been eliminated by most modern philosophers: spirituality, a concept essential to his idea of the life of reason. In his definition, "Spirituality likes to say, Behold the lilies of the field! For its secret has the same simplicity as their vegetative art; only spirituality has succeeded in adding consciousness without confusing instinct."[13] The way Santayana uses the term spirituality links him quite clearly to the New England transcendentalists. Like Emerson or Potter, Santayana was indeed a maverick but one who believed that it was the great majority who had departed from the true path of reason.

If one would catch the true transcendental note in Santayana, he must look at such incidental essays as "A Brief History of My Opinions" in which the philosopher sums up his vision of the arts and his philosophical purpose. Santayana speaks the language of transcendentalism when he writes that "a society will breed the art which it is capable of, and which it deserves; but even in its own eyes this art will hardly be important or beautiful unless it engages deeply the resources of the soul." The key word here is *soul*, that source in humans of the powers that make true art possible. With a full awareness that culture was dissolving, he wrote the next oft-quoted sentence: "The arts may

---

[12]Ibid., 224.
[13]Ibid., 191.

die of triviality, as they were born of enthusiasm."[14] Aiken and others who
were experiencing the new modernist movement sensed the emergence of a
vast artistic triviality, but they also felt an enthusiasm of creativity in modern
art—a feeling, as Aiken himself later said, that a great new creative period
was getting under way.

For Santayana reason was the synthesizing power within man. He believed that even in a time when societies are dissolving, the man of reason
will still know the transports of rational life that are—as they were for Plato
and Aristotle—moments of contemplation. Thus for the man of reason, if the
arts die in triviality, there is still the life of reason: "there will always be beauty,
or a transport akin to the sense of beauty, in any high contemplative moment.
And it is only in contemplative moments that life is truly vital, when routine
gives way to intuition, and experience is synthesized and brought before the
spirit in its sweep and truth."[15] Clearly, then, for Santayana the life of reason
is not a life devoted totally to cogitation, as most today would take it to be,
but it is an achieving of essential insights. At the end of "A Brief History of
My Opinions," Santayana thus sums up the aims of all his philosophical efforts: "The intention of my philosophy has certainly been to attain, if possible, such wide intuitions, and to celebrate the emotions with which they fill
the mind."[16] Instead of intuition Aiken would use the term *vision,* and he
would speak of the "evolution of consciousness" as an extension of human
vision. As for emotion, Aiken would center on what he considered the most
basic of emotions: love. Thus Aiken's own pursuit of the life of reason led
him to seek a path that Santayana pointed out to him in those early years. Aiken always admitted his indebtedness to Santayana, but he would find at least
one other master even closer to him because he was more modern, more in
tune with Aiken's own suffering. That master was Sigmund Freud.

I will discuss later the precise uses made of Freud's thinking by Aiken,
but suffice it to say here that Freud helped Aiken to be a transcendentalist in
modern intellectual dress. The fact that Freud was a medical doctor and natural scientist helped to endear him to the son of a doctor and a lover of science. Freud dealt fearlessly, as no Olympian master of the poet's early
inspiration would do, with sex and its observation, including those painful
struggles between parents and children. Freud encouraged, demanded even,

---

[14]Ibid., 20-21.
[15]Ibid.
[16]Ibid.

as necessary for sexual healing, an extended talking out of psychic problems. Defying all Victorian reticence and stoicism, he proclaimed an age of soul-baring, and nothing probably appealed any more to Aiken—who would himself become a confessional poet. Freud was a man of reason in the generally accepted sense of this century, which means that he honored the conscious reasoning process without affirming reason in the Greek sense of a unifying principle in human activity. But Freud also accepted as real the emotional and instinctive life of humans, and he sought by scientific methods to increase not only the power of sexual love but of all the love life of humanity. As it was for the classic Greeks like Aristotle, and for Santayana following in their path, human happiness was to be based in this new theory on the idea of a harmonious life as the goal of living. James Joyce rightly thought it was fitting that his surname in Irish had the same meaning as Freud's in German: joy. The release of the creative emotions of love and joy was Freud's goal, and his method to accomplish it was twofold: confession and dreaming. Since Aiken honored vision almost as much as love, Freud's doctrine of the dream enthralled him. Charmenz S. Lenhart recalls that years after first discovering Freud, Aiken "could scarcely wait at night to see what dreams he would have." Although Lenhart thought that Aiken was intellectually indebted to Freud, "he explored the unconscious to a degree that links him . . . with Jung."[17] The transcendentalists, who by no means rejected concepts, honoring as they did all intellectual activity, still put vision, intuition, and emotion at the top of their value system. But these qualities seemed to have faded by the end of the century, and Santayana honors them without exhibiting them very often in his own work, so much so that many students of philosophy would not even think of him as having transcendental connections. Freud, however, helped to bring a consideration of dreams back into life, even everyday life. The visions contained in certain dreams came not as the result of transcendental rapture but as the normal flow of the psyche, whose observation Freud recommended for everybody. Like Freud, Aiken was a psychological democrat: a creative dream life existed for everybody, he believed, who observed their own dreams. Freud thus helped Aiken make a step beyond his transcendental forebears, a step into the world of everyday psychopathology, which could, along with the insights provided by dreams, reveal a strange world of sexual struggle and sudden delight.

---

[17]Unpublished letter to author.

Freudianism, as most people know, began to overshadow Freud's theories not long after they were enunciated. But Aiken was never really a Freudian, as Percy was for a time. By 1917 Aiken had discovered Nicolas Kostyleff's *Le Mecanisme Cerebral de la Pensee,* and he announced in a review that the Kostyleff work had gone beyond Freud on matters of art. Two years later Aiken in his critical work *Scepticisms* would, according to Martin, give no person such authority as Kostyleff, though Freud would be quoted more often. For Kostyleff poetry results from cerebral mechanisms that are sometimes accidental, sometimes induced.[18] Doubtless, with his own emotional shocks at an early age in mind, Aiken saw Kostyleff as a theorist who understood aspects of the psychological side of poetry not yet explored. In fact, Aiken's interest in Kostyleff's work reveals that as a critic he very early was interested in the nature of language itself. And, as Martin has suggested, the "unique part of Aiken's theory of language is the psychological analysis which he imposed upon his Platonic foundation."[19] The relationship of his theory of language and his literary criticism to his entire work I will analyze in another section because an understanding of this side of his work is necessary to understand his role as man of letters.

Aiken's study of Kostyleff is but one aspect of the poet's efforts to reclaim his transcendental background. Freud, Kostyleff, and the archaeologist Flinders Petrie, whose Egyptian studies greatly helped the poet in formulating his personal philosophy, all were fully modern and rational in the twentieth-century sense; and each one helped him to continue a long philosophical and literary apprenticeship into old age. Aiken was always a student, particularly of his grandfather's sermons because they were, in a sense, the original impetus of his life apprenticeship, but he was always finding new and deeper ways of looking at life and art. Aiken early was forced to struggle with the agonies of his own life, and he turned to art, to vision, and to knowledge to find ways of rising above its limitations. At the same time, he sought—though not always successfully—to escape being imprisoned in the palaces of art, vision, and knowledge. The escape route lay in a return to the agonies and joys of the individual self. What made it possible for Aiken to hold together opposites like life and art was his thorough grounding in the visionary life of transcendentalism as he first found it in Potter, then as he saw it modified in Santayana's vision of the life of reason, and finally as he followed the understanding

---

[18]Martin, *Conrad Aiken,* 78-79.
[19]Ibid., 134.

of Freud, Kostyleff, and Petrie in developing his own transcendental insights. If one should ask what is the essential meaning of Aiken's transcendentalism, I would answer by quoting Frederick J. Hoffman: "The key to Aiken's appraisal of transcendentalism is his view of it as supraphenomenal."[20] Hoffman backs up this statement by quoting Aiken himself on the subject: "It was a mode of apprehension that transcended one's sensory knowledge of the phenomenal world and all the experiences of the senses."[21] Alongside this definition of transcendentalism, one must place a key concept of Santayana's: harmony. But before dealing with the centrality of that concept in Aiken's work, it is necessary to examine in some detail Walker Percy's apprenticeship.

IV

From various remarks Walker Percy has made, it seems obvious that the strong influence of W. A. Percy led to his choosing medicine as a career. That one choice seemed to close off a budding interest in literature in particular and the humanities in general. Like Aiken, he found in his teen years that writing poems was an almost natural activity for him. But when he entered the University of North Carolina, he was engulfed by courses in chemistry and biology, though he did find time to write articles for the University's literary magazine. "All I can say," he told interviewer John Carr, "is that I was interested first in philosophy, in writing essays, although I never took a course in philosophy at Chapel Hill."[22] Aiken's father had been a medical doctor, a poet, an inventor, in fact, a kind of Renaissance man; but by the thirties the intensity of specialization was necessary for young men like Walker Percy who wanted professional careers. He would not be free of that intensity until tuberculosis forced him to give up medicine shortly after receiving his M.D. He reports a sense of relief at being freed from specialization. His real education, his real apprenticeship, that is, began in a sanitorium in New York state when he began to read philosophy seriously. Dostoyevski and existential thinkers like Sartre and Camus helped to open up Percy's mind, but it was

[20]Frederick J. Hoffman, *Conrad Aiken* (New York: Twayne Publishers, 1962) 34.
[21]Ibid.
[22]John Carr, "An Interview with Walker Percy," *Georgia Review* 25 (Fall 1971): 318.

finally in the early fifties that he discovered the philosopher to whom, in his own words, he would "owe the greatest debt," Søren Kierkegaard.[23]

Percy is like Aiken in having a family member who passed on a strong philosophical tradition: this figure was Will Percy, who gave his own version of Southern stoicism to his young relative. Also, as Aiken found Santayana, Percy would discover a dominant philosopher, Kierkegaard. But here the similarity ends. Percy rebelled against stoicism, though he would never fully free himself from it, and Kierkegaard for him provided material for his own growing inner revolt against the secularized, scientific humanism that dominated most people's thinking by the time he had entered medical school. Percy would never rebel against either science or medicine; indeed, he would seek ways of viewing them both as part of the larger field of philosophy, to which they once belonged before specialization became intense. But Percy is by nature a kind of rebel. He told John Carr that "I've always found . . . my main motivation, the wellspring of my writing, I hate to say it, is usually antagonism, disagreeing with somebody and wanting to get it right."[24] Behind what was probably a necessary rebelliousness to break the too tight hold Will Percy and scientism long had upon him, there is a polemical and even prophetic nature that drives him, particularly in his novels, to declaim against the triviality of modern life. Just as the link between New England and Aiken's transcendentalism is clearly evident, so the link between the prophetic Protestantism of the Deep South and Percy's longing to polemicize is not hard to discern. Percy became a Catholic after marrying in 1946; in this decision and what follows it, we see Percy seeking to overcome through a sacramental view of life the rift in his own psyche springing from his anger at the modern world. After all, existentialism is in part the philosophy of the intense individual— the perfervid individual, as Walter Kaufmann calls him—and Percy found it necessary to hold to writers like Sartre and Kierkegaard in order to maintain his individuality against a strong family past and a stronger modern system of thought that seemed to demand total allegiance. Kierkegaard in particular answered questions that the other two thought systems Percy had long lived in did not even consider. One is the problem of despair, which modern man is always denying, and the other is the mysterious nature of the individual, which scientific abstractions cannot deal with. Science is concerned with cate-

---

[23]Bradley R. Dewey, "Walker Percy Talks about Kierkegaard: An Annotated Interview," *The Journal of Religion* 54 (July 1974): 297.

[24]Carr, "Interview," 318.

gories—man, for instance, in relationship to his environment—but it does not explain the role of man as man, a creature who continually refuses to consider himself as only another organism who must adapt to a physical environment.

Percy absorbed the full impact of Kierkegaard and could finally speak thus of the Danish theologian's essay "The Difference between a Genius and an Apostle": "If I had to single out one piece of writing which was more responsible than anything else for my becoming a Catholic, it would be that essay of Kierkegaard's"[25] But Kierkegaard's extreme subjectivity was too great for him. Kierkegaard was too much the man alone, too much the Protestant, and too much the romantic rebel. To counteract the strong influence of Kierkegaard, Percy began to read seriously the Jewish existentialist Martin Buber, a critic of Kierkegaard's doctrine of the single one, and the Catholic existentialist Gabriel Marcel, whose empiricism appealed to him. Both Buber and Marcel emphasize a category of human experience called in philosophical circles intersubjectivity, a term Percy often uses that refers to human relationships. Marcel, in fact, would become an important thinker in the apprenticeship of Walker Percy, possibly even more important than Kierkegaard in spite of Percy's protestations. He was for Percy what Santayana was for Aiken. Instead of the term *spirit,* which Santayana uses, the philosophical term *Being* is employed by Marcel to name the element in existence that transcends sensory experience. For Santayana and Marcel, both of whom were imaginative writers as well as philosophers, the transcendent element has a mysterious quality and can be only occasionally glimpsed. Also for both, all aspects of man's nature—conscious reason as well as intuition and emotion—are involved in the relationship to spirit, or Being. Through a relationship to Being, man's radical alienation is overcome, and intersubjectivity becomes possible.

Percy's greatest single subject is alienation and the despair that results from it. The essay he selected to provide the title for the book that gathers his diverse efforts in the essay form deals specifically with alienation. "The Message in the Bottle" presents man as a castaway but suggests that only a few individuals are even aware of their alienation. Yet the end of the essay suggests the possibility of escape from the "castaway" condition through acceptance of the "news" concerning Being. In this central essay, published in 1959 and reflecting many of the discoveries made on his long apprentice journey, Percy puts St. Thomas alongside Kierkegaard and finally agrees with St.

---

[25]Dewey, "Percy Talks," 282.

Thomas that knowledge and faith do not have to be viewed as inseparable, as the Danish theologian is always suggesting. In speaking of this affirmation of knowledge and reason, Weldon Thornton in his excellent analysis of Percy's studies of language says, "This belief in the value of reason is consistent with and lies behind Percy's aims as an essayist."[26] Thornton goes on to suggest that Percy still is more Kierkegaardian than anything else because in his essays and novels he often satirizes modern man's approaches to his problems as being simplistically reasonable. But this satire is directed at the misuse of reason that springs from the adherence of most men to a "rational" system like that proposed by the philosopher Hegel, who was so often the subject of attack by Kierkegaard. The true use of reason, as Marcel and St. Thomas would teach Percy, can spring only from man's relationship to Being. When man ignores Being and creates a "system" of reason by which to live, he debases reason and drives out love, the power that makes intersubjectivity rewarding and meaningful. In interviews Percy sometimes calls himself a bad Catholic, but his mastery of two Catholic theologians, St. Thomas and Marcel, suggests that he is really very close to the unified thinking of earlier centuries.

One must not, however, lose sight of Percy the rebel, Percy the ironist, Percy the angry man still partly in flight from much in modern civilization. This side of him was always strong, but, as most of his writing and much of his life will show, it is not his dominant side. In fact, some of his best fiction represents a successful attempt to purge himself of this side. But anyone like Aiken and Percy who feels driven even from an early age to find a vision of new and creative life must suffer the pangs of alienation due to revolting against the dominant thought systems of an age. The nineteenth century in the name of progress saddled humanity with the machine system and mechanistic science, and many serious modern artists and thinkers have addressed themselves to the problem of achieving personal and social release from mechanistic systems as well as mechanistic thinking. For Percy, Kierkegaard and French existentialists like Sartre and Camus provided the impetus for revolt. Percy's tuberculosis was itself possibly an unconscious revolt against the confining specialization of his medical training, which had tied him hand and foot to a system. By revolting then and continuing to revolt as a thinker and an artist, Percy achieved an individualism rare in modern authors. This individualism

---

[26]Weldon Thornton, "Walker Percy on Language," *The Art of Walker Percy*, ed. Panthea R. Broughton (Baton Rouge: Louisiana State University Press, 1979) 189.

reminds us of that of many nineteenth-century transcendentalists, who were in one sense the existentialists of their day in that they sought answers to specifically human problems as opposed to the problem of how man could become a cog in the machine system. But the creative artist cannot revolt forever and continue to be creative. Otherwise, he will die before his time, like Kierkegaard, or become old and bitter, like Sartre. The creative artist who achieves his own individuality in a time of revolt and withdrawal and then returns with renewed understanding and vision brings with him powers that are often both creative and fructifying, though it may take people a while to find out the importance of this artist's gifts. Percy is fortunate that the discovery of this healing power in his work began to occur during his lifetime.

Marcel, before Percy, had made the same return. When his own powers as a thinker and artist reached their peak, Marcel realized he was no longer an existentialist and refused to call himself by that name. He had indeed been a Catholic existentialist, but, though it was a necessary period in his life, Marcel had to move on to become a celebrator of Being. He had struggled with the problem of freedom, along with his fellow French existentialists, and some of his best writing is about man's loss of humanity. He asks, when man frees himself from the machine, what does he do? What is he for? Marcel's answer is that he is free to participate in Being. In the following passage Marcel repudiates the negativism of existentialists like Sartre and proclaims his vision of the creativity inherent in Being:

> These liberating flashes of lightning serve to assure us or to confirm us in the assurance that no matter how much a proud and blind philosophy claims that there exists only an emptiness, a nothing; there is on the contrary a fullness of life, the marvelous resources of a world where promises abound, where everything that exists is called to universal communion, where no possibility, no chance is ever irretrievably lost.[27]

The generous tone, the sense of fullness of life in the above passage is worthy of the best of the earlier transcendentalists. Yet in Marcel there is a strong sense of conscious reason as well as of ritual—far more than is found in the earlier transcendentalists. Marcel, in short, provided Percy with a kind of viewpoint that in time would help him achieve in both his essays and his fiction a unifying vision that would at least occasionally look beyond what he

---

[27]Gabriel Marcel, *Tragic Wisdom and Beyond* (Evanston IL: Northwestern University Press, 1973) 142.

called in his first published essay "the disastrous effects of the mind-matter split."[28]

Marcel is central to Percy's quest for understanding, but like Aiken he never stopped with one or even two masters. His long apprenticeship was performed in relative silence for years, but when he finally entered print in 1954 with "Symbol as Need," he began to achieve recognition as a thinker and philosophical scholar. From 1954 to 1961 he wrote twenty-four articles for such journals as the *Sewanee Review,* the *Journal of Philosophy, Commonweal,* and *Psychiatry.* As Aiken had done when beginning his philosophical studies, Percy concerned himself primarily with problems of language and symbolism. References to Marcel and Kierkegaard are not as frequent in these essays as one might expect. Like Aiken's turning to the empiricism of Kostyleff, Percy often quotes approvingly both empiricists and behaviorists. George Mead and even B. F. Skinner are used to back up some of his best insights. Percy is obviously making overtures to the contemporary sciences of linguistics and semiotics. And yet I agree with Thornton that the chief value of his essays on language "lies in their attempt to win certain basic questions about language, about meaning, about human nature, back from those specialists who have claimed them but neglected them."[29] The essays in *The Message in the Bottle,* which are chiefly about language and meaning, are *attempts* (the original meaning of *essay*) to work out a deeper anthropology than any we have had in this century. What is the nature of man is the question that rings throughout them. The essay form, however, could never be enough for Percy, and that is why in the late fifties we find him, spurred as he tells us by the example of Sartre's *Nausea,* attempting to write philosophical fiction. In *The Moviegoer* and the books that follow it after 1962, Percy would make use of many of those insights he had found in Marcel and Kierkegaard. But above all he would introduce a view of life based on a deep reading of Sigmund Freud. Percy has told us that he was early in his life so caught up in Freud that he inevitably revolted. Therefore, Freud is sometimes the object of satire in his fiction. But mainly what is attacked is Freudianism: that seemingly rational system of explaining humanity that becomes another mechanical trap for the psyche. Yet Percy's novels are, as philosophical fiction, based on his own reading of certain philosophers *and* on insights gained from Freud at first and later from Jung. His novels *Lancelot* and *The Second Coming* are,

---

[28]Percy, *The Message in the Bottle,* 292.
[29]Thornton, "Percy on Language," 190.

as I will later demonstrate, heavily dependent on Jungian insights. Like Aiken, Percy would use certain findings of modern depth psychology as a strong element in the development of his understanding, and this developed understanding would be one of the distinctive features of his imaginative literary work. What emerges in these works is greater than any of the findings of the long apprenticeship and still awaits our full investigation. The philosophical artist often has to wait for the deep meaning of his work to emerge in the imaginative re-creations of his best readers. We are now only just entering upon that emegence as Percy continues to find the good readers every creative writer hopes to have.

V

Childhood trauma acting upon two sensitive intelligences accounts in large part for the devoted apprenticeships of Conrad Aiken and Walker Percy. Both early felt the need to search deeply in science, philosophy, and literature for answers not only to personal problems but to human problems generally. Both had obvious literary talents from an early age on, and it was natural for them to turn to language itself for the purposes of philosophical speculation. But their apprenticeship was more than a search into science, philosophy, and literature; it was an apprenticeship to life in the tradition of the *bildungsroman,* of which Goethe was probably the greatest practitioner. The young apprentice in this tradition always asks the essential question: how to live? It is the question Stein in Joseph Conrad's *Lord Jim* phrased for Marlow as the two discussed the life apprenticeship of the young Jim. It is, in Stein's words, how to be. The intense concern of both writers with this great question led them to create imaginative works that at their best deal quite seriously with this problem.

The apprentice novel as developed in German romanticism inevitably led to the often misunderstood movement called existentialism, a movement that Percy was and is very much a part of. Because the term *existentialism* was not introduced until 1929 by F. H. Heinemann, Aiken was not familiar with the concept in his formative years, and thus he never thought in strictly existial terms. Existentialism is a movement associated mainly with France and central Europe, and Aiken's interest in continental literature was centered primarily in Spanish literature. But Percy was early inspired by existentialism, and to him it does not primarily represent a "perfervid individualism," as it does for Walter Kaufmann.[30] Essentially, Percy tells us, it is a view of "man in a predicament." Speaking thus to John Carr, he said:

> The philosophy I was interested in was what was called then existential phi-
> losophy. Of course, the word no longer means much. It still means a concrete
> view of man, man in a situation, man in a predicament, man's anxiety and
> so on. And I believed this view of man could be handled very well in a novel,
> and I was interested in phenomenology, which is very strongly existentialist:
> the idea of describing accurately how a man feels in a given situation. And
> that's certainly novelistic.[31]

Here Aiken and Percy, in spite of the differences in their terminology, are really at one: both would, after writing philosophically about language and literature, center their main attention on imaginative works in which central characters with backgrounds and attitudes very similar to their own struggle against inertia and push back and sometimes overcome the forces of chaos working within them and against them from the outside. Many think of Percy as primarily a Catholic novelist, but this term is misleading. Although Aiken was a Unitarian all his life and Percy has been a Catholic since 1946, religion as such is not central to either's work. What is central is what Percy in the Carr interview calls the "idea of transcending everydayness."[32] The fact that he would use the term "transcending" suggests how much he belongs to the tradition of transcendentalism, which Aiken clearly subscribed to. Percy is not Emersonian, as is Aiken, but transcendentalism was and is an interna-tional movement whose primary emphasis is placed on that element in man and the universe that transcends the experience of the senses. How much Percy, drawing from Marcel, is a part of this tradition can be seen in the answer he gave when Carr asked him if existentialism proposes the salvation of man. "I'm thinking now about your and Marcel's peculiarly Catholic existential-ism," Carr says as he asks the question. Percy replied,

> I think it would be the idea of transcending the everydayness, of transcending
> being so caught up in the everyday world that even religious reality, espe-
> cially religion, becomes a sort of stereotype and something you go through
> everyday. And Marcel speaks of something he calls 'recollection.' That is, a
> man recollects himself, so he can recover things anew and afresh.[33]

---

[30]Walter Kaufmann, *Existentialism from Dostoevsky to Sartre* (New York: Meridian Books, 1956) 11.

[31]Carr, "Interview," 322.

[32]Ibid.

[33]Ibid.

Both Percy and Aiken are part of that branch of modern existentialism that is still attempting to carry on the old romantic transcendentalism by giving it new life in imaginative letters. The old transcendentalism of the last century played itself out in a kind of remote, idealistic speculation, or else it became enshrined in the Hegelian system of thought, which tended to eliminate the individual in his uniqueness. The new realistic, scientific spirit of the later nineteenth century sought to banish idealism and transcendentalism altogether. Comte, Marx, and Spencer created materialistic systems on the ruins of idealism, and the new empirical and analytical thinkers of this century sought to eliminate all forms of transcendentalism with various linguistic and positivist methods of thought. For positivists transcendental problems are pseudo-problems that are all couched in terms considered to be meaningless. But, as F. H. Heinemann has said, "existentialism arose because the solutions proposed by Hegel and Marx proved ineffective for overcoming the fact of alienation."[34] In this century we have turned more and more to artists, psychologists, and politicians to deal with the problem of overcoming alienation. Actually, it is a problem all three must deal with to be effective in their appointed tasks. Many artists have despaired of the task and have themselves been overcome by their own sense of alienation. But not all artists have been so overcome, though their number is few. Those who have made progress in overcoming alienation have found themselves, often without knowing it, adopting attitudes that are both transcendental and existential. Aiken and Percy are among the very few who knew what their philosophical and scientific roots were and acted accordingly. They are probably the only two of international reputation in our time who are wholly or partly Southern and who have at the same time identified themselves with particular Southern cities.

But what do we learn from the imaginative works themselves? This is the essential question. In the analysis of these works that follows, I hope to demonstrate their discoveries of different ways alienation is overcome. And, finally, because they were so deeply involved all their lives with science, art, philosophy, and religion, I hope to point out ways in which they see the possibility of all these human activities working together. For Aiken and Percy alienation was an early fact of life, and as they grew up they continually saw evidence of it in all human activities. Their own efforts toward healing the split nature of modern life were carried on most intensely in their imaginative creations, and it is to these that we must turn for their insights.

---

[34]F.H. Heinemann, *Existentialism and the Modern Predicament* (New York: Harper Torchbooks, 1958) 12.

Narcissism and the
Way of Pilgrimage

Chapter IV

I

The most obvious similarity between Conrad Aiken and Walker Percy is
that they both see the human being as a wayfarer or pilgrim. Both are intensely aware that most people in this century are afraid to accept this traditional image of man because of a certain inertia. In fact, they record their
own strong feeling of inertia, but they also reveal a conscious choice made
over and over to struggle against inertia in order to become a pilgrim. Their
work is a study not only of the nature of pilgrimage but of the quality of
psychic inertia, which in Freudian terms is called narcissism.

Aiken collected most of his important early poems under the title *The
Divine Pilgrim* with the significant transitional poem ''Changing Mind''

serving, as he tells us in the Preface to the *Collected Poems,* as the coda for his early poetic work on the subject of pilgrimage.[1] "Changing Mind" was written in 1925, the same year his first volume of stories, *Bring! Bring!,* was published. His first novel, *Blue Voyage,* begun in 1922 and published in 1927, is clearly a statement, paralleling *The Divine Pilgrim,* of the author's personal pilgrimage with the short stories serving, as several critics have noted, as a preparation for the first novel. For Aiken the image of the voyage would always be his chief way of depicting the path of the pilgrim. Clearly then, most of the important literary work of Conrad Aiken before 1930 was centered on the concept of human pilgrimage.

Walker Percy was just as clear in his own mind about the subject of pilgrimage as Aiken. His essays on language from the beginning reveal his concern with anthropology, the subject of man's nature. Language for Percy was only a key to man, that most important of subjects. In spite of Aiken's Unitarianism and Percy's Catholicism, both men followed Alexander Pope's dictum that "the proper study of mankind is man." And for both, an understanding of the two psychologists who most influenced them— Freud and Jung—is necessary. Neither could really be called Freudian or Jungian, yet what they are doing in both their fiction and nonfiction is the sort of thing best understood by reference to modern depth psychology.

The origins of the two authors' concepts of pilgrimage are somewhat different: Aiken's lies in his adherence to the transcendentalism of the last century while Percy's has two chief origins, Thomas Aquinas and Gabriel Marcel. Percy has made this quite clear in the Carr interview along with his own thoughts about the relationship of his work to Catholic dogma.

> I think my writings reflect a certain basic orientation toward, although they're not really controlled by, Catholic dogma. As I say, it's a view of man, that man is neither an organism controlled by his environment, nor a creature controlled by the force of history as the Marxists would say, nor is he a detached, wholly objective, angelic being who views the world in a God-like way and makes pronouncements only to himself or to an elite

---

[1]In his Preface to *Collected Poems* (New York: Oxford University Press, 1953) Aiken explains his arrangement of his poetic work up to 1953 and tells why he includes nothing from his first book of poems, *Earth Triumphant.* From his second book, *Turns and Movies,* he retains only the title poem, and from the third book, *Nocturne of Remembered Spring,* only one poem is retained. The poems included under the heading *The Divine Pilgrim* are mostly those he called the "Symphonies," but "Changing Mind" clearly provides a bridge for those later poems of the thirties he called the Preludes.

group. No, he's somewhere between the angels and the beasts. He's a strange creature whom both Thomas Aquinas and Marcel called *homo viator,* man the wayfarer, man the wanderer.[2]

Percy made this statement four years after the publication of his second novel, *The Last Gentleman.* In the year of its publication, he told Ashley Brown that Will Barrett, the hero of *The Last Gentleman,* "is what Gabriel Marcel calls a wayfarer—like an old-fashioned pilgrim on a serious quest."[3] At the very beginning of his first novel, *The Moviegoer,* Percy has his hero, Binx Bolling, declare that he is a seeker of God, that is, an old-fashioned religious pilgrim in modern dress. *The Moviegoer* itself represents the culmination of attempts by the author during the fifties to write two novels dealing with the nature of man. Even as he was publishing some of his best essays in the late fifties, Percy had come to see that only in the story form could he really deal with man the pilgrim as well as with the problems of his own traumatic childhood.

Almost from the beginning of their careers, both Aiken and Percy found critics who understood their vision of the pilgrim. In fact, Aiken was one of the first modern poets to have a full-length study devoted to his work. In his *The Melody of Chaos* (1931), Houston Peterson grasped the essential fact about the archetypal pilgrim in Aiken's prose and poetry, which is that he pushes into both an internal and an external chaos and finds there a certain harmony, or melody, that sustains life. Even more to the point is Henry Murray's essay on the subject of the paradoxical element of creativity to be found within the dissolution of chaos. In taking up the theme of the pilgrim in Aiken, Murray rightly relates it to the meaning of myth, pointing to a "continuous yet protean-eyed, far-ranging consciousness of a mythic poet, unexampled in history yet representative of our age; in fact, the unique but universal consciousness of Conrad Aiken himself."[4] This is extremely high praise from a well-known psychiatrist. Percy received similar high praise from another notable figure, Robert Coles. In one of what is a long series of remarkable similarities, we find that Coles and Murray both are in many ways alike and even had similar backgrounds, both being psychiatrists with varied activities to their credit and both be-

---

[2]John Carr, "An Interview with Walker Percy," *Georgia Review* 25 (Fall 1971): 325.
[3]Ashley Brown, "An Interview with Walker Percy," *Shenandoah* (Spring 1967): 7.
[4]Henry A. Murray, "Conrad Aiken: Poet of Creative Dissolution," *Wake* 11 (1952): 97.

coming after a time professors at Harvard University. Both were personally involved with the two authors they studied, and Coles in his *Walker
Percy: An American Search* says that *The Moviegoer* changed the direction of his entire life: "Walker Percy's novel gave hope to me, helped me
feel stronger at a critical time, when I was somewhat lost, confused, vul-
nerable, and it seemed, drifting badly."[5] Yet Murray and Coles, strangely
in that they were both psychiatrists, do not trace the sources of the two authors' urgency in insisting on the necessity of the pilgrimage to their early
traumas. Webster Schott noted in a review of Coles's book that the author
"for a psychiatrist . . . passes up many a probe."[6] The reason is possibly
that Murray and Coles were too close to their subjects. In fact, as Percy in
the eighties becomes an established success among literary critics, particularly in universities, *and* at the same time a popular success as a book-of-
the-month club author, there is a danger that certain basic questions about
this remarkable writer's works will not be asked. In fact, Percy's statement
that man is a wayfarer should be challenged. Man often finds it more to
his convenience not to be a wayfarer. In some ages the pilgrim is a central
figure, and in others he is peripheral or nonexistent. We may ask if the
theme is not again becoming important. If not, why in the seventies and
eighties does a writer with such a serious theme as Percy's find such a ready
audience?

Aiken possibly understood the problems of the pilgrimage better than
Percy because his childhood shock seems to have been greater and because
from very early in life he sought answers to the meaning of this shock. Percy
writes more simply and directly about pilgrimage, but has his popular success in the seventies and eighties sometimes been a curse? Yet, Aiken himself often longed to have the kind of wide attention Percy began to receive
as early as 1970. Possibly it began on a national scale with Alfred Kazin's
article "The Pilgrimage of Walker Percy" in 1971.[7] Always the shrewd
literary observer, Kazin centers on the concept of pilgrimage and gives the
reader both biographical detail and real insights, but already we find a soft-
ening of the tone of inquiry that also appears the next year when Coles pub-

---

[5]Robert Coles, *Walker Percy: An American Search* (New York: Atlantic-Little, Brown,
1972) 74.

[6]Webster Schott, "Marriage of Two Minds," *New York Times,* 17 February 1973, 15.

[7]Alfred Kazin, "The Pilgrimage of Walker Percy," *Harper's* 243 (June 1971): 81-86.

lishes his book and Martin Luschei comes out with his study.[8] For one thing, Percy's vision of modern man's predicament is far deeper than Kazin, Coles, or Luschei indicates. *Malaise* is certainly not the right word for the problem Percy studies. But Percy himself, as he became a well-known essayist, publishing in *Harper's* and other periodicals in the late seventies, would at times lead readers in the same direction—toward the concept of social malaise. He had by this time begun to exercise the function of man of letters, but still his deepest insights remain to be found in his novels, the central core of all his work.

Percy's novel *The Moviegoer* does deal with the vague uneasiness that is malaise, but it is only a prelude to his later studies of the basic sickness of modern man—which springs from nothing less than his desire to kill himself or to kill somebody else. The often repressed suicidal impulse of humanity is the basic sickness analyzed by both Aiken and Percy, and few modern authors were better equipped to perform this task. The job required a plunging into their own psyches and a bringing up of the contents of the unconscious mind, both their own long repressed suicidal impulses as well as what they would both find within the unconscious—a healing power that when released would make it possible for them to deal with the destructive contents of the mind. The long record of modern artists who have committed suicide or come to some other destructive end is dreary indeed. That Aiken and Percy could emerge victorious from a prolonged struggle with powers of destruction in themselves is a sign they did find healing energies. It is finally the chief fact in their lives that made them powerful writers as late as their sixties and, finally, enabled them to emerge late in life as significant American men of letters. As such, they were able after having achieved integrated lives to understand the relationship between the death wish in humans and the warfare that exists within the split consciousness of most people.

The fact that they were both willing to undergo a long apprenticeship to philosophy and to life accounts in part for their overcoming the death wish latent in themselves and in everyone. Also, the fact that they became early in their lives fully aware of the seriousness of the modern predicament—resting as it did on the reality of large-scale warfare in world society and in the individual unconscious—and resolved to surmount their

---

[8]Martin Luschei, *The Sovereign Wayfarer: Walker Percy's Diagnosis of the Malaise* (Baton Rouge: Louisiana State University Press, 1972).

own deadly tendencies toward retreat and death helped to make them aware of the necessity of seeking a way of dealing with their personal problems. Both discovered that problems of the mind are overcome by continuing to grow and by not remaining fixed in one place. The seemingly natural tendency of humans to remain fixed in one place is based on narcissism—falling in love with oneself and one's activities—and this narcissism keeps man from being a pilgrim. In a period when the surfaces of life seem stable, it is the way of most people *not* to be pilgrims. But a few like Aiken and Percy come to see, sometimes early in life, that psychic growth means moving on a psychic journey. The problems caused by what Freud called fixations—either on the conscious self or on one's parents—cannot be solved simply by confronting them, although that is a necessary first step. Rather, they can be solved by outgrowing them because fixation itself, as many psychiatrists and psychologists since Freud have demonstrated in working with patients, represents the individual's refusal to move on beyond a particular stage of his development. The pilgrimage in the works of both Aiken and Percy is, more than anything else, a moving beyond the problems of their own traumatic childhoods. If they had not begun this movement, they doubtless would have, like many of their colleagues, ended their careers long before they reached their prime, which came for both after age fifty.

An apprenticeship to life, as I have already suggested, leads the writer in the direction of literary works that can be called mythic in the sense of recording the author's own quest or pilgrimage. Both Aiken and Percy would, however, find that the difficulties of dealing with the painful materials of their own lives would force them to serve, along with their life apprenticeship, a long literary apprenticeship, which I will deal with as I take up their various imaginative works. Aiken's literary apprenticeship began with his efforts to become one of the new modern poets in the second decade of the century, working as he was with friends and associates like T. S. Eliot, William Carlos Williams, and John Gould Fletcher.[9] But the real leap forward in his literary career came with his discovery of Joyce's *Ulysses* in 1922. That same year he began his first novel of pilgrimage, *Blue Voyage*. Concerning Joyce, Aiken wrote Selden Rodman, "As for

---

[9]For a discussion of literary influences on him when he began to write poetry, see Aiken's letter to Houston Peterson of 8 June 1928 in Joseph Killorin, ed., *Selected Letters of Conrad Aiken* (New Haven: Yale University Press, 1978) 145.

Joyce—*Ulysses* was a landmark in my life."[10] From 1922 on, in both his poetry and his fiction, the theme of pilgrimage became the overriding one in his major work. There is also reason to believe that it was Joyce who gave the deepest impulse to Percy's mythic writing. I have already referred to Percy's statement concerning the influence of writers like Sartre and Camus in getting him launched as a novelist. Sartre's *Nausea* showed Percy that it was possible to write a novel with ideas in it, yet one that would not be a novel of ideas in the usual sense; but it was Joyce who showed him how to write about a protagonist who lives out his ideas. Percy's essential subject is the existential struggle of the hero. In a remarkable essay called "Notes for a Novel about the End of the World," he first lays out in apocalyptic terms what his fiction is pointing to: "A serious novel about the destruction of the United States and the end of the world should perform the function of prophecy in reverse. The novelist writes about the coming end in order to warn about present ills and so avert the end."[11] Then he proclaims himself an eschatological and a Christian novelist and propounds the problem of the Christian novelist: "How does he set about writing, having cast his lot with a discredited Christendom and having inherited a defunct vocabulary?" The answer is that he turns to Joyce: "He does the only thing he can do. Like Joyce's Stephen Dedalus, he calls on every ounce of cunning, craft, and guile he can muster from the darker regions of his soul. The fictional use of violence, shock, comedy, insult, the bizarre, are the everyday tools of his trade."[12]

Joyce thus showed the way to both Aiken and Percy in their efforts to give an aesthetic as well as an ethical meaning to the chaos they had had to endure much of their lives. Joyce analyzed in *Dubliners* and *Ulysses* the problem of the modern city—and therefore of the world's civilizations, which are based on city life—as being that of paralysis. In his story "The Dead," people are trapped in their own narcissistic and parental fixations. Stephen Dedalus almost alone in Dublin seems to know the answer, which is to get moving on a journey or pilgrimage that will be in effect part of the general growing of humanity into a new life and a new city. I will now take

---

[10]Killorin, *Selected Letters of Conrad Aiken,* 183.

[11]Walker Percy, *The Message in the Bottle: How Queer Man Is, How Queer Language Is, and What One Has to Do with the Other* (New York: Farrar, Straus and Giroux, 1979) 101.

[12]Ibid., 118.

up how Aiken and Percy each in his own way achieved this vision of pilgrimage.

II

Aiken's chief literary problem was always how to deal with the suffering of his traumatic childhood without being overcome by all that was purely personal in his life. A similar problem is posed for the literary critic who examines a confessional writer like Aiken. To deal almost exclusively with purely personal and biographical material is always tempting, especially in a time when for many people literary biography is the chief approach taken toward poetry, fiction, and drama. But the good critic will always remember that it is what the author does with his material in literary terms that really matters as far as the function of criticism is concerned. We will always ask what the writer is really saying, what is the value of what he said, and how did he say it. In other words, interpretation, evaluation, explication—these tools cannot be ignored by the critic. And as both critic and poet, Aiken knew his work, if it was to have literary value, would always have to rise above the personal. Yet for him the personal was absolutely essential. How then to be personal and still achieve that aesthetic detachment that James Joyce and T. S. Eliot—both great influences on Aiken—demanded of the best modern literary artist? Aiken deals in part with this problem in his preface to *3 Novels,* written as late as 1965. Of *Blue Voyage* he says, "Naturally, therefore, the novel is autobiographical: every bit of it is based on fact."[13] But earlier in this preface he has stated what it is for him that gives aesthetic meaning and artistic detachment to the literary work. "And, of course, the vision was the thing, as it was and always will be: without that no amount of observation, or cataloging, or mere naming . . . can ever add up to any sort of totality of response to the universe with which we are faced, outer and inner."[14]

When the concept of vision is invoked, the question must arise as to what the imagination, or visionary function, as Blake called it, really is. Obviously, at his best, Aiken gives us a vision of modern chaos, as do many other writers. But it would be better to say that he gives us insights into chaos. Vision for Aiken, I believe, is essentially an awareness of what

[13]Conrad Aiken. "Author's Preface," *3 Novels* (New York: McGraw Hill, 1965) 3.
[14]Ibid., 2.

Santayana calls harmony. Without this awareness, Santayana believed, the life of reason could not be led. And reason for Santayana was at the center of philosophical life. In "A Brief History of My Opinions," Santayana centers on the principle of harmony after first telling us that "in philosophy I recognize no separate thing called aesthetics." He then says, "Harmony, which might be called an aesthetic principle, is also the principle of health, of justice, and of happiness."[15] There is then, Santayana says, joining with the transcendentalists, a principle of health, balance, and joy at the center of human existence. For Aiken this principle is often symbolized by the harmony of music; at the same time, the sense of harmony is accompanied by love.

In his own life, as well as in his studies of Freud, Aiken found love; but he also found the powers of chaos, even to the point of their being part of his own deepest desire. The everyday insight of humans inevitably confronts a dualism consisting of such opposites as life and death, love and hate. And so Freud, after twenty years of theorizing about the nature of Eros, finally posited his second great principle, death, in his study *Beyond the Pleasure Principle*. However, he was never able to go beyond this dualism because he adhered to a mechanistic theory of science that allowed for no unifying principle in the cosmos. But Aiken, always deeply influenced by Santayana, was seeking in his own early work a vision of harmony that would unify the disparate elements of existence. The fact that he occasionally found it is noted as early as 1931 in *The Melody of Chaos* by Houston Peterson, who, by the way, devotes space to Santayana's influence. The very title of Peterson's work suggests Aiken's awareness that even in chaos, it is melody—symbolizing the underlying harmony—that he seeks and often finds. In fact, it is through the acceptance of chaos that one overcomes the war of the dualistic opposites. This acceptance enables one, in Nietzsche's phrase, to pass "beyond good and evil." Others have noted this juxtaposition of harmony and chaos in Aiken. It is, of course, at the center of Henry Murray's term "creative dissolution," which he uses to explain the profoundest element in Aiken's work. Later, Arthur Waterman, in contrasting Aiken's modernity with Eliot's "retreat to the past, to tradition and the church," says that the poet "insists on looking within the modern chaos for the solution that will account for the chaos and resolve

---

[15]*The Philosophy of Santayana*, ed. Irwin Edman (New York: The Modern Library, 1936) 20.

it."[16] The plunge then into the problem of inner and outer chaos is necessary for the human to find that melody, or harmony, that makes it possible to overcome the threatened destruction of chaos.

There is, however, always the danger of accepting a false harmony, of trying to seize an image of harmony and flee chaos altogether, of living in a palace of art or in a schizophrenic world of one's own creation or in a world created by drugs. The dangers will spring from the problem that Aiken is always showing us in his "Symphonies," the desire to remain fixated on one's own image and on the images of one's parents. Yet one is called to seek a greater harmony than one has previously known. The seeking, the journeying, is absolutely necessary for the discovery of this true harmony. Because of his increasing awareness all of his life of his own pilgrimage, Aiken in 1949 rearranged and revised the "Symphonies" in the work he called *The Divine Pilgrim*. Among other reasons, he did this to bring out what he himself called the "problem of personal identity, the struggle of the individual for an awareness of what it is that contributes to the consciousness; an attempt to place himself, to relate himself to the world of which he feels himself to be at once an observer and an integral part."[17] The key words here are "consciousness" and "integral." For the pilgrimage to be meaningful, there must be an evolution, an expanding of consciousness; and if this process takes place, then one has a sense of becoming, at least some of the time, integrated with the harmony of life. That Aiken's pilgrimage was authentic can be seen in the fact that in some of his best works there is the visionary glimpse of harmony that lifts one above the ordinariness of existence. No better statement of this sense of universal harmony is found in Aiken's work than the one at the close of *Ushant:* "we rise, ourselves now like notes of music arranging themselves into a divine harmony, a divine unison, which, as it had no beginning, can have no end—."[18]

For those who know Aiken's fiction and poetry well, there are many small and large moments of harmonic insight. There is in his work the awareness of harmony that George Santayana thought to be a basic element in the life of reason. We today usually take reason to mean simply

---

[16]Arthur Waterman, "The Evolution of Consciousness: Conrad Aiken's Novels and *Ushant*," *Critique* 15 (Winter 1974): 69.

[17]*A Review's ABC,* ed. Rufus A. Blanshard (New York: Meridian Press, 1958) 130.

[18]Conrad Aiken, *Ushant* (Cleveland: The World Publishing Company, 1962) 365.

the orderly working of the conscious mind. We believe that people called poets and visionaries live in a separate world where the conscious mind is always deranged but that the so-called "mystic" side of humanity is cultivated to bring forth farfetched imaginative (and because imaginative therefore meaningless for the "reasonable" world) works for the idle hours of human existence. But this idea of reason is based on the old split order between head and heart that is at the bottom of modern repression and the violence that springs from it. The philosophical mind like Aiken's rises above this split to encounter the integrative power of reason, harmony, and spirit in the classic Greek sense that Santayana recognized as the basis of our Western culture. Thus Aiken can at his best know true vision, but also he can in conscious "rational" terms outline intellectually the whole course of his journey as a philosophical poet.

In 1968 Aiken made one of the important statements of his career as a literary critic about the meaning of the life of reason for the philosopher, or for anyone living the philosophical life. Note that in this statement categories like spirit, wonder, knowledge, love, and admiration are all accepted as parts of an integrated whole, a fact which shows that Aiken as man and author lived that rare thing in our time: an integrated life.

> Of course I do believe in this evolution of consciousness as the only thing which we can embark on, or in fact, willynilly, *are* embarked on; and along with that will go the spiritual discoveries and, I feel, the inexhaustible wonder that one feels, that opens more and more the more you know. It's simply that this increasing knowledge constantly enlarges your kingdom and the capacity for admiring and loving the universe.[19]

Many of Aiken's best critics—Jay Martin and Douglas Robillard, for instance—have insisted on his similarity to Goethe, yet others have rejected such an idea. Obviously, Aiken did not have artistic gifts as great as Goethe's, but a study of Aiken and Goethe and then a study of Santayana's teaching about the philosophical poet will show an essential similarity between the two.

Yet even as one becomes aware of Aiken's accomplishment as a philosophical poet and novelist, he also becomes aware of the price Aiken had to pay to achieve this distinction. The pilgrimage cannot be an easy one or else there is no real evolution of consciousness. For consciousness to de-

---

[19]"Conrad Aiken: An Introduction," *Paris Review* (Winter/Spring 1968): 119.

velop, there must be a purging of destructive elements in the unconscious mind. Freud taught Aiken much about the cathartic nature of dreams, and much of the best of Aiken's *The Divine Pilgrim* contains dream-like scenes of many of the deepest agonies of his traumatic life. Douglas Robillard in an excellent essay on supernatural elements in Aiken's poetry discusses the "dreams of evil events" in the "Symphonies."

> To the extent that dreams of evil events serve to offer emotional balance to the individual, they serve the function that Aristotle ascribes to tragedy, that of a catharsis. As the conscious mind can work upon the materials presented to it within the formal contexts of tragic spectacle, the unconscious performs a similar act; but it goes further in compiling and presenting its own materials. It performs an artistic and creative function that is usually denied to the ordinary person. Dreams are the poems of the unpoetic.[20]

Robillard has captured in this discussion both the Freudian concept of catharsis Aiken used as well as the Jungian idea (which was also a transcendentalist concept) that the unconscious mind, or psyche, contains a creative power that can overcome the destructive forces that have been repressed from earliest childhood but must be faced if they are to be purged. The reason they continue being repressed is that the hero of the "Symphonies"— who is at once Aiken and Everyman—does not have a sufficient belief in the creative powers that can banish the forces of destruction. For this reason images threatening death swim up out of the unconscious to terrorize the dreams; or else, as Freud showed, they are projected onto others, who are forced to assume one's anger and lust.

Aiken's unconscious mind leads him in the early narrative poem to use images of a deadly woman who appears in the guises of a witch, a vampire, and a lamia: that snake-like creature of Greek myth who with her woman's head can drain a man of his life force. Possibly his most compelling figures of evil in the "Symphonies" are his vampires. Using Theophile Gautier's story "La Morte Amoureuse" in *The Jig of Forslin,* he has a narrator tell of a beautiful woman who takes him for rides on supernatural horses. But instead of being the lover he thinks she is, she is the vampire who asks for "One little drop . . . / One little bubble from his red vein."[21] The narrator wakes and finds himself lying on her grave. He goes

---

[20]Douglas Robillard, "The Supernatural in the Poetry of Conrad Aiken," unpublished paper.

[21]Aiken, *Collected Poems,* 85.

to a priest, and together they sprinkle holy water on her body. After telling this vampire story, Forslin asks: "Why do we muse upon them, what secret's in them? / Is it because, at last, we love the darkness, / Love all things in it, tired of too much light?"[22] These lines should be put alongside the following lines written by Aiken's father on a prescription form that was found in his room after his death.

> *Like a garment soft and warm,*
> *Grateful to my shrinking form—*
> *Promise of the welcome sleep,*
> *Free of dreams and oh! so long and deep.*[23]

Hoffman says of one of the "Symphonies," *The Charnel Rose*, that its "essential heart" is "the struggle with death, the refusal to give in to it."[24] This could be said of all of *The Divine Pilgrim* and of some of Aiken's other works. As a reader of Poe from his early years, Aiken knew that a poet or anyone else who allows images of death to become dominant in his dreams and thoughts is moving toward early death. Marie Bonaparte, one of Freud's chief disciples, has analyzed with full approval of her mentor the dark labyrinth of Poe's mind, showing how the dark images of death are related to his fixation on the mother and his desire to follow the mother into the darkness of the tomb. Freudian analysis works well for poets like Poe, and since the days of early Romanticism many poets can be viewed in the Freudian context with great profit. How else, for instance, can we understand the life and art of Sylvia Plath without studying her Electra complex? Yet there is a mechanistic aspect of Freud that makes Freudian analysis of literature and life seem like a deterministic trap. Aiken early realized as both critic and artist that he would have to use some of Freud's ideas to preserve his art and even save his life. However, he also knew that the other depth psychologists he was reading along with Freud had important ideas about man's creativity that were connected with knowledge he had already made his own from his work with the teachings of Grandfather Potter and George Santayana.

The problem for one like Aiken who had worked long in the Freudian tradition was this: how is creativity to be released? Confession alone is not

---

[22]Ibid., 86.
[23]Quoted by Alexander A. Lawrence in "228 Habersham Street," *Georgia Review* 22 (Fall 1968): 332.
[24]Frederick J. Hoffman, *Conrad Aiken* (New York: Twayne Publishers, 1962) 94.

enough, and denouncement of evil cannot stop the vampire in his search for blood. This problem is related to what makes the pilgrimage, or quest, authentic. Without authenticity a quest can degenerate into aimless wandering. Aiken found that one must make a conscious choice, which is also the teaching of most of the existentialists and is at the heart of Walker Percy's concept of pilgrimage. One must choose to recollect, as Marcel would say, that there is a transcendent element that will unify the diverse forces at work in oneself and in the world and that this element is a fullness and at heart a joyfulness. In attempting to recollect, or recall, the fact of transcendence, one relies on past teachers. Certainly the young Aiken relied on the recollections of those like Potter and Santayana who had gone before him and had not been defeated by the forces of death lingering in everyone's psyche.

But why does one seek death anyway? Freud went so far as to posit a death wish or instinct. But in doing so he was working solely within the biological and mechanistic traditions of the past century, and therefore he never answered the chief questions about death to the satisfaction of very many. Why should a young and gifted man like Conrad Aiken feel such strong desires to die, until finally in 1932 he would make a serious attempt to kill himself? It took Aiken most of his life to fully answer this question. In *The Divine Pilgrim* he gives some answers, and the most pertinent ones have to do with narcissism and the Oedipus complex. The deadly woman of many forms is finally the possessive mother and wife that Aiken will also write about in some of his best fiction. He longs to possess and be possessed by her because of the loneliness and pain resulting from an intense narcissism. In the "Symphonies," his best statement about the connection between sexual possessiveness and narcissism is to be found in *Priapus and the Pool*. Priapus, the classical god of male procreative power, is a symbol of modern man bound by a possessiveness that causes him to turn women into objects of his own gratification. The poet shows that this lust is always springing up because the narcissistic lover has fallen in love with his own image reflected in a pool. But not only does the lover desire to possess, he desires to be possessed. Finally, however, the pilgrim sees the true nature of the woman he wants to possess and who in turn wants to possess him: she is Medusa who "could not see / The world she turned to stone and ash. / Only herself she saw."[25] In recognizing the witch who has tempted him in many guises, the pilgrim in *Priapus* cries out:

---

[25] Aiken, *Collected Poems*, 395.

Out of my brain
Take back your voice that lodges there in pain,
Tear out your thousand golden roots
That thrust their tentacles in my heart
But bear no fruits.[26]

But then he realizes the witch herself is isolated and that it is her loneliness that drives her to possess and devour. Finally, he sees that he is no different: the isolation caused by his narcissism has made him, like the witch, a possessing individual. But possession, bearing no fruits of love, brings with it despair—the hopelessness of never finding that love the heart longs for. From this despair springs the longing for death.

In Aiken's first "Symphony," *The Jig of Forslin* (1916), the narrator is shown realizing that to overcome his narcissism he must give up the attempt to make his life a juggling act. Now "growing older," he says, "I wanted something better. / To do the impossible!"[27] In succeeding "Symphonies" he will see himself as a pilgrim moving on into a new life, passing through the desolation of his own soul described in *The Charnel Rose*, published two years later. In the deepest sense, the last of the "Symphonies" is *The Pilgrimage of Festus*, published in 1923. Here the theme of pilgrimage is everywhere central. We see the poet turning to the great religious masters of the past: to Confucius, the Buddha, and particularly to Jesus, who is also invoked in earlier "Symphonies" like *The Jig of Forslin* and *The Charnel Rose*. Yet the most powerful poem of the collected "Symphonies," which Aiken entitled *The Divine Pilgrim*, is "Changing Mind," written in 1925. Aiken considered this work a coda for the collection. It leaps beyond the "Symphonies" in its power and its terse, direct diction, marking as it does a bridge to that metaphysical poetry of the thirties Aiken would call the Preludes. In "Changing Mind" he leaves behind the styles and attitudes of a late and overripe romanticism and moves on to a kind of incisive verse that has caused an increasing number of critics to compare his best poetry to that of T. S. Eliot and Wallace Stevens.

The impact of the intense style of "Changing Mind" is paralleled by a depth of understanding about the relationship between pilgrimage and narcissism. To be freed from narcissism, the pilgrim discovers, one must fight and suffer every day. "Changing Mind" is based on one of those re-

---

[26]Ibid., 396.
[27]Ibid., 58.

markable dreams Aiken always had at crucial points in his life, a dream about a boxer that he in his late seventies once described to me in terms so vivid that he might have dreamed it only the night before. The poem begins with the protagonist being called under the water into the darkness, that is, to descend into his soul. Within the soul he finds what Aiken in his preface to the poem calls "the constituent particles of himself."[28] These particles are various psychic forces that he has inherited as part of what he refers to as the racial memory. But also under the water he finds an imprisoning power called Narcissus, which has trapped the power of his psyche: "O Alba! Look! While thus Narcissus sleeps / Under the river, and beside him keeps / Conscious and yet unconscious my bright soul!" A new power, or "god," appears at once: "Out of the east / the blue god looms, and with him come new worlds."[29]

The new "god" is for Aiken the power that helps him overcome the dark power that is called Mephistopheles; and this power, now under control, shows him a crucified woman, symbol of the wounded feminine powers of the soul. The way to a reviving of these powers is for the pilgrim to fight against the giant and to accept his blows. By thus accepting the suffering inflicted by the giant, powers spring to life, crying: "Alas, Narcissus dead, / Narcissus daily dead, that we may live!"[30] With the renewal of the psychic powers, the pilgrim also discovers dwelling in his soul both Socrates and Christ. Both come in the pilgrim's soul to a place called Golgotha, a scene of the daily crucifixion of the poet. At last the pilgrim identifies with the man in the soul who fights every day, though always weak and sick: "Daily I fight here, / Daily I die for the world's delight / By the blow on my visible heart!"[31] In "Tetélestai," the most important poem before "Changing Mind," Aiken speaks of "guarding his heart from blows," referring both to himself and his father, with whom he often identifies himself, especially in "Changing Mind." But now the poet can accept the blows on the heart, and by living with psychic pain he can begin to be both creative and loving. Thus he frees himself, slowly as part of a life project called pilgrimage, from both narcissism and the accompanying despair and longing for death.

---

[28]Ibid., 272.
[29]Ibid., 281.
[30]Ibid., 287.
[31]Ibid.

"Changing Mind," with its shadow and anima archetypes, requires explication in the terms of Jung's psychology, but since it marks the beginning of Aiken's new poetry of the thirties I will reserve my interpretation of its Jungian aspects until I discuss the Preludes. Actually, Aiken would not be able to push forward with his new poetic insights after 1925, when "Changing Mind" was written, because he was deeply involved with *Blue Voyage,* begun in 1922 and published in 1927. This first novel was written under the almost total influence of James Joyce and Sigmund Freud, too much so for it to be a good novel. But Aiken doubtless felt that he needed to confess himself in terms more concrete than those used in the poems of *The Divine Pilgrim.* And confess himself he does, possibly too much for the sake of good art. Yet there are moments of vision in the novel that will be carried over into later and better novels and finally into the incomparable *Ushant,* an autobiography written like a novel, using stream-of-consciousness techniques borrowed from Joyce as early as 1922 for use in *Blue Voyage.*

Blue Voyage is about a young literary man named Demarest (very much like Aiken) who is traveling on shipboard to England. In first class, above him in all ways, is his love Cynthia, who on the voyage ignores him. He is stunned by being rejected and retreats into that solipsism that is characteristic of the narcissist when he is thwarted. But using techniques learned from Joyce, he transforms the solipsism into a kind of dream-vision in which he confesses himself, with the help of his mentor Freud. He discovers that Cynthia is a mother-substitute and that he desires both to possess and be possessed by her. Her rejection becomes the oft-feared castration by the parents, and his anger springs from those narcissistic demands for total attention that the eldest child (as Aiken was) usually makes more strongly than other children because he has, as the first child, been put on a pedestal by doting parents. All of this breaks through him in painful flashes, but doing anything about it often seems impossible. Yet with growing self-knowledge, Demarest gradually renounces Cynthia as mother-substitute and faces his own egotism, which seems to be an impossible chain to break.

The voyage of Demarest is transformed into a pilgrimage by his own authentic choice to find himself and his own creativity. In his poems Aiken depicted the inner struggles of the pilgrim, but in *Blue Voyage* he shows that pilgrimage is both an inner and an outer journey. Indeed, the facts of the inner and the outer journey become in a deeper sense inseparable. As forces in the soul miraculously aid the pilgrim in putting down Narcissus in "Changing Mind," so a helping figure appears in the form of a chewing gum merchant named Silberstein who briefly plays the role of psychoanalyst and Jungian "wise old man," giving the pilgrim some of his own strength in a weak moment. Another passenger, Smith, is like an image of death encountered in "Changing Mind," and the wounded woman of the poem is paralleled by a flawed widow named Faubion. Finally, Demarest seeks the Christ within himself, briefly identifying with His suffering and selflessness.

As a result of his own choice to confess himself, to accept pain, and to reach out to others, Demarest receives not a final solution to his problems—which never comes to anyone—but a psychic growth that partially frees him and his creative powers from the fixations of narcissism. The result is that he can finally renounce Cynthia and all mother-substitutes and can begin to have a sexual relationship based not on possessiveness but on love. At the end of the book, the widow Faubion comes knocking on his cabin door, drawn to the fruitfulness of his newfound sexual powers after he loses his fixation on Cynthia as a mother-substitute. Aiken makes it clear, in keeping with Freud's ideas about Eros and sexuality, that creativity and sex are intimately linked and flourish together. Also Demarest experiences those brief moments of harmony given to the true pilgrim: "We accept everything. We deny nothing. We are, in fact, imagination: not completely, for then we should be God; but almost completely. Perhaps, in time, our imagination *will* be complete."[32]

Blue Voyage, once considered an important experimental novel, has rightly now shrunk in the estimation of the critics, but it does contain many of Aiken's basic philosophical and psychological ideas that would flower again in the thirties in his more successful novels, *Great Circle* and *King Coffin,* and in the most powerful poetic works of his career, the Preludes. In following Joyce's lead, Aiken was seeking to bring into being a new American philosophical novel based on the theme of pilgrimage. But in a larger sense, Aiken was still caught up in the modern American tradition of realistic and naturalistic fiction. Hawthorne and Melville had brought forth in America a new philosophical fiction, but the tradition of realism that came to dominate American fiction after the Civil War snuffed out what might have been a great tradition of the philosophical novel of the kind that

---

[32]Conrad Aiken, *Blue Voyage* (New York: Scribner's, 1927) 250.

continued in Russia until the early twentieth century. American poetry at its best would continue to employ philosophical concepts, and Aiken would, with the help of inspiration from modern French and Spanish verse, continue the tradition of philosophical poetry in America. It would at last remain for novelists in that final phase of modernism we call the contemporary period to develop a philosophical novel in America. Among them one of the most important would be Walker Percy.

III

Like most of the important contemporary novelists, Walker Percy would be at once less experimental in technique and generally more careful in construction than novelists who came into their own between 1900 and 1940. Consequently, a writer like Percy—or, for that matter, Saul Bellow, John Updike, or John Barth—seldom rises to the artistic peaks of the best modern novelists before 1940, but then such a writer seldom sinks to the depths a Hemingway or Faulkner might reach at his worst. Conrad Aiken as a poet, short story writer, and novelist took many more chances as an experimentalist than did Percy, and sometimes his visionary insights are more striking than anything found in Percy. But in all of Percy's published fiction there is a consistency of artistic value not generally seen in the writers of the twenties and thirties. Thus the period after 1945 has been one of consolidating artistic and technical values established in earlier phases of the modernist revolution, going all the way back to the second half of the nineteenth century. There is undoubtedly a waning of artistic energy that accompanies the technical excellence of contemporary writers, but at the same time there is an underlying longing to move on into what is now generally referred to as the postmodernist period.

In spite of both personal and literary differences, there is a strange underlying similarity between the essential literary accomplishments of Aiken and Percy. It exists because both are writing about the same kind of pilgrimage, and both are aware that only through taking this pilgrimage could they overcome both narcissism and a strong inherited death wish. What is particularly significant in discussing the similarity between their pilgrimages as we see them described in their works is that, due to their determination to push on into the depths of problems that were at once both personal and entirely characteristic of the modern age, they have written books whose protagonists are representative of three parallel stages of development: the period of early maturity before forty, the period of middle age between forty and the late fifties, and the period after sixty, which is one of summing up. Percy's first two published novels, *The Moviegoer* and *The Last Gentleman*, are paralleled by Aiken's *The Divine Pilgrim* and *Blue Voyage*. The protagonists of both *Blue Voyage* and *The Last Gentleman* in fact have their lives continued in the most important works (so far, that is, for Percy) of the third period. Thus Demarest is the protagonist of both *Blue Voyage* and *Ushant*, and the story of Will Barrett in *The Last Gentleman* is continued in *The Second Coming*. Aiken was sixty-three when *Ushant* was published in 1952. *The Second Coming* was published in 1980, when Percy was sixty-four. Both of these late works represent an optimistic and joyful summing up of long lives of pilgrimage. For the middle period Aiken's two best works, *Great Circle* and the Preludes, parallel Percy's *Love in the Ruins* and *Lancelot* and deal with extremely painful psychic material. It is during this middle period that the greatest plunge into the repressed contents of the unconscious occurs. In terms of the mythic journey, it is the descent into the cave or the plunge into the sea to be lost for a time in the belly of the whale.

Both authors began their works of pilgrimage with a strong anchoring in the two philosophers who influenced them most: Santayana and Kierkegaard. Both were deeply influenced by Freud, though Percy sometimes satirizes a kind of Freudianism that has often fallen into absurdity in the contemporary period. Percy himself underwent psychoanalysis for a time in New York, and Aiken boarded ship with the intention of being psychoanalyzed in Vienna by Freud himself (an admirer of Aiken's work) but was dissuaded during the voyage by Erich Fromm, who suggested to him that one should never undergo analysis unless it is absolutely necessary. Yet in spite of their complex backgrounds and wide reading, Aiken and Percy never let philosophy or psychology become paramount in their best work: the human on a pilgrimage seeking a new and better life always is at the center of their writing. The same was true for Joyce, and for that reason he was a literary inspiration for both, possibly as far as their fiction is concerned the greatest single influence. Aiken, Percy, and Joyce were always at heart medical students seeking to understand how life works and what human health and disease really are.

Percy does not, like Aiken, plunge into the abyss of human sexual disturbance in his early work. This comes later in his dark masterpiece, *Lancelot*. His first novel, *The Moviegoer*, begins with a depiction of the protagonist, Binx Bolling, living very much on the surface of life. Beginning the book in the late fifties, Percy captures a sense of the so-called "silent generation" of that decade. It was a period in which most people clung to the surface of life and was to give way to a new rush of energy in the early sixties when the book was at last published. But Bolling is very much a man of the fifties who feels at home in a suburb of his native New Orleans. He is fully urban, a man who has accepted the false stasis of pleasurable existence. In fact, he is a man well adjusted to what everyone around him calls "the good life of contemporary America." Instead, as Bolling gradually comes to see, his life is actually based, in the words of British psychologist R. D. Laing in *The Politics of Experience,* on "our alienated social reality," alienated because contemporary man is separated from what Laing calls "inner archetypal mediators of divine power."[33] It is not that Bolling has no religion; it is that he has no religious experience that makes him aware of anything greater in life than his own experience. He perceives life as a great emptiness in which "everydayness," or ordinariness, is the enemy to be warded off by successful business endeavors, reading, casual lovemaking, and, above all, moviegoing. At the center of all his activities is an image of himself as the only object of real adoration with pleasurable sensation as the proof that his existence is real. But from the beginning of the book, Bolling realizes something is wrong because he is possessed by a strange apathy.

Much of *The Moviegoer* deals with the aimless wandering of its protagonist in his efforts to overcome the apathy of ordinariness, and it is this aspect that has helped to attract many readers to what for some is Percy's most successful novel. For a smaller group of readers it is the theme of the pilgrimage leading beyond narcissism and alienation that marks the book as a distinctive novel of the early sixties. Percy, like Aiken in *Blue Voyage,* shows his hero in states of lust and flight—all based on a largely hidden despair—but at the same time he shows him consciously choosing to begin a search for a better life based on faith in God. Even as the book begins, he is coming to terms with that strange apathy that increasingly since the fifties has been called depression. The pleasures of the narcissistic personality no longer give joy; women used as sex objects lose the power to tantalize. He is at that place where a turn to religion seems called for, but when he contemplates that prospect he finds that most Americans believe

---

[33]R. D. Laing, *The Politics of Experience* (New York: Ballantine, 1976) 168.

in God and that this fact does not cause most of them to live much differently from himself, except that they have not discovered their own apathy. The answer is that one must seek something that will give new meaning and joy to a life that is drying up. Thus Bolling poses the problem to himself by writing in his notebook, "What do you seek—God? You ask with a smile."[34] Bolling is too "sophisticated" not to treat the matter with some irony and detachment. But he goes on to say that his choice to seek God leaves him out of the kind of statistics that social scientists regard as the ultimate knowledge concerning man: thus he answers himself by writing that Americans have already "settled the matter for themselves" because "polls report that 98% of Americans believe in God and the remaining 2% are atheists and agnostics—which leaves not a single percentage point for a seeker."[35] But Binx does make the choice to believe and to seek, and very soon his life begins to change. Yet even as his life changes, he continues his flight from ordinariness as well as from the God that he really seeks.

As Flannery O'Connor has shown in her stories and particularly in her two novels, *Wise Blood* and *The Violent Bear It Away,* the choice to encounter any authentic religious experience that would change one's life often leads the individual to flee from the very experience he seeks. O'-Connor's characters often flee God by plunging into a religious experience that is a kind of destructive fanaticism. Percy's Bolling flees in search of the ultimate moviegoing experience, and he carries with him to Chicago a girl friend named Kate, whom he would force into a partnership in losing the self in moviegoing. His imprisonment in narcissism at the beginning of the novel has driven him primarily to search for sexual pleasure, but his drive to lose himself is too great to be satisfied by sex. In his flight to Chicago with Kate, he pins his hopes on a movie palace that he calls the great Urwomb. The narcissist in despair at his alienation from others madly seeks to possess and to be possessed. Binx's apathy is so great that he lacks the power to possess the women he merely flirts with. But Kate is different. Her instability demands care and concern from Binx. And because he has made a sincere decision to search for transcendence, he gives up his desire to lose himself in what he realizes is nothing more than the immersion of himself in the remembered pleasures of the mother. The narcissist seeks

---

[34]Walker Percy, *The Moviegoer* (New York: The Noonday Press, 1961) 13.
[35]Ibid., 14.

an ever deepening fixation on his own image, but if he does not move forward on a pilgrimage that is in effect a psychic growth, then in time he must retrogress, moving back to the remembered womb. The full meaning of this theme Percy will explore in *Lancelot,* his fourth novel, but in *The Moviegoer* it is enough for Binx to see the meaning of his plunge into the Urwomb. He draws back in time and accepts the spiritual task at hand, which is helping Kate on her journey. When he returns to New Orleans, his faith, growing as his search has continued, enables him to accept the death of his half brother Lonnie without cracking and in fact to accept Lonnie himself as a full brother in faith. At the end of the book, we see Binx, like Kierkegaard's knight of faith, accepting the role of spiritual guide to his other brothers and sisters and agreeing to take up a profession even to the point of accepting his Aunt Emily's advice to enter medical school.

Most critics of Percy have pointed out how the author uses Kierkegaard and Marcel to give philosophical meaning to *The Moviegoer.* Binx, as Percy himself said in the Carr interview, moves from the Kierkegaardian aesthetic stage to the stage of faith without going through the ethical stage. Binx's either/or decision to believe in and to seek God creates in him a capacity for the kind of intersubjectivity that Marcel believed was the sign of the life of the Christian wayfarer. But those many readers who have lived, sometimes for years, with Binx Bolling in their devotion to this work (a minor cult in itself) do not look first at the philosophical concepts but rather at the lived experience that Percy records in the book. When this is said, it must be recognized that Binx is only making a beginning, that the great tests of his faith still await him, that in fact he is still very much at odds with the everydayness that is his enemy. Percy himself knew he was writing about the beginning of a pilgrimage; and in one sense all of his novels are about a beginning, except *Lancelot,* which is about a continuing retrogression, though even at the end of the book the protagonist thinks he is making a new beginning. Clearly, *The Last Gentleman,* which lacks the poetic beauty of *The Moviegoer,* is a deeper study of a pilgrim whose plunge into his own psyche as well as into his painful past leads him to a clear understanding of his role as knight of faith.

I have already discussed Will Barrett's descent into the deep South of his youth to face the fact of his father's suicide in order to purge that experience from his mind. Binx at the end of his story still has New Orleans and his family to face and overcome before he can establish his full individuality. Barrett, on the other hand, faces the region and culture of the

South, which has left him with a deeply scarred psyche, only after preparing himself for the journey in the city of his exile, New York. There,
ironically, he has adopted the role of a technician, intellectually embracing
the dominant scientism of the nation but at the same time actively engaged
in seeking the archetypal powers that would make it possible for him to
achieve full humanity. From the beginning of his pilgrimage, Will realizes
that these powers for most people must be mediated through ritual, and here
we see the emergence of the Catholic side of Percy. Like Binx, Will makes
a Kierkegaardian leap of faith; and, as Marcel recommends, he works out
his religious quest through intersubjectivity by becoming involved with a
psychically wounded young girl named Kitty Vaught. Still, his mind turns
continually to a question that modern anthropologists and mythologists have
devoted much effort to in the last fifty years: where are the effective rituals
that make true growth possible? The pilgrim seeks the new life for himself,
and through rites he often receives those powers that give him the strength
to continue his journey. Thus early in the novel Will Barrett thinks,

> When he was a youth he had lived his life in a state of liveliest expectation,
> thinking to himself: what a fine thing it will be to become a man and to
> know what to do—like an Apache youth who at the right time goes out into
> the plains alone, dreams dreams, sees visions, returns and knows he is a
> man. But no such time had come and he still didn't know how to live.[36]

A tribal society, as Will sees, has a prescribed path that leads a person to
full maturity, that guides him beyond both the narcissistic fixation on his
own image as well as beyond fixations on parental images. C. G. Jung and
younger psychologists like Viktor Frankl and R. D. Laing have noted the
failure of modern society to provide those true rites of passage that enable
individuals to fully experience all the stages of their lives. Will Barrett lives
out his psychological perception by asking the right questions about ritual;
having done this, he admits that there are not clear-cut ritual paths for
modern man to follow. Yet he decides to set out to find a way of personal
growth through belief in transcendence. The rest of the book reveals how
that decision sets into motion certain events that lead him into a ritual participation through which he begins to receive some of the archetypal powers he associates with Apache tribes. Yet because he is a modern man and

---

[36]Walker Percy, *The Last Gentleman* (New York: Farrar, Straus & Giroux, Noonday
Editions, 1966) 11.

because he does participate in Catholic ritual, there is a richness and depth of experience not found in tribal life.

There is also a mystery lurking beneath the jagged surfaces created by money-seeking half-people that Will is always encountering, first in New York and then in that equally commercialized "New South" he painfully drags himself into. His decision to accept the way of pilgrimage has led him into the intricacies of the money-making way of life by involving him in the affairs of the Vaught family, whose Confederate Chevrolet Agency in a city much like Birmingham, Alabama, fuels their lives. But even as Barrett is moving, through his involvement with Kitty, into the intricacies of modern economic life, he is also moving into a ritual encounter with transcendence. The most important process in the book becomes his association with Val, a member of the Vaught family, who has become a nun. This association leads to his participation in the baptism of Jamie, Kitty's younger brother, who is dying. Like Binx after he has accepted the process of pilgrimage, Will finds he has loving concern for those he meets on his life's journey. It is this concern that causes Jamie to trust Will enough to believe Father Boomer's words concerning "the truth of religion" simply because Will believes them. Thus Barrett plays a decisive role in the dying Jamie's salvation. What has occurred is the act that Charles Williams calls substitution, which is the performing of an act of spiritual aid, and Percy's literary handling of this act reminds the reader of similar events in some of Williams's novels. As in Williams's books, one good, or bad, act sets off ripples leading to other good, or bad, acts.

Will's concern for Jamie thus leads to the final encounter of the book, which is with Kitty's older brother. Sutter Vaught, the medical doctor and defeated idealist, has withdrawn from intersubjectivity in his anger at the world and is contemplating suicide. But Will's concern for Jamie has made it possible for Sutter to accept that same concern for himself. This acceptance causes him to delay his suicide. Both Will and Sutter recognize in each other their hidden selves. Will sees his own suicidal self that was faced when he returned South again and relived his own father's violent death but that still waits like a beast ready to leap. On the other hand, Sutter is awakened to the possibility of beginning a journey that will lead him out of his own frustrated idealism, which is based not so much on his unselfish desire to help people as on his own narcissistic worship of himself as a great benefactor of man. The example of Will, the pilgrim with human concerns, jolts Sutter temporarily out of his narcissistic delusions. It is impossible to say what Sutter will do in the future, but at the end of the book he at least sees the possibility of overcoming his death wish.

No resolution exists for any of the problems of people in *The Last Gentleman,* except Jamie's problem of belief, which is solved by his acceptance of God through the rite of baptism, an acceptance made possible by the mutual faith Jamie and Will have in each other. That faith, which leads to an acceptance of God and His love and mercy, makes both Will and Jamie face and overcome the fear of death in a similar but deeper version of the overcoming of death by Binx and Lonnie in *The Moviegoer.* But the continuing necessity of the pilgrimage for the living is emphasized in *The Last Gentleman,* and the key word in the last sentence is "waited." A car waits for Will. He leaves Sutter still struggling with his death angel, and he sets off to return to Kitty and possible marriage and an ordinary job selling Chevrolets in a modern Southern city. The pilgrim moves but only as he receives the mysterious promptings of the transcendent principle; these come mainly through other people in Percy's books and not directly from prayer or revelation, a fact that has made some people challenge Percy's right to be called a Catholic or even a religious novelist. Percy, in fact, does not in one important sense really fit either category. He has made it clear in interviews that he does not want to write about "religion" as such because the novelist in our time cannot bring off artistically the so-called "religious" experience. After all, even Flannery O'Connor, who considered her Catholicism the most important fact of her existence, told Granville Hicks that "I'm not interested in sects as sects; I'm concerned with the religious individual."[37] Percy, who learned some important lessons from O'Connor, has shown agreement in what he has written: his best characters are always religious individuals on a pilgrimage. The key act for Percy, then, is to choose to accept pilgrimage and then to wait for signs that spring not so much from voices on high as from the promptings of events and people encountered on the journey. Through this interchange come small moments of visionary insight and a sense of human closeness that makes loving concern not so much a matter of duty but of a gift springing from the acceptance of the journey.

---

[37]Granville Hicks, "A Writer at Home with Her Heritage," *Saturday Review* 16 (12 May 1962): 22.

IV

The most basic similarity between Aiken and Percy is that their best imaginative works, dealing as they do with pilgrimage, continue to go deeper into the subject because their authors continued their own pilgrimages right on into old age. A work or two reflecting the pilgrimage of an author is not uncommon in this century, but very few writers are able to continue bringing forth deepening works on the subject. One reason Aiken and Percy could, as I have suggested, is that they felt an urgency to continue because of their early resolve to overcome pressures of intense childhood trauma. For them, to live meant to have creative relationships with other people. But they also show that what Marcel called intersubjectivity—which for him was necessary if true pilgrimage was to continue—is not as simple a matter as the French philosopher seems to say. Human relationships are fraught with great dangers. Love too easily becomes hate and possessiveness. And what is taken to be human concern is sometimes really selfish manipulation.

What enables Aiken and Percy to deal with problems of intersubjectivity on through middle age and even into old age is that they work within a tradition of transcendence. Aiken represents a continuation of the tradition of American transcendentalism, but that tradition was seriously vitiated by the middle of the last century because of too deep an involvement with the concept of immanence. As a strong part of the romantic revival, transcendentalism in Europe and America preserved a concept, or a principle, that worked to unify the disparate elements in life. Or, as Saul Bellow has his character Herzog write: ''Romanticism guarded the 'inspired condition', preserved the teachings and records of transcendence and the most generous ideas of mankind, during the greatest and most rapid of transformations, the most accelerated phase of the modern scientific and technological transformation.''[38] But the transcendentalists ''fell in love'' with themselves as beautiful souls and then projected that love onto persons they called ''heroes.'' Even in the twentieth century we see this old-time transcendentalism practiced by powerful artists like G. B. Shaw and D. H. Lawrence; the result is ''hero-worship.'' Aiken, following Joyce and Eliot in this matter, turned to the antihero as pilgrim; yet he maintained the

---

[38]Saul Bellow, *Herzog* (New York: The Viking Press, 1964) 165.

idea of a transcendent principle working throughout all existence, a principle imbued with a mysterious quality that cannot be identified with one individual or one group. Thus for Aiken, and Percy after him, the transcendent principle takes on qualities traditionally associated by theologians with what is called "transcendence," defined by one encyclopedia as "denoting the superiority and independence of Deity, as contrasted with immanence."[39] Immanence always puts great emphasis on the close connection between Deity and creation and tends to become pantheism if not checked by a strong sense of transcendence, although too great an emphasis on transcendence can lead to a removal of the power of God from creation altogether.

Aiken and Percy both solve the problem of immanence by continually suggesting that man knows the action of the transcendent principle by observing it in the flow of love between humans. Although transcendence may once have regularly expressed itself by a voice from a cloud or by a prophetic vision, we see in our century its working as an agent unifying the individual soul and unifying individuals themselves in harmonious and creative relationships. Those who do not know Percy's thought and art well might argue that his Catholicism places him outside of this kind of interpretation, based as it is on romantic and modern transcendentalist conceptions. The influence of Marcel, himself influenced by William James, was decisive in the development of Percy's thought and imaginative powers. Marcel works within a stream of Catholic thought that links him with the mainstream of romantic religious thought. And though F. H. Heinemann rightly calls him a "mysterious empiricist," Marcel was always careful not to fall into the traps set by the immanence of nineteenth-century transcendentalists. I myself heard Marcel lecture in 1964, and at the time, making one of his last public appearances, he stressed the need to speak of God not *in* man but working *through* man.

The foregoing discussion may seem unnecessarily abstract, but it vitally concerns many critics and readers. Critic John Romano brings it to the fore in his review of *The Second Coming* in the *New York Times:* "The doubt, excited by Percy's characteristic concerns, is whether a transcendent religious conviction and an ultimate attachment to other people are

---

[39]E. Royston Pike, *Encyclopedia of Religion and Religions* (New York: The Meridian Library, 1958) 378.

not finally incompatible."[40] The problem of the narcissism of all enthusiasts, particularly those in the religious area, is invoked often in this century because of the human failure of so many earlier romantic individualists. Narcissism is at the bottom of this failure, and narcissism was early an important problem in the lives of Conrad Aiken and Walker Percy. What their best works would continue to investigate was how narcissism could be overcome. *The Last Gentleman* goes far in this investigation, but it would not be until *The Second Coming* that many readers' questions concerning narcissism and transcendence would be answered, just as *Ushant* would finally resolve many similar problems posed in the early work of Aiken. Essentially what both writers were seeking to realize in imaginative terms was how a concept like transcendence could be reconciled with the everyday concerns of feuding individuals and how adherence to it could lead to an overcoming of narcissism.

---

[40]John Romano, "A Novel of Powerful Pleasures," *New York Times Book Review,* 29 June 1980, 29.

Apocalypse and the Middle-aged Man

Chapter V

I

Lionel Trilling saw the role of New York intellectuals like himself as being to challenge certain aspects of liberalism. In spite of the fact that the life of contemporary liberalism, like that of a novel, is periodically declared at an end, liberalism in all its many forms is still a movement in American life. Conrad Aiken always thought of himself as a thoroughgoing liberal, and when I saw him shortly after the 1968 presidential election, he told me with great happiness how Hubert Humphrey had called to thank him for his letter in the *New York Times* on behalf of Humphrey's campaign. Walker Percy is not so obviously a liberal. Indeed, because of his Catholicism and his attacks on various aspects of modern life dear to some liberals, he is sometimes thought to be a conservative. But Marcel's strong influence on Percy and Percy's own continuing involvement with science, contemporary philosophy, and the everyday life of ordinary people place him in one contemporary branch of the liberal tradition.

A term like liberalism must for the sake of any discussion be defined. Its continental roots are in seventeenth century England and Holland; its early emphasis was on personal and political liberty (but not to the extent of anarchism), the use of science and technology for the betterment of life, and the belief that more wisdom resides in the general run of people than in some elite or ''aristocratic'' group that would impose its will on the majority. These ideas were basic to the thinking of the cultural architects of America—men like Franklin, Washington, Adams, and Jefferson. Each century since the seventeenth, however, has seen challenges to various aspects of the liberal position. In the nineteenth century Emerson and the New England transcendentalists challenged the lack of emphasis in eighteenth-century liberalism on spirituality. Emerson maintained, as Marcel and Percy would do in our century, that the ordinary life of all people would be impoverished if only the utilitarian aspects of liberalism (which Emerson generally approved of) were present in society. Attention must be paid, Emerson said, to the element in existence that transcends all sense experience and that, when properly apprehended, gives joy and hope to life. The transcendental tradition—whether represented by Emerson, Wordsworth, Carlyle, Hugo, Fichte, or Tolstoy—had a far greater impact on nineteenth-century life than many people imagine. That impact continues in this century through the influence of modern transcendentalists like G. B. Shaw, D. H. Lawrence, or even Saul Bellow. The transcendental tradition, however, created problems. It often emphasized ''hero-worship'': Anglo-American industrialists, for instance, influenced by Carlyle, put such an emphasis on individualism and ''heroism'' that the collective side of life suffered. Continental individualists influenced by Nietzsche identified the transcendent principle with power. The result was a worship of energy and power for their own sake without regard for the needs of the powerless. The reaction to extreme individualism produced a growing emphasis on a new tradition of liberalism inspired by the thought of men like John Stuart Mill, who would emphasize the enhancement of all individuals through collective action. Liberalism then for many in the twentieth century would come to be thought of as collective government action.

When Lionel Trilling at the end of his life speaks of his own challenge to American liberalism after 1920, he means that he fought a liberalism that was putting more and more emphasis on the power of the collective, so much so that many were becoming Marxists. Marx, whose political thought is similar in some ways to that of Hobbes, emphasized the kind of government by elite (the dictatorship of the proletariat) that liberals had fought against in the seventeenth century. What Trilling and his followers devoted themselves to was an exaltation of individual intelligence as the means for both individual and social improvement, two basic goals of most branches of liberalism. But the dominant strain of liberalism in this century has placed such a great emphasis on the collective body (which is of course necessary for most individuals to flourish) that the individual has been neglected.

Inevitably, the needs of the individual would be brought forward again; and Trilling, Aiken, and Percy are clearly part of this movement, though all three accept the needs of meaningful collective life. Where Aiken and Percy disagree with Trilling and others who have represented the dominant strain of Anglo-American liberal intellectualism is in their insistence on the necessity of taking fully into account in both thought and action the principle of transcendence called variously Spirit, Being, or God. Aiken's transcendentalist vision, as I have shown, springs from Potter and Santayana, and Percy's from Kierkegaard and Marcel. What ties both authors to the New England and New York transcendentalist tradition is the Harvard philosopher who was for a time the chief influence on both Santayana and Marcel. That philosopher is, of course, William James, who was probably the chief link between early Northeastern transcendentalism and the realism and naturalism of the modern world. Santayana was greatly influenced by James but found that later his former teacher did not put enough emphasis on transcendence. Therefore, Santayana drew closer to Greek and continental metaphysics, and thus in some ways he resembles the modern religious existentialists. Marcel, throughout his philosophical career, was influenced by James; but also because his metaphysics was Catholic and continental, Marcel is far more oriented toward the concept of Being than James ever was. However, Aiken and Percy, who have continental influences in their background, are far more in the American grain than either Santayana or James. They fully accepted realism as a viewpoint and as a literary technique. Like James, they turned happily to the democratic embrace of all types of people and to the acceptance of the plain speaking of everyday man, including even such language channels as comic strips (Aiken loved them) and television programs (Percy watches them nearly every night).

What is most deeply like William James in both Aiken and Percy is their "cash value" attitude toward transcendence, or Being. The oft maligned term "cash value" is William James's most famous phrase and is the key to the meaning of his pragmatism, from a worldwide standpoint the most influential of American philosophies. William Barrett has put James's concept of "cash value" in a proper context in his seminal work *The Illusion of Technique*. Reaching the peak of his philosophic endeavor at the end of the last century, James saw clearly what was happening to the concept of Being in modern thought: it was being wiped out. As Barrett puts it, modern philosophers "have let the idea of Being disappear from their thinking. More than this: they would bar us from even entertaining the idea by erecting barriers of language against it."[1] Thus Barrett examines that school of philosophy generally called "analysis," taking Wittgenstein as its representative thinker, and to it he opposes James's "cash value" attack. What James did, he says, can be summed up in this way:

> The rejection of the idea of Being, in recent times, has been made by philosophies that turn one way or another around the analysis of language. Very well; we shall defend this idea by showing that it has a distinct "cash value," that it is in fact indispensable for our comprehension of language as a human phenomenon.[2]

Both Aiken and Percy in effect began their literary careers with the serious study of language. Their concern with childhood trauma inevitably made them ask basic questions about that most intimate of language scenes, the family. For example, why is some language effective and other language an utter failure? This led to the further question: what provides the underlying unity that makes close human relationships possible on the family and other intimate levels? Humans cannot be creative without fruitful emotional relationships. Their absence means depression leading to schizophrenia or else a paranoia leading to delusion and possible violence. F. H. Heinemann has written that one problem above all others "haunted

---

[1]William Barrett, *The Illusion of Technique* (Garden City. NY: Anchor Press/Doubleday, 1979) 174.
[2]Ibid., 175.

all the existentialists, i.e., to overcome the alienation of man.''[3] Alienation between people is the essential problem in the imaginative work of Aiken and Percy. For them it is overcome through participation in Being. Therefore, for them the ''cash value'' of Being is that only through participation in it can moments of human unity be achieved. Some readers of Percy in particular have complained about not finding anything specifically ''religious'' in his work. The answer to their complaint is that the nature of God, or Being, is revealed in his work, as it is in Aiken's, as the unseen energy that reunifies disparate elements of life. Thus in emphasizing effective human community as central to that experience called ''religious,'' both writers are working in a tradition of spiritual pragmatism.

Aiken and Percy had chaos thrust upon them early in life, and by the time they had reached middle age they were, because of their spiritual pragmatism, ready to deal with its effects on their lives. But their struggle with darkness as reflected in the work of what I call their middle age by no means negates their liberalism; it merely corrects certain aspects of it. Dostoyevski, who like them suffered family violence, began his career in the liberal tradition of his day but became eventually a conservative and finally a reactionary. On the other hand, Aiken and Percy took full account of their personal chaos and absorbed it into their liberal vision. Like William James, they accepted the commonplace experiences of life and eschewed the elitism of Harvard cultural leaders like Charles Eliot Norton and those who followed him. For James, Aiken, and Percy, people in many walks of life are capable of intelligent activity and cultural participation, and no one group has a monopoly on intelligence and culture. Trilling fought Marxism, but he himself sometimes seemed to succumb to that branch of elitist liberalism that denies one of the basic premises of early liberalism. For eighteenth-century liberal thinkers like Franklin and Jefferson, the philosopher was not essentially a person of some city or college or geographical section or nation but a man who belonged to the entire world. Here Aiken and Percy are in tune with early American liberalism, and like Jefferson and Franklin they are fully able to feel at home in various cities and areas. It is primarily because of their acceptance of the world that they can also be at home as men of letters in particular cities and geo-

[3]F. H. Heinemann, *Existentialism and the Modern Predicament* (New York: Harper Torchbooks, 1958) 142.

graphical areas. Thus Franklin and Jefferson were firmly rooted in Philadelphia and Virginia, but at the same time were at home in Europe.

The problem of elitism always haunted Jefferson, who was at once founder of the Democratic party and a slaveholder. We see now, knowing much more about him, that he was always a split man. The kind of split that Jefferson hid from the world endangers liberalism everywhere that it appears in the twentieth century. Most liberal thinkers have despaired of solving the problem, and many have developed the habit of denying that there is a problem. The nature of the relationships between the democratic "common man" and the cultural leader is the great problem addressed by Aiken and Percy in the middle period of their creativity. During this time they dealt in much of their best work with the middle-aged man and his struggle with the chaotic powers of the twentieth century. In their first period the two authors are clearly drawing on experiences from their own lives; in their work of the middle period they draw not only upon memories of personal chaos but also upon an awareness of the general chaos experienced by everyone.

II

Aiken's middle period begins just as the decade of the Great Depression is beginning. Early in the period Aiken is still wrestling with the demon of self-destruction that haunts his early poetry; this struggle finally comes to a climax in 1932, September of that year marking, as Killorin writes, "his year of discouragement."[4] With attempted suicide behind him, he plunges into the writing of his deepest poetry—work containing his finest visions of the overcoming of chaos on both a personal and a cosmic basis. The decade of the thirties was for America and for world civilization a time of great danger, and Aiken's poetry and fiction reflect this fact. Percy's middle period, similarly, parallels a danger period in American life as well as in the life of the world, coming as it does in the late sixties and early seventies when America was caught up in the agony of race riots, youth revolt, and the Viet Nam debate. The fear of revolution, spreading war, and nuclear holocaust provides a feeling of apocalyptic doom that Percy uses well in his two powerful and very successful novels of this pe-

---

[4]Joseph Killorin, ed., *Selected Letters of Conrad Aiken* (New Haven: Yale University Press, 1978) 157.

riod, *Love in the Ruins* and *Lancelot*. At this time he was living a fruitful life with his wife and two daughters in Covington, an exurb of New Orleans. His youthful struggles to find a place for himself as a thinker and a writer had ended in relative success. Yet even as he deals in his novels of this period with national and even worldwide problems, he still shows his protagonists wrestling with the question of suicide. But his firm grasp of social problems of the late sixties and early seventies makes it possible for him in these novels to see personal chaos in the larger terms of apocalyptic violence.

In a time when most novelists and even most poets have, because of their acceptance of the attitudes that accompanied the styles of realism and naturalism, found themselves describing modern violence without showing ways of overcoming it, Aiken and Percy depict the middle-aged man as antihero facing apocalyptic terrors without being overpowered. In fact, it is their successful facing of inner and outer violence that allows them through acceptance of their full humanity to define the role of everyman in a liberal, democratic society. To accomplish this task Aiken and Percy had to develop a deeper psychological understanding of human beings in this century.

Freud was the psychological guide of the two writers as young men. Percy in fact tells us in an interview that once he had elevated Freud "far beyond the point that even [Freud] would place himself."[5] And Freud, of course, launched Aiken's psychological investigations. But, as Jung has pointed out, Freud's ideas and findings were applicable to people before age thirty-five since nature had destined young people to be more concerned with sex and procreation than with anything else. After thirty-five, as Jung has suggested, the human finds the problem of death to be more important to him than procreation. Aiken read Jung, but he never really understood how Jungian much of his late work is. Percy, on the other hand, undertook a study of Jung during the seventies; by the time he had written *The Second Coming,* he had a full realization of the Jungian viewpoint and wrote with a clear grasp of Jung's theory of archetypes. But more of this later because Jung is really a psychologist as well as a philosopher who deals with the essential problems of old age—death and rebirth—and his explorations of the mythic understanding of these matters must be examined closely in connection with the third period of the two authors' work.

---

[5]Barbara King, "Walter Percy Prevails," *Southern Voices* (May/June 1974): 22.

The psychologist most needed for an understanding of the middle phase of life and of the way Aiken and Percy handled it is Alfred Adler. Both writers probably underestimated Adler, but his viewpoint is crucial for understanding the chief problem of the middle-aged person: how to find a full belief in one's own importance without falling into delusions of grandeur. This has also been the chief problem of modern liberalism, and it is fitting that Adler in suggesting at least a partial solution was working within an international liberal tradition. Yet Anglo-American liberalism could not absorb the teachings of Adler to any great extent; at best it grasped only one side of his teachings, that having to do with the inferiority complex. Freud, as Trilling has said, taught modern man how to strike through the mask, that is, how to look beneath surface appearances, and liberalism absorbed this teaching. But the liberal failure that two mavericks like Aiken and Percy would seek to rectify in their work lies primarily in the area Adler deals with, which concerns the individual's reaction to his deep sense of unimportance in a mechanized world. This reaction is often one of violence, and in fact it is on the rock of violence that the whole ship of modern liberalism, as well as modern civilization itself, threatens to founder. The best solution many liberals can think of for this problem is to deny its importance.

As I will now suggest in discussing the chief work of the middle periods of Aiken and Percy, the problem of modern violence is closely connected with the deep concerns of the ordinary man reaching the well-known "mid-life crisis" of his forties. The middle-aged man asks who he really is at this critical period of life; and if he is not established as a member of some particular group, or even if he is, he often finds himself crushed by what seems like the terrible ordinariness of his existence.

III

Conrad Aiken in both his poetry and fiction of the thirties addressed the problem of the ordinary man facing the ultimate life crisis: whether he should go on living at all. Aiken himself lived out his own crisis in those early years of the thirties while writing his best novel, *Great Circle* (1933); some of his finest stories, which were published in *Among the Lost People* (1934); and his poetic drama, *The Coming Forth by Day of Osiris Jones* (1931). He had already begun in the late twenties that series of metaphysical poems he would call the Preludes, which would reach their artistic peak in the thirties and early forties. In all of these works, in one way or another, Aiken would pose the problems of humans who feel left out of the mainstream and who at once feel in themselves deep potentialities and a sense of meaninglessness and purposelessness. In one sense he was mirroring the difficulties of man caught up in the Great Depression, and in another he was probing his own feeling that, in spite of some literary successes and a certain amount of recognition, his career was stalled. Aiken thus considers in much of his work of the early thirties the classic problem of the inferiority complex formulated by Alfred Adler. Freud had thrown Adler out of his little circle for suggesting that the desire for power could play a role in sexual intercourse—Freud preferred his sexuality theory uncontaminated by other drives—but later psychological studies do show, in fact, that the need for power and prestige, or ego-gratification, plays a role in everything a human does. Indeed, the basic drive of man may not be as much for sex as for status. T. S. Eliot late in his career seems to have reached something like this conclusion. In *The Cocktail Party* Edward confesses to Harcourt-Reilly, the psychologist, "But I am obsessed by the thought of my own insignificance." Harcourt-Reilly replies, "Half of the harm that is done in this world is due to people who want to feel important."[6]

As *Great Circle* begins, we see the hero Andrew Cather becoming suddenly aware of his own self-destructiveness. He tells himself, "You are deliberately seeking a catastrophe—you are yourself in the act of creating a disaster."[7] Cather's whole life is falling apart with his career at a standstill and his wife having an affair with his best friend. A sensitive man, Cather is too moral to project his anger and his own sense of unimportance on others but instead turns his fury on himself. On his way through Boston Cather sees the police investigating a suicide in the Charles River; he takes it as a symbol and admonishes himself, "Cling to life, you poor bastard."[8] For Cather, as he goes through Boston to confront his adulterous wife in Cambridge, sex is the one aspect of his life that seems least important: "Sex! Good jumping Jesus, to think of the nuisance, and nothing but nuisance sex had been."[9] Although Aiken depicts the struggles of a man caught in a crisis in which self-importance is everything, particularly with his wife

---

[6]T. S. Eliot, *The Complete Poems and Plays* (New York: Harcourt, Brace and World, 1952) 348.
[7]Conrad Aiken, *Great Circle* (New York: Charles Scribner, 1933) 8.
[8]Ibid., 38.
[9]Ibid., 45.

kicking the last props from under his shaky ego, the solution to Cather's problem is achieved by Freudian means and with the help of Freudian knowledge.

Freud kept *Great Circle* in his waiting room, probably because he believed it to be psychologically accurate, but the discoveries that Cather makes in the novel are of the sort that have a basis in the views not only of Freud but also of Adler and Jung. Controlled LSD experiments conducted in the seventies by psychiatrists in California indicate that the psyche contains various layers, certain of which could be called Freudian, Adlerian, and Jungian. But the motives of a human, as Aiken shows in *Great Circle,* are knotted together in such a way that no one authority could give a final explanation of the nature of the psyche. However, Aiken also demonstrates in this novel—and this pleased Freud and continues to please psychoanalysts—that the Freudian method, which utilizes confession (or "talking out") and dream interpretation, does yield results in psychic terms. The novel was written with the symphonic form in mind ("constructed in four parts, like a symphony, each section with a different key and movement of its own," Aiken tells us).[10] Its first movement, psychologically speaking, is Adlerian. At the end of this movement Cather, overcome by his powerlessness, sinks into drunkenness. In section two the Freudian theme is sounded as Cather dredges up from his unconscious mind with the help of the releasing power of whiskey the repressed childhood memories of his own mother's adulterous affair with his uncle. Section three continues the Freudian theme with Cather visiting a psychoanalyst, who helps him see that his own sadistic wounding of his wife springs from his hatred of his mother. Section four takes a step beyond Freud into an area that must properly be called Jungian. Cather realizes that his psychic wound cannot be healed simply by confessing his problems and by interpreting his dreams. He sees that he must perform certain ritual actions on his own with no one's help. And thus section four deals primarily with his returning to the scene of his mother's death in search of an exorcism of his childhood trauma. This fictional return would be paralleled three years after the publication of the novel by Aiken's own return to Savannah to face fully his own parents' death, a return he would describe in *Ushant* as marking a milestone in his psychic rebirth. Aiken and Cather then became mythic pilgrims who accept a journey in which the demons of one's past are met and overcome

---

[10]Conrad Aiken, "Author's Preface," *3 Novels* (New York: McGraw Hill, 1965) iii.

by believing in the healing powers contained within the psyche itself. Cather thus can begin to cry out as he awakens from dreams of his long repressed suffering, which has caused him to hate the intimacies of marriage: "You in the flesh again, redivius."[11] And then as he sees what the process of exorcism will mean, he thinks: "It would be good to touch, for the last time, that agony, and to exorcise it . . . the strange and exciting mixture of astonishment and suffering with which—at a moment of discovery— one loses oneself in order to create oneself! The end that is still conscious of its beginnings. Birth that remembers death."[12]

The fact that Aiken, even while he was moving toward attempted suicide, could be writing a novel like *Great Circle* in which he dug deeper in his fiction than he ever had before, using some of his own most powerful and revealing dreams, shows how deeply he was devoted to the concept and the reality of pilgrimage. And the fact that *Great Circle* ends on a note of hope with a vision of rebirth indicates that Aiken had definitely accepted the kind of mythic thinking found in the psychology of C. G. Jung. This is not to say that Jung was the primary influence on Aiken in his development of the "mythical method," as Eliot called the mythic way of perceiving experience in his review of Joyce's *Ulysses* in *The Criterion*. Aiken, of course, had admitted Jung's influence on his work, but it is certain that Joyce, who was greatly influenced by Jung, also provided Aiken with Jungian ideas. Even closer to Aiken was T. S. Eliot, who after 1920 was firmly committed to the mythic viewpoint. Aiken wrote Houston Peterson:

> (Incidentally, I have known Eliot ever since my second year at Harvard, intimately, and the extent of cross-influence here is incalculable; Eliot and I have always in a curious sense kept our eyes on each other; anyway, I've always kept my eyes on him, and I fancy he has increasingly kept his eyes on me.)[13]

Eliot's work shows little direct influence by depth psychologists like Freud and Jung; but, as Elizabeth Drew has demonstrated, Eliot's concept of the "mythical method" is much the same as Jung's: "The central experience which informs most of the poetry of Eliot is this same age-old pattern of

---

[11]Aiken, *Great Circle*, 303.
[12]Ibid., 342.
[13]Killorin, *Selected Letters of Conrad Aiken*, 145-46.

symbolic death and birth, lived through as an intense personal experience and accepted as a central truth of a religious faith.''[14]

Eliot through extensive reading in literature and anthropology worked out a vision of myth for himself, which of course had an effect on Aiken. But at the same time, Aiken himself was working out, all during the twenties, his own mythical insights not only through literary and psychological studies but also through reading about archeological work, particularly in the field of Egyptology. Probably the most mythic work of his middle period is *The Coming Forth by Day of Osiris Jones,* which has as its background some of the archeological discoveries of Flinders Petrie. By 1931 Aiken had already worked out a mythic vision that had at its core the concept of death and rebirth, which he makes ample use of in *Osiris Jones.* The concepts that went into this expressionistic poetic drama were those of death and psychic rebirth and were essentially optimistic. They had to be for Aiken to go on living at all at the end of the twenties and the beginning of the thirties. Not only were there the troubles of America as well as personal financial problems for Aiken, there was also his long personal involvement with the deranged poet John Gould Fletcher, who in 1932 attempted suicide and was committed to Bethlehem Hospital. But even more basic to Aiken's life crisis at the pivotal age of thirty-nine were the loss of a teaching position at Harvard and his wife's desertion of him for another man, events that form the basis for *Great Circle.* In a letter to Eliot from Cambridge on 31 March 1928, Aiken sums up without a trace of self-pity those two shattering blows to what was always a fragile ego.

> As for me, I've been fired for moral turpitude. . . . Next? I don't know. I may go to New York. I was planning to return to my abandoned family in Rye, in June; but [Martin] Armstrong has beaten me to it. He is going to marry Jessie.[15]

Yet even as Aiken is going through years that can in some ways best be described in terms of Adlerian psychology, he is working at his deepest level of creativity on mythic verse and on the drama *Osiris Jones.* In 1927 he began the Preludes and completed them in 1931. In all, there were sixty-three poems in this series. He had first called them *Preludes to Attitude,* but they were published in 1931 under the title *Preludes for Memnon.* Ai-

---

[14]Elizabeth Drew, *T. S. Eliot: The Design of His Poetry* (New York: Charles Scribner's Sons, 1949) 14.

[15]Killorin, *Selected Letters of Conrad Aiken,* 142.

ken undoubtedly realized as early as 1927 that he was moving toward a climax of crises that would finally culminate in his attempted suicide late in 1932. His efforts to find a mythic view that would aid him in putting his past behind him were in fact successful, and he would write years later in *Ushant* that after his failed suicide attempt the past "had been, in some uncanny fashion, finished."[16]

Aiken's awareness of his own death wish was always closely related to a growing perception of a worldwide death wish. Out of the world pain of the Great Depression, there grew in the thirties a sense of world apocalypse. Many felt that the next great war, should it come, might mark the end of man himself. As the thirties continued to see the expanding totalitarian regimes of Germany, Italy, Russia, and Japan, the belief grew that a new world war was inevitable. Liberals in Western Europe and America, even as they sprang to the defense of the infant Spanish republic in its struggle against fascism, were never more disheartened, caught as they were between Mussolini and Hitler on one hand and Stalin on the other. Aiken as a liberal felt the tug of political loyalties throughout the thirties and early forties, but he knew that his deepest commitment would have to remain that of writing the poetry and prose that marked his journey upward to a new life after the low point of his suicide attempt. The way in which that development of new life would take him at last to the celebration of human existence as he passed from middle age to old age I will discuss in the next chapter. Now, however, it is necessary to see how he dealt with world apocalypse in two great but still neglected works, *The Coming Forth by Day of Osiris Jones* and "The Poet in Granada."

Appearing in 1931, *Osiris Jones* reflects Aiken's awareness of a growing world apocalyptic mood following the crash of 1929. But the play also reveals his own application of his deepest metaphysical principles to both world problems and the personal problem of a mid-life crisis. The results of this application of principles led him to the affirmation of life renewal contained in *Osiris Jones*. Mircea Eliade's statement that myth is essentially a process of life-death-rebirth is well illustrated by the play. Furthermore, Aiken, in showing why rebirth is possible, solves the problems of the nature of man himself that were posed by certain conflicting ideologies of the century. Yet his newfound insights did not immediately relieve him of his painful feelings of unimportance. Aiken was being driven

---

[16]Conrad Aiken, *Ushant* (Cleveland: The World Publishing Company, 1962) 225-28.

toward suicide even while he was writing *Osiris Jones*, largely because he deeply felt this sense of personal worthlessness. The rising totalitarian powers in the thirties were announcing that man by himself was worthless and that only by his adherence to an all-encompassing state could he find his real worth. The Western liberals continued to emphasize the unique worth of the individual but could not point to where this worth resided. Adler offered hope to the liberal cause by proposing a new educational system, but finally he could suggest as a way of life no more than social cooperation and life adjustment. In a time of totalitarianism and apocalyptic social collapse, how could these remedies work? Aiken had long pondered the problem of man seen in terms of classical liberalism. His answer in *Osiris Jones* is that no matter how ordinary, or "common," any man might be, nevertheless he has the potential to be the god Osiris—or as his Grandfather Potter had said, everyone can become a god. This was one of Aiken's most basic premises, and he made a point of emphasizing it in the interview conducted by the *Paris Review*.[17] His protagonist, Osiris Jones, then is everyman, who is at once "the common man" but who, seen in his true light, is the god-man in the making. The good society for Aiken is one that helps, in all ways it can, the ordinary person achieve the life of godhead. Through a study of Flinders Petrie he thought he had found in ancient Egypt just such a society, and with the help of the *Egyptian Book of the Dead* he composed *Osiris Jones*.

The great question for liberalism in the thirties was how could the good society that stood for "life, liberty, and the pursuit of happiness" be achieved. Aiken's answer in *Osiris Jones* is the same as that given by James Joyce in *Finnegans Wake*. In fact, when Joyce saw the title of Aiken's work, he realized, as Richard Ellmann tells us, that here was a statement of the basic theme of his own masterwork still in progress. Joyce immediately felt the need to read *Osiris Jones* but never got around to it.[18] Aiken and Joyce in *Osiris Jones* and *Finnegans Wake* announce the inevitability of the death of the common man in the chaotic period that Vico, Joyce's chief philosophical guide, tells us every civilization must pass through. But the agony of the death process—or apocalypse as it is experienced in social terms—forces individuals to find what is deepest in themselves. For this reason the profoundest statement in the play is probably "Chaos—hurray!

---

[17]"Conrad Aiken: An Introduction," *Paris Review* (Winter/Spring 1968): 118.
[18]Richard Ellmann, *James Joyce* (New York: Viking Press, 1959) 745.

— is come again'' because it announces the full acceptance of the apocalyptic period in history as a necessary prelude for the new life in which the common man is transformed once again into the uncommon man, or god-man.

Joseph Campbell tells us that in the world's mythologies the deaths of both microcosm and macrocosm are basic events in the story of the continuing recovery of heroism. In *Osiris Jones* Aiken tells us that Everyman ''must go forth to the outer darkness / And die, and pick the deathless asphodels.''[19] Finally, Everyman after his journey into darkness declares his true devotion to the one great task, becoming a god: ''I have not shunned the god at his appearance. / I am pure. I am pure. I am pure. I am pure. I am pure'' (*CP*, 601). Following this the stars announce ''Chaos—hurray!—is come again'' (*CP*, 606). Then they cry ''Great Circle!,'' a symbolic statement of the fact that once again, as so many times before, the god-man appears speaking the true language of universal love, restoring paradise on earth. Then a few lines later Jones's death is announced; however, it is not death as extinction but as the passage to new life. The drama ends by showing the image of a wounded woman who awaits the return of Jones. She is Isis waiting for the return of Osiris. Interestingly enough, Joyce ends *Finnegans Wake* the same way: an old woman awaits the return of the Irish mythical hero Finn. Both Aiken and Joyce thus fulfill one of the roles of the shaman by invoking visions of a once and future paradise.

Aiken believed that there was a single god-power at the center of each human and that this power could be gradually awakened as one followed the footsteps of another, like Osiris, who had identified himself with the god within. The full awakening, leading to the restoration of an earthly paradise, would follow a chaotic period when life would be threatened with extinction. Aiken shows no real concern for the aspect of traditional Christian theology that speaks of the Word coming down from heaven and dwelling in the flesh among men. His view of the universe, based in part on the findings of natural science, excluded for him the possibility of a heavenly realm. Nevertheless, he believed in a divine dimension and that it was man's destiny to discover, by passing through death and chaos, the nature of this dimension. Osiris, Buddha, and Christ are among the great images of godly life in his poetry; but as Aiken grew older, Christ became

---

[19]Conrad Aiken, *Collected Poems* (New York: Oxford University Press, 1953) 599.

the central figure for him, as we can see in the work called *Brownstone Eclogues and Other Poems* (1942).

The opening poem of *Brownstone Eclogues,* "Sursum Corda," rehearses many of his poetic themes of the thirties but does so in specifically Christian terms. Man, as we are told, continually experiences Christ's death. We experience, the poem says, a separation from Christ, and "we faint in darkness for an age." But the time of reunion with Christ returns and then

> *We wear the rainbow and the rain, and see:*
> *We break the numbers and the names, and see:*
> *We are thyself, the heart of light, and see.*

> (*CP,* 780)

Frederick J. Hoffman rightly says about this poem that "Aiken's gift, here admirably controlled, has no better evidence of what it may do."[20] Yet Hoffman relegates to a footnote Aiken's greatest religious poem, "The Poet in Granada." Virtually ignored by Hoffman, Martin, and other commentators, this work, included in *Brownstone Eclogues,* marks the most decisive step Aiken took beyond Unitarianism in his vision of the role of Christ in the redemption of man, yet it repudiates in no way his earlier metaphysics.

Aiken himself spoke at some length to me about the importance of "The Poet in Granada" to the whole body of his work. For him it contained the essence of the ritual tradition of Catholicism. Certainly more than any other work it represents that other pole of his metaphysical view, a pole that was anchored in his attachment to Spanish culture and to the viewpoint of George Santayana. This long poem is at once a metaphysical statement and a tribute to García Lorca, the great Spanish poet put to death by the fascists. It is a statement about the coming of the Spanish Civil War, that opening explosion of European conflagration. The poet Lorca must die, Aiken tells us, but his essence is Christ; and, like Christ, his words will rise again to form a new language that will, through its inherent Logos power, once again bring order and goodness to the world.

The poem opens with a vision of an incomparable natural beauty surrounding the city of Granada. The time is Palm Sunday; Christ's entry into Jerusalem is being reenacted in the midst of the urban ugliness and chaos

---

[20]Frederick J. Hoffman, *Conrad Aiken* (New York: Twayne Publishers, 1962) 144.

of a once great city. By the miracle of a ritual performed with belief, the presence of Christ is summoned: "And Jesus, the poet, the condemned man, self-condemned, / Had entered the Street of the Catholic Kings" (*CP,* 652). But only a few who believe can experience the presence of Christ in modern Granada. Most of the city's inhabitants cling to a ritual of their own, the bullfight. In re-creating in the poem a modern bullfight, Aiken shows us how what was once a mythic ritual ("the dedication of the undying to death") has become a destructive pseudo-ritual dedicated to Priapus and Bacchus. Out of the orgies of the crowds at the bullfight come "the harvest of murder" and "the illusion, the dreadful and desperate dream" (*CP,* 658).

Man lives by some form of ritual, but the pseudo-ritual enhances his powers of destruction, which in time must erupt in apocalyptic fury, destroying civilizations. This is because the human mind is asleep and the language of poetry—the one language that can make the good society possible—is unheard.

> *The poet, the veiled recumbent, lies sleeping, lies solitary,*
> *While human returns to human;*
> *The god, the veiled mystery, lies watchful, lies waiting;*
> *lies fertile, while the human sleeps.*

(CP, 655)

The poem ends as it began with a view of the beauty of nature, symbolic of the surrounding metaphysical dimension.

Aiken thus answers the fears of liberals who saw in the death of poets like Lorca the crushing by totalitarian governments, based as they are on the absolutizing of certain ideas, of all aspects of a free society. People caught up in false rituals bring on the meaningless slaughters of apocalypse; they surrender themselves to a totalitarian madness because of their blindness. Yet the poet in the role of shaman must at last awake to announce restoration of the paradise, symbolized in the poem by the harmony of nature. The pain of seemingly endless suffering at last brings the poet and his audience to metaphysical awareness and prepares humanity for the emergence of a new and better world.

It is fitting that *Brownstone Eclogues* should appear in 1942: the year of greatest apocalyptic battles in Russia and a time when the world might well have descended into a permanent Nazi nightmare. Although he would publish *The Soldier: A Poem* in 1944, *Brownstone Eclogues* marks the high point of Aiken's apocalyptic vision, which began to appear as a major statement in 1931: the year when both *Preludes for Memnon* and *Osiris Jones* were published. After the war a theme that was present as early as *Preludes for Memnon* comes to full flower: the celebration of the growing insight and joy springing from the acceptance of the personal forces of apocalypse that had so long haunted Aiken and that had reached their peak in the suicide attempt of 1932. After 1945 Aiken no longer will be concerned with world apocalypse but will deal at his best with the spiritual fruit springing from his growing triumph over the forces of darkness. There is a world apocalypse, the myths of various cultures tell us, that in time leads to a new golden age; but there is also the personal apocalypse, which if survived, leads to a relatively joyous old age that is primarily concerned with wisdom. Works like *Ushant* and *A Letter from Li Po and Other Poems* would contain the fruits of the postwar wisdom of Conrad Aiken, found, for instance, in *Thee,* a work of the late sixties.

IV

Walker Percy shortly before and during World War II would find himself suffering from a sense of isolation and feelings of inferiority that inevitably would be felt by a student from the provinces living in New York and by anyone isolated in a tubercular world. He never sank to the suicidal depths that Aiken knew in the early thirties, but in New York he did fall into his old habit of too much moviegoing and for a time accepted psychiatric assistance. Like Aiken, Percy would seek to face his own problems in the best of his early fiction; but by his third novel, *Love in the Ruins,* he had come up squarely against the apocalyptic theme he saw reflected in the social disruption that America experienced in racial conflicts and the struggles centering around Viet Nam. This strife came to a peak with the Kent State massacre in 1970, a year before *Love in the Ruins* appeared. As one consciously working in the continental existentialist tradition, Percy was deeply connected in viewpoint to the twentieth-century apocalyptic vision, of which intellectual historian F. L. Baumer has said: ''The 'crisis thinking' so prevalent in Europe today feeds upon the wars and rumors of war, the concentration camps, the tyranny, the economic and social dislocation and . . . the Big Machine—the big state, party, business, labor union, the ultimate military weapon—which reduces the individual to insignificance."[21] The sense of both individual and social crisis is strong in all of Percy's fiction, but in *Love in the Ruins* he plunges into the heart of the problems caused by disruption. His answers to the problems are by no means as gloomy as one might expect, and they are couched in terms often witty and sometimes ambiguous. Yet underneath it all, the novel's protagonist, like those of his two earlier novels, is a man who is seeking a wholeness of existence he can find only in a religious commitment. The chief differences are that Tom More is a middle-aged man much more deeply sunk in psychic turmoil than Percy's young protagonists and the society depicted in the novel is one of the future in which full-scale social disintegration has occurred.

Love in the Ruins lacks that depth of insight into character so highly prized by the admirers of *The Moviegoer* and *The Last Gentleman*. For one thing, Percy sacrifices psychic exploration (which he returned to in his next novel, *Lancelot*) in order to present a large-scale picture of society in decline and the particular decline of one man—all done in terms of the novel of the absurd as written, say, by Joseph Heller. There is much wit, much sharp and satirical insight into attitudes that might be called pseudo-apocalyptic. Yet Percy does present the suffering of a man seeking a new life beyond the depths of his own depravity. Surely J. Gerald Kennedy is wrong when he says that the novel's revelation "comes to us finally not as the confession of a fellow sufferer but as the clinical diagnosis of an angel orbiting earth."[22] Looking at *Lancelot*, published six years after *Love in the Ruins,* we see the profound suffering of a man who cannot escape his fixations, but in *Love in the Ruins* we see this same individual overcoming disintegration by accepting the path of pilgrimage. Yet the protagonist is placed in a context of social satire. Much has been made by critics of the fact that, as Kennedy says, "Walker Percy likes to compare his role as a novelist with that of the physician or diagnostician."[23] *Love in the Ruins* is probably the author's best novel of diagnosis, and because so much effort is placed upon diagnosis the protagonist cannot, given the fictional

---

[21]F. L. Baumer, "Twentieth-Century Version of Apocalypse," *European Intellectual History since Darwin and Marx,* ed. W. Warren Wager (New York: Harper Torchbooks, 1967) 115.

[22]J. Gerald Kennedy, "The Sundered Self and the Riven World: *Love in the Ruins,*" in *The Art of Walker Percy,* ed. Panthea R. Broughton (Baton Rouge: Louisiana State Press, 1979) 136.

[23]Ibid., 115.

terms Percy has chosen to work in, have his inner depths revealed. In other words, *Love in the Ruins* is not primarily a psychological novel like *The Last Gentleman* or *Lancelot* and should not be so judged.

Love in the Ruins should be valued as Percy's finest fictional statement of the problems that have developed around modern science and liberalism in the late twentieth century. As a medical diagnostician Percy indeed probes the attempts of certain modern people to use both science and liberalism to dehumanize man. In showing how these attempts are made, he succeeds in defining both science and liberalism in terms of metaphysics, to place them, that is, in the metaphysical setting out of which they emerged in the late nineteenth century. The two groups—contemporary scientists and liberals—are placed in an imaginary city called Fedville. In fact, the protagonist, Dr. Thomas More, is caught up in helping the other scientists, who "are mostly liberals and unbelievers," control individuals and their environment so far as it is possible in a chaotic society where government has only a limited power.[24] But as a Catholic who still remembers his metaphysical training, Percy sees that many liberal scientists lack a belief in man as free and essentially related to the divine source of existence. The result is that scientists who are given power over people seek to give man's life meaning by organizing him so that he can be "adjusted" to an environment created by scientist-engineers whose liberalism consists in continually professing concern and even "love" for the people they are constantly manipulating "for their own good."

As the novel progresses, More begins to face the fact of his own shadow side. He has invented a machine to probe the souls of people with which he hopes to "help" people and to win the Nobel Prize, that great symbol for him of scientific achievement. Yet his remembered Catholicism allows him to see the folly of his warped vision, to see that in fact he has poisoned the lives of the two people nearest him: Doris, his wife, and Samantha, his daughter. Their deaths rest upon his conscience. Unlike the scientists of Fedville, who regard the conscious, reasoning mind as the only part of man worth considering, he cannot project his shadow onto others different from himself. For him the shadow side of the psyche, which the Fedville scientists deny exists, is very real. Thus he must face the turmoil in his own soul, and he comes in time to accept his own destructiveness.

---

[24]Walker Percy, *Love in the Ruins: The Adventures of a Bad Catholic at a Time Near the End of the World* (New York: Farrar, Straus and Giroux, 1971) 15.

By accepting responsibility for the destructiveness of his own earlier repressed shadow, More can experience one of those classical confrontations with evil that often mark the beginning of pilgrimage. Percy shows him encountering the shadow in the form of Art Immelmann (who can be seen as either internal or external or both). More tries to hate the "diabolical abuse" of this shadow figure but is told that the shadow is powerless except as he is allowed power by the individual himself. He tells More: "We only help people do what they want to do. We facilitate interaction in order to accumulate reliable data" (*LR*, 363). Art offers to get More the Nobel Prize or anything else he freely chooses. And then More suddenly sees that life is essentially so many free choices and that it is the free choice to follow God that gives an individual the power to rid oneself of domination by the shadow. More makes the essential choice; thus his Catholicism, instead of being only a memory, becomes at last an active force at work in his life.

As he moves onto the path of pilgrimage, More does not cease to be either a scientist or a liberal, nor does he lose immediately all his desires to "help" the world and become famous. But once he has been on the path of pilgrimage for a short time, he can look back and see how he has changed: "It took religion to save me from the spirit world, from orbiting the earth like Lucifer and the angels . . . it took nothing less than . . . eating Christ himself to make me mortal man again and let me inhabit my own flesh and love . . . in the morning" (*LR*, 254). As Kennedy points out, by taking communion, More "once again touches the vital thread which can bring the sundered self together."[25] The healing of the split self means that More can again make a human use of his reasoning powers and at the same time enter into a creative emotional relationship with others, particularly his new wife. The end of the book finds him living "with love" the ordinary life amidst the ruins of the old "Auto Age," before the shopping centers were covered with vines. We see him wearing sackcloth, barbecuing a chicken, drinking bourbon, and singing popular songs from the dead time when he lived in a suburb called Paradise Estates. His priest, Father Smith, sums up the good life of the new age when he tells More that we must "like doing our jobs, you being a better doctor, I being a better priest, showing a bit of ordinary kindness to people, particularly to our own families . . . doing what we can for our poor unhappy country" (*LR*, 399). As a man on pilgrim-

---

[25]Kennedy, "The Sundered Self," 127.

age More accepts the daily tasks given him by God, becoming a better scientist and doctor and even taking part in a new version of liberal politics.

Like all of Percy's novels, *Love in the Ruins* deals with the subject of
religious pilgrimage, but probably the central subject of the novel is the
modern apocalypse that Percy discusses in his essay "Notes for a Novel
about the End of the World." The novel is primarily, as I have suggested,
a lighthearted satire that does not dig deeply into the modern disintegrating
soul, as *The Last Gentleman* and *Lancelot* do. Its satire lacks the profundity of a Swift or even an Orwell. Yet in dealing with his own vision of
modern apocalypse, Percy makes some very serious points, in a sometimes lighthearted manner, about the death and rebirth both of the individual and society. In doing so he is working in the tradition of that master he
tells us in "Notes" he early selected, James Joyce. Like Joyce, Eliot, Yeats,
Aiken, and other serious modern authors, he uses the "mythical method"
to show that it is possible for individuals and societies to die and be reborn
without total catastrophe. What is probably unique about Percy among the
important modern writers of mythic and religious pilgrimage is that he
shows in a book like *Love in the Ruins* how it is possible for a society to
suffer the total death of one culture and enter a new age in which culture
is reborn and social institutions are recreated. Percy also suggests some of
the actual details of such a transformation. Here, I believe, we see the profoundest side of his comic vision, which manifested itself at times in *The
Last Gentleman* and will appear again in *The Second Coming* but which
has its apotheosis in *Love in the Ruins*.

What Percy means by apocalypse is clearly stated in "Notes" as "the
passing of one age and the beginning of another," and this is the process
he describes in *Love in the Ruins*.[26] Yet he shows an interest in the ultimate
apocalypse of Christianity as well as the mythic concept of the return to a
golden age that Aiken, for instance, deals with in *Osiris Jones*. Unlike Aiken, he shows the dangers of becoming possessed by ideas of ultimate
apocalypse. *Love in the Ruins, Lancelot,* and *The Second Coming* all deal
with this matter, and they suggest that a repressed self-destructiveness often
leads to a morbid concern with the end of the world because the individual
cannot face creatively the ordinariness of most of life. As Percy suggests

---

[26]Walker Percy, *The Message in the Bottle: How Queer Man Is, How Queer Language
Is, and What One Has to Do with the Other* (New York: Farrar, Straus & Giroux, 1979)
114.

in an essay, the problem of modern man is not so much what will happen if the atomic bomb falls but what will occur if it does not. Yet he implies that there is for the Christian a connection between the ultimate apocalypse of St. John the Divine and the ordinary apocalyptic situations that occur when one age dies and another begins. The Christian always has in mind the possibility of Christ's return but knows that no dates have been set for him; yet in the apocalyptic statements of both Christ and St. John, the Christian sees the need to face the devil both in one's life and in a dying world. By facing the power of destruction with faith, not once but many times, the Christian in Percy's novels can encounter a series of rebirths leading him to wholeness of life. Thus Percy, like Aiken, suggests ways in which the individual in achieving psychic wholeness can be his own shaman. At the same time, Percy implies the coming of a new age of love.

In all of Percy's novels the problem of suicide, whether with a razor or with immersion of the self in movies or drugs, is one of the chief issues. In *Love in the Ruins* Percy asks, why is all of society in the late twentieth century so self-destructive? The answer is that people seek to be either angels or beasts, not knowing what being human really means. When angelism produces destructive results, humans blame not themselves but their activities. Thus they believe that either science or technology or religion or liberalism (or conservatism) is at fault. Percy clearly shows us that the human being is at fault because he has rejected the path of pilgrimage or does not even know such a path ever existed.

Cleanth Brooks in his essay "Walker Percy and Modern Gnosticism" analyzes angelism as depicted in *Love in the Ruins* and *Lancelot* as an aspect of modern gnosticism. Brooks selects Eric Voegelin as the leading authority on that contemporary way of thinking called gnosticism, which leads man to forget the metaphysical foundations of both humanity and the universe and urges him to solve human problems by his own means, preferably those of science and technology. The protagonist of *Lancelot,* Brooks tells us, believes "that man is not responsible for evil and that his salvation depends on his own efforts."[27] This statement sums up the actions of More before his return to the path of pilgrimage and all of Lance's actions. But what is the relationship between gnosticism and self-destruction? The answer, Percy says, is that in working for one's own salvation and that of

---

[27]Cleanth Brooks, "Walker Percy and Modern Gnosticism," in *The Art of Walker Percy,* 270-71.

others, one in time absolutizes what he considers to be his own best self. Thus the scientist who is also a gnostic will absolutize his science. Reductionism follows, and everything is seen in terms of one's own particular science. Thus aspects of the self are forgotten, and one projects one's shadow onto those who seem to be enemies. Finally, like More, one sees himself as an angel, or even a Messiah, circling the earth with the great cure for all ills. Yet, like More, one is constantly trying to kill himself or kill somebody else because his angelism has left him in a profound state of isolation.

Brooks is right in seeing Voegelin as one of the great authorities on modern gnosticism, but Percy himself was awakened from a view almost totally based on science by one of the great dissecters of this way of thought, Kierkegaard, who saw in Hegelianism all the dangers of modern gnosticism. Hegel's system was in many ways the beginning of the practice of replacing the Christian God with ideology. Europeans, Kierkegaard saw, were beginning to live under the Hegelian dispensation in which an idea system would provide painless answers for all problems. No longer, the modern gnostics believed, would the painful path of the religious pilgrimage be necessary. Hegelian ideology (later to develop into Marxian and other idea systems) would spell the end of any consideration of the mysterious subjective life of humanity. And by ignoring that aspect of existence, man would experience, along with the loss of the pilgrimage, the absence of love: his soul's greatest desire. In America Nathaniel Hawthorne saw the gnostic element in much of American transcendentalism and recorded its rejection of pilgrimage in favor of gnosticism in his story "The Celestial Railroad." But Kierkegaard is credited with being the founder of the philosophical school of existentialism because he wrote so deeply about the subjective life, that side of humanity from which spring the deepest ethical and artistic intuitions.

A close examination of the plight of Thomas More before his return to pilgrimage and also that of Lance Lamar throughout all of *Lancelot* will reveal an understanding of gnosticism that comes in part from Dostoyevski, whose work Percy read along with Kierkegaard's during his period of recovery from tuberculosis. Dostoyevski in *Crime and Punishment, The Idiot,* and *The Brothers Karamazov* reveals in detail, and probably with the greatest intensity ever brought to the subject by a novelist, what can happen to someone who follows modern gnosticism to its ultimate conclusions. Raskolnikov in *Crime and Punishment* becomes a manic-depressive who sees himself alternately as a louse and a superman above all laws. The political conspirators in *The Idiot* become depraved criminals, and Ivan Karamazov becomes so isolated in his intellectual arrogance that finally he is led to a confrontation with the Devil himself. Dostoyevski's answer to gnosticism in all three books is the Christian pilgrimage: the only way, he believed, that man can find the love necessary to overcome the isolation that must inevitably spring from the consequences of seeing oneself as the center of the universe.

Percy deals with all of the above existential problems in a relatively humorous and satiric manner in *Love in the Ruins* and in a darker, more sober manner in *Lancelot,* a book in which the protagonist moves into satanic corridors as frightening as any in Dostoyevski's writing. Studies of Percy in relationship to the continental existentialists make it clear he is working the same vein of philosophical ore, but the question that needs to be asked is what he gives his readers that other existentialists do not. He cannot, of course, compete with Kierkegaard and Dostoyevski in sheer imaginative power, nor can he deal as brilliantly with the absurd and futile aspects of existence as Sartre and Camus. He takes into full account their findings concerning the deep subjective life ignored by gnostics, but his chief contribution to existential literature is that he can show us how humans can develop fruitfully as they proceed down the path of pilgrimage. Even the greatest existentialists, like Kierkegaard and Dostoyevski, rebel so much against the pseudo-rationalism of gnostic systems like Hegel's that they deny the role of reason and abstract thinking in the full development of the individual who is on pilgrimage. Percy's work, as it matures, seems to say that we must cultivate reason and science even while we are developing the subjective aspects of existence. His pilgrimage involves a search for the unified vision in which the objective and subjective aspects of existence work in some degree of harmony. As a modern shaman he often points to the possibilities, through continuing pilgrimage, of a unified existence for individuals and for societies.

Percy will show the fruits of the pilgrimage in terms of unified existence most extensively in his fifth novel, *The Second Coming.* But it is in his fourth novel, *Lancelot,* that he digs deepest into the mind of a man who clings to his heroism as an ideal but who is gradually taken over by the shadow forces without being aware of it. Lance Lamar in *Lancelot* has done all the things contemporary American society expects of its conventional heroes. He has been a great athlete, achieved wealth and a beautiful wife and children, and devoted himself to doing good works for his fellowman through the pursuit of old-fashioned liberal politics, even to the point of politically helping blacks in a South that would deny them full citizenship. But this heroism is not enough for him; he must take the reins of power into his own hands and destroy the bad and exalt the good. In short, he must play god. Finally he tries to become a pseudo-shaman by creating through his own unaided efforts the earthly paradise.

By the end of the novel Lance has passed from the old liberalism to a kind of gnostic "liberalism" that became important in America in the late sixties and early seventies and has played throughout the century a growing political role in the world in the form of terrorism. Like Hegel, Lance arms himself with a theory of history; and, like Marx, he adopts an apocalyptic view of modernism that says the good people will soon kill off all the bad people and then will establish the perfect life on earth. Lance sees himself as beginning the "Third Revolution," or "new order," with his own forces of light contending with the forces of what he calls "buggery," which for him is the shadow. He strikes the first blow by destroying a hated Hollywood director who has seduced his wife and by burning up his own ancestral mansion as if to cleanse himself of a dead past. He is confined as a homicidal maniac but expects to be released, having been pronounced "cured." After his release, Lance will go to Virginia to found a new Eden with the perfected woman, who for him is a young woman confined in the next room who believes that she has been made innocent by being raped and forced to engage in fellatio. Thus Percy shows his protagonist to be at once a Manichean (one type of old-fashioned gnostic) and a believer in a doctrine found in various forms of Satanism that says purity can be found only through depraved sexuality. Thus Lancelot, by repressing his shadow and refusing pilgrimage, turns shamanism upside down.

Lancelot is the story not only of Lancelot Lamar but of his friend Percival, the priest who is hearing the story of Lance's life from his own lips. The irony running throughout the book is that gnosticism in all its forms has become so strong that most people would regard Percival as a kind of harmless or even dangerous lunatic, mainly because he is on the path of pilgrimage, and Lancelot as a great man gone wrong but who can be "cured" by psychotherapy and sent back into the world to do good. We see Percival mainly through Lance's eyes, but when we begin to understand Lance's madness we can see the progress Percival has made on his pilgrimage. And we can see, as Cleanth Brooks says, that Percy is presenting in Kierkegaardian terms an either/or situation. In the final analysis, Percy is telling us, life in our times must be either Lance's way or Percival's way. One way leads to paranoid destruction and the other to a celebration of life that sees Lance's destructiveness but refuses to condemn the man.

What ultimately is the source of this destructiveness? The life and work of another founder of modern existentialism, Friedrich Nietzsche, must be invoked to explain the pathological conditions of the protagonists of *Love in the Ruins* and *Lancelot*. Nietzsche was haunted by the emptiness of modern life and attributed this sense of emptiness to what he called the "death of God." What follows when the "death" is apprehended is stated in Nietzsche's formula that if God is dead, then I must become God. Nietzsche's way of becoming God was to invoke a god from the past whom he called Dionysus and to announce the coming of the higher man (superman) who could create a new way of life, and with whom he identified himself, even to the point of madness. In a seminar on the subject, Barbara Hannah said, "Jung made it abundantly clear that Nietzsche had become insane because of his identification with the Superman."[28] Nietzsche, like several nineteenth-century writers, identified with the power of some shaman of the future who would announce a new age. He could not see himself as a modern shaman moving on a path toward higher shamanistic experiences, one who must see himself as an antihero in many ways.

The great problem that deeply concerns Percy and many of the existentialists before him is that of nothingness, which the antihero sometimes experiences. For Percy the one existentialist philosopher above all others who dealt successfully with that problem is Marcel, yet Marcel did not work out his solution in terms of ordinary contemporary experience as Percy did. Therefore, Percy is as important as Marcel in dealing with nothingness and the journey beyond it. In the seventies Percy turned to a serious study of Jung; and in writing *Lancelot,* possibly his profoundest novel, he deals with the form of superman identification (angelism, as one of his mentors, Allen Tate, called it) that has become a commonplace in modern gnosticism. But behind what Jung calls archetypal identification lie a sense of isolation and the awareness of nothingness. An exploration of nothingness and an

---

[28]Barbara Hannah, *Jung: His Life and Work* (New York: G. P. Putnam's Sons, 1981) 227.

encounter with the archetypes mark Percy's deepest fictional efforts in the seventies and early eighties.

V

In a large sense Aiken and Percy were always writing about problems caused by a sense of isolation. It well might be that isolation is the great unadmitted subject of modern literature. Angel Medina in an important meditation on the novel and modernism (one influenced by the deconstructionists) says that "silence becomes a framework for the text, not just an element of it." "Thus," he goes on to say, "the darkest elements of the expressive process become the principal factors to be interpreted in a text."[29] The dark elements of the expressive process take over center stage from the elements of "light," as represented often by science and liberal politics in some of the best work of Aiken and Percy. Yet, unlike many modern artists, Aiken and Percy found it impossible to live primarily with their conscious thoughts and their personal knowledge of the dark element of experience. The reason was that they had suffered too much from the shadow side of life as a result of family disintegration. To live and to create at all, they had to push beyond their own deep awareness of modern silence and isolation. To do this meant to invoke the metaphysical realm not in terms of an idea system or a reasoned argument but rather in the language of concrete belief and choice, the language springing from their own shamanistic efforts to preserve their creativity. What Heinemann says of Marcel's philosophy can be applied to both: "Consequently the lonely isolated individual which formed the basis and starting-point of modern philosophy is replaced by a person standing in vital relations with others, and the *I think* by *we are.*"[30] Yet the ability to say genuinely "we are" is based on the continuing act of faith that Marcel, following Kierkegaard, took to be the essential act necessary for overcoming isolation and the sense of nothingness. Where Aiken and Percy most resemble Marcel is in their mutual belief that individuals can overcome their alienation by accepting relationships with others and that the conscious reason, Descartes' ego thinking, must also be taken into full account by the pilgrim who seeks transcendence.

---

[29]Angel Medina, *Reflection, Time and the Novel* (London: Routledge and Kegan Paul, 1979) 3.

[30]Heinemann, *Existentialism,* 146.

Celebrations
of Life after Sixty

Chapter VI

I

The path of pilgrimage is the constant in the best work of Conrad Aiken and Walker Percy. Both men reveal a continuing absorption with this their major theme and, as they matured as artists, increasingly show the fruits of pilgrimage. Both eventually put behind themselves the traumatic events of childhood. Yet both reveal in their work that pilgrimage at any age means a continual facing of the shadow side of life. In two important works that come at the advent of old age, there is at once greater emphasis on the fruits of pilgrimage and a deeper awareness of the struggle with opposing psychic forces than we see in earlier works.

As previously mentioned, *Ushant* was published when Aiken was sixty-three, and Percy brought forth *The Second Coming* in his sixty-fourth year.

Both reveal in these works their deepest apprehension of the problems of self-destruction, but also apparent in each is a sense of liberation that springs from putting aside self-destructive impulses. The very word *Ushant* means for Aiken "you shall not," the words of the castrating powers that threaten the pilgrim, telling him he must stop at one level of development and not push on to experience that unified personality and creativity the shaman eventually comes to know. Yet no other work of Aiken's is filled with such joyful wisdom as this book contains. The title of Percy's book reveals the problem of the pseudo-apocalyptic shadow in the life of his protagonist. This shadow, along with the protagonist's own unpurged self-destructiveness, hangs over his quest for self-fulfillment and love. Percy makes some telling statements about conservative and liberal aspects of religion in the South and suggests that organized religion itself in an age of affluence is sometimes one of the castrating powers barring the pilgrim on his journey. Yet no book of Percy's is as sunny, as genuinely comic, as wise in its insights into both individual and social problems in contemporary times as this novel.

Both *Ushant* and *The Second Coming* are works that continue the progress of protagonists in early novels. Both authors seem to be taking up an unfinished problem of pilgrimage. In fact, in Aiken's first novel, *Blue Voyage,* he shows the problems of pilgrimage at its beginning; but in *Ushant,* nearly thirty years later, he is as much interested in the fruits of discovery after years of pilgrimage as he is in the forces arrayed against the pilgrim. Percy's protagonist, Will Barrett, is a young man who enters upon the path of pilgrimage in *The Last Gentleman;* but whereas Aiken in *Ushant* presents a picture of continuing pilgrimage, Percy shows Barrett as a man about to enter old age who has forgotten his original quest and must begin again. Yet Percy shows far more of the fruit of continuing pilgrimage here than he does in any other novel. There are thus significant differences in the way Aiken and Percy reach the ripe wisdom found in these works of their sixties. What is similar is that they both see their pilgrimages as a path leading to the continuing discovery of glimpses of a metaphysical realm whose underlying presence makes possible the psychic development of the individual. Neither author is concerned with attempting to portray the extraordinary visions of pilgrims in religious traditions of earlier times—the sort, for instance, that occur in medieval romances. Instead, the sign for both that the metaphysical dimension has been manifested is the appearance of a lasting love between people. It is the occasional moment of metaphysical apprehension that also makes possible the loving and human use of knowledge (or science), the creation of imaginative works, and the development of meaningful social and political life.

I will continue to emphasize certain differences between the two authors. To do so, it is necessary, before analyzing their first important works of beginning old age, to trace the development of those aspects of their work that deal with the fruits of the pilgrimage. Aiken's work is obviously more diffuse and varied than Percy's. There is a concentration of purpose in Percy's five novels and in his essays, including the book-length essay *Lost in the Cosmos,* that is not found in the work of Aiken, who often experimented with the different genres of literature and with various forms within a particular genre. No modern writer's work requires greater critical discernment than Aiken's because of the uneven quality of some of it; whereas Percy, who has written less, maintains a relatively high standard of performance throughout his published work. But the older writer, just because he did take a good many chances, sometimes plunges—particularly in his verse—into depths not touched by the younger writer. Yet one thing they both have in common is their growing awareness after sixty that life can be, at least some of the time, a celebration. Present also in their work is always the pilgrimage, which means the continuing facing of shadow forces and the shamanic awareness in moments of epiphany of a realm of both joy and love.

II

Aiken's deepest awareness of the shadow forces of life was probably experienced in the early and middle thirties. It can be seen as early as *Preludes for Memnon,* published in 1931. The greatest fictional statement of this awareness is to be found in the story "Mr. Arcularis" (later to be turned into a play in 1951) and the novel *King Coffin.* The former is one of Aiken's great artistic achievements; the latter is an interesting failure. *King Coffin* (1935) is the closest that Aiken ever comes to the sort of existentialist fiction Percy has written, and in many ways its theme is the same as that of *Lancelot.* Frederick J. Hoffman rightly says of it that "its hero, Jasper Ammen, descends from Dostoevsky, Poe, and Nietzsche; and, in each case, he loses much from the inheritance."[1] Ammen, like Lance Lamar,

---

[1]Frederick J. Hoffman, *Conrad Aiken* (New York: Twayne Publishers, 1962) 53.

is seized by the hero image and orbits above the earth, looking down on a despised humanity. Both Ammen and Lamar despise, like Nietzsche, the antiheroic wherever they find it, in themselves or in others. The result is that Ammen moves ever deeper into shadow possession, projecting his own self-destructiveness onto others until at last he decides to commit the perfect crime by killing someone he does not know, someone who will represent all the pettiness in human life that, Nietzsche-like, he rails against. But in the process of plotting murder, he begins to discover both his own humanity and that of his victim. By the end of the novel, he is moving beyond shadow possession to an acceptance of ordinary human limitations, which he has tried to deny in himself and has despised in others. The failure of this book is due largely to a lack of depth in characterization. Aiken is obviously writing about a side of himself, as he was in *Blue Voyage* and *Great Circle,* but he does not delve deeply into his own paranoid tendencies. It is quite possible that he preferred to deal with them more indirectly in the Preludes. Certainly Aiken in the area of a fictional treatment of human destructiveness shows in *King Coffin* none of the courage and probing intensity Percy displayed in *Lancelot,* a book he obviously prepared himself for over a period of some years. But Percy is primarily a novelist, and Aiken is not.

It well may be that Aiken by 1935 had grown tired of the novel as a form for expressing his deepest thoughts and feelings. Certainly he would never again attempt a work of fiction as extensive as *King Coffin.* The two novels that would follow, *A Heart for the Gods of Mexico* (1939) and *Conversation: Or, Pilgrim's Progress, a Novel* (1940), would be relatively slight efforts when seen in relationship to his best work, though both would have virtues of their own. What had happened is that in the thirties Aiken was digging into his own life with increasing intensity in the best poetry he would probably ever write, *Time in the Rock: Preludes to Definition* (1936) and *Brownstone Eclogues and Other Poems* (1942). It is inconceivable that even the greatest man of letters could be at his best in both verse and fiction at the same time. Also, Aiken in putting his deepest efforts into poetry was no doubt, at least on the unconscious level, preparing himself for a new form of prose narrative. He would not come fully to grips with this new form until after World War II, when he would be writing possibly his greatest work, *Ushant.* Aiken called this work an essay; but it has more correctly been called an autobiographical narrative in that it is part novel (being a continuation of *Blue Voyage*), part autobiography, and, indeed, part essay.

Aiken's best novels are in a sense a preparation for *Ushant;* but his stories stand on their own as, at their best, important fictional statements of psychic exploration. One more of these stories needs to be discussed: "Mr. Arcularis," one of Aiken's fictional triumphs. In it he deals with man's encounter with the infinite quality of the universe and with the fact of death. Both the story and the play that grew from it show Aiken's sense of awe before infinity and the uncharted journey beyond death. The epitaph he chose for his own grave—"Cosmos Mariner/Destination Unknown"—reveals his continuing interest in the individual's movement into a dark cosmos, with no set destination before him but with a firm sense of a life of the soul that can be found through spiritual pilgrimage. The protagonist, Mr. Arcularis, is a modern antihero not unlike Joyce's Leopold Bloom in his love of the small pleasures of life. Yet in a voyage seemingly ordered for his health, he finds himself confronted both with nature's immensity and with the fact of death embodied in a coffin in the bowels of the ship. The story possesses a sense of the urgency of the metaphysical quest, a sense of life being suddenly transformed from the ordinariness of antiheroic existence to the extraordinariness of life seen from the standpoint of one being drawn into a pilgrimage in which the inner essence of both humanity and the cosmos is miraculously touched. Yet the protagonist dies before he can enter into the fruit that awaits the continuing pilgrimage.

It well may be that Aiken would turn more and more to poetry after "Mr. Arcularis" because only by doing so could he speak in depth about a journey into his own psyche. By the time he began *Ushant,* he had evolved a style of autobiographical narrative that would allow him to write of his own life as if it were a fictional journey yet also a true journey of everyman's pilgrimage. Certainly in *Preludes for Memnon* (1931) and *Time in the Rock: Preludes to Definition* (1936), he was writing verse at his top form, seeking to show at once his own descent into the maelstrom of personal and national suffering as well as his awareness of a newfound joy. Mainly these two volumes record both the pilgrim's encounter with the shadow and his refusal to be overcome by its powers. This refusal, coupled with an affirmation of the divine essence underlying and working through all people and things, leads him beyond shadow encounters to find increasing visions of renewed life lived at intense levels of joy and love. Yet the visions are momentary, giving way to new encounters with destructiveness.

In *Preludes for Memnon* Aiken is particularly concerned with the shadow images in his own unconscious mind. Thus he announces "the uprush of angelic wings, the beating / Of wings demonic, from the abyss of the mind."[2] The shadow makes its most dreadful appearance to the pilgrim as chaos, which threatens total obliteration: "Ice: silence: death: the abyss of Nothing" (*CP*, 501). The apprehension of nothingness brings with it bad dreams, which are in effect the necessary visions of the hidden sickness of the soul: "O God, O God, let the sore soul have peace. / Deliver it from this bondage of harsh dreams" (*CP*, 501). As in other volumes, we find Aiken crying out to God to give him power to overcome forces that threaten annihilation. The result of this invocation is that he does receive a renewed energy that enables him to move deeper into his soul. At last in his psyche the pilgrim glimpses love: "Love, be that glory and that sense of brightness. / You are what chaos yielded. Be my star" (*CP*, 520). In *Preludes For Memnon* Aiken continually maintains that "the maelstrom has us all" (*CP*, 520). Yet the continuing pilgrimage makes it possible to receive both insights and emotional powers that allow the quester to celebrate the creative life. In his second volume of Preludes, *Time in the Rock,* Aiken puts his major emphasis on this celebration of creativity that occurs as the human heart relates to the divine essence in both itself and in nature. In fact, Aiken used the line "Time in the rock and in the human heart" (*CP*, 551) from *Preludes for Memnon* to provide both the title for the second volume of Preludes and for a sonnet sequence called *And in the Human Heart* (1941). Thus, Jay Martin tells us, "Aiken stressed the affinity of all three volumes," though I cannot agree with Martin that the two volumes are a "prelude to death."[3] Actually, they announce the triumph of the individual over the shadow. This triumph is gradual as one learns that there is an immortal "Time" in both the heart and the rock. Thus Aiken says in the first volumes of Preludes, "Keep in the heart the journal nature keeps" (*CP*, 520, 547). It is this essential admonition that is at the heart of the second volume of Preludes, in which Aiken reaches out to both nature and humanity.

In *Time in the Rock* Aiken defines the pilgrimage and clarifies the meaning of its destination. The pilgrim for a long time knows little of his journey's destination; but at last he begins to see that though the final destination is obscure, he nevertheless is moving toward the growing experience of love and

[2]Conrad Aiken, *Collected Poems* (New York: Oxford University Press, 1953) 499.
[3]Jay Martin, *Conrad Aiken: A Life of His Art* (Princeton: Princeton University Press, 1962) 170.

light: "And it is you: toward the light you move / as silently, as gravely, as a ship / counters the evening tide" (*CP*, 755). With the growth of visionary light comes an understanding of the shadow forces that must be faced along the way. The suffering is necessary to refine the heart:

> *the suffering, the shame,*
> *the pity, and the self-pity, and the horror,*
> *that all these things refine love's angel,*
> *filth in flame made perfect.*   (*CP*, 736)

The full acceptance of the journey means, among other things, a reaching out to nature and to people met on the journey. Thus Aiken ends *Time in the Rock:*

> *Simple one, simpleton,*
> *when will you learn the flower's simplicity—*
> *lie open to all comers, permit yourself*
> *to be rifled—fruitfully too—by other selves?*
> *Self, and other self—permit them, permit them—(CP,* 756-57)

It is the power of love that makes possible the opening of oneself both to the inner essence Aiken calls Self and to the other selves, who also are part of the one Self.

For Jay Martin "caritas" is the great virtue proclaimed by Aiken; through it the pilgrim can celebrate all of life. Through the personal struggles and continued pilgrimage of the thirties, Aiken had moved into an awareness of the centrality of love. This belief, as Martin notes, finds its way into his literary criticism of the forties. "By 1940 Aiken's criticism reflected the new emphasis upon self-extension and caritas in his work." Aiken will even attack the tradition of Pound and Eliot and proclaim that "it is the nature of English poetry to be romantic."[4] In 1941 he would define poetry "as the very act of loving, the profoundest sort of acceptance."[5] Yet *And in the Human Heart,* the third volume of what Martin calls in effect a trilogy, lacks the poetic power of the first two volumes. A sonnet sequence, *And in the Human Heart* praises love but shows little grasp of the creative act of love itself. The same is true for his novel *A Heart for the Gods of Mexico* (1939), which Martin tells us is "the first book in which he attempts to register directly the emotion of a caritas completely understood and completely accepted."[6] Yet Aiken cannot

---

[4]Ibid., 156.
[5]Conrad Aiken, "Poetry: What Direction?" *New Republic* 4 (1941): 281.
[6]Martin, *Conrad Aiken,* 178.

communicate his sense of caritas in fiction, and Martin's judgement echoes the view of other serious critics that *A Heart for the Gods of Mexico* is his least successful novel. The outflowing of love, the subject attempted in this book as well as in *And in the Human Heart,* is not really Aiken's great subject, nor for that matter is it any important writer's subject in this century because there has been no great outpouring of love during this time. Aiken's real subject is the discovery of love and joy in certain auspicious times amidst the general confusion of a century caught up in the chaos of transition from one culture to another. *Brownstone Eclogues,* of all his works of the late thirties and the forties, represents what he could achieve in his best writing. Martin rightly says that "this book seeks to illustrate the means of finding joy in the midst of horror."[7] It and *Skylight One: Fifteen Poems* (1949) are probably Aiken's most meaningful preparations for his masterwork, *Ushant.*

Mary Rountree in her acute study "Conrad Aiken's Heroes: Portraits of the Artist as a Middle-Aged Failure"—the very title of which sums up much that is basic to *Ushant*—tells us that the autobiographical narrative is an official "selfportrait" that "marks a culmination of a process, a completion of Aiken's own great circle, which has fictive portraits the artist had adumbrated and, in a sense, urged forward."[8] *Ushant* is at once a statement of the author about himself and a portrait of a representative man: the artist who seeks through pilgrimage to achieve a wide-ranging consciousness. It is written from the vantage of an incipient old age (sixty being the turning point into old age) but with full awareness of a middle age just being left behind. The major outward fact for Aiken of the middle-aged existence is worldly failure in the chosen field of letters. On one level Aiken is writing a book about people he knew well like Ezra Pound, T. S. Eliot, and Malcolm Lowry, who had achieved greater individual literary accomplishments than himself and even a measure of the fame that had always eluded him. He even hoped this aspect of the book would draw sufficient readers to make it sell, yet this he knew was only a surface level. In fact, D., the narrator who is the William Demarest of *Blue Voyage,* states his purpose in telling the story of his life in *Ushant* as "a breaking-down of reality into its so many and so deceptive levels, one under another, one behind another, as if one were peeling off the seven or eight layers of time, and language, and meaning, in a thousand-year-old palimpsest—the

---

[7]Ibid., 186.

[8]Mary Rountree, "Conrad Aiken's Heroes: Portraits of the Artist as a Middle-Aged Failure," *Studies in the Literary Imagination* 13:2 (Fall 1980): 82.

personalities and the situations alike altering as the light upon them altered—that project, outlined in the dream.''[9] Failure on one level has been D's life, but success at the deepest level has been achieved in that he has accomplished the most important task he set himself—which in one sense is, he sees as he enters old age, the only task that has real meaning for him. This is the task, shamanic in nature, of achieving ever increasing consciousness and with it enough love and joy to enable him to celebrate the past, the present, and the future.

Using the psychic details of his own life, Aiken in *Ushant* has moved from his own "Portrait of the Artist as a Young Man" in the novel *Blue Voyage* through the fiction and poems of mid-life that parallel Joyce's *Ulysses* to a dream-epic like *Finnegans Wake*. Joyce's final work—still largely misunderstood—is about the passing away of Finnegan, the antihero at the center of modern life, to make way for Finn, the new heroic figure of the next age. Aiken thus is completing in *Ushant* the task he began twenty years earlier in *The Coming Forth by Day of Osiris Jones*. But he does not write in the expressionistic terms of this earlier work nor in the complex symbolistic manner of Joyce's last great work. Instead he writes in an impressionistic, poetic manner that retains a respect for basic facts of the past but continually rises to the level of musical harmony. For Aiken music is an artistic statement for humanity of the nature of cosmic experience. By the end of *Finnegans Wake* Joyce shows the completion of the move from antihero to hero; but, more realistically, Aiken shows us a representative man in his narrator D. moving past the threatening forces of the shadow to realize in particular moments the power of the hero energy, which makes possible the author's celebration of life.

Demarest, as the book progresses, shows the reader that modern man must accept the occasional failure of his powers. Just as the archetype of hero is a fact of existence, so the antihero is always present; and in an antiheroic age such as ours, the antiheroic archetype must often be predominant. The danger is that one will identify with this archetype and think that he is doomed to failure, or at least to actions the opposite of anything heroic. Yet through pilgrimage, in which the quester consciously chooses to confront the deepest part of himself and to accept the challenge of all those powers that threaten him, one is continually encountering the power of the hero, or the great man as primitives call him, while at the same time having to combat the ever present

---

[9]Conrad Aiken, *Ushant* (Cleveland: The World Publishing Company, 1962) 322-23.

forces arrayed against the pilgrim. The tone of *Ushant* is that of a person who
has won certain victories and therefore has earned the right to celebrate them.
He also celebrates those companions who have traveled with him part of the
way. Most of all, he celebrates the love and self-knowledge that grew out of
his individual pilgrimage and his associations with others on that journey.
Ushant, then, represents a stocktaking for Aiken just as he is beginning to
enter old age, which he believes will be for him a time of the flowering of
hard-earned wisdom.

In *Ushant* Aiken never says that he has arrived at any destination but suggests that he is moving toward a distant experience yet to come for mankind
as a whole: an experience best represented by the archetype of the golden age,
or paradise, as Eliade calls it in his studies of shamanism. That he had this in
mind can be seen throughout the book. It can also be seen in his choice of
epigraphs for the book. From Coleridge he chose a passage asking the question "What hast thou, Man, that thou darst call thine own?" ("Self-Knowledge"). Here he suggests the metaphysical teaching, so emphasized by his
Unitarian background, that the divine essence is everywhere and that it unites
us all but that it must be continually evoked and sought. It and one's biological heritage constitute the basic nature of one's life and cannot ever be completely altered. From Nietzsche's *Ecce Homo* he chose a passage about "that
undiscovered country, whose frontiers no one has yet seen, a land lying beyond all other known lands and hiding-places of the ideal, a world so over-
flowing with beauty, strangeness, doubt, terror, and divinity." The Nietzsche
passage is a good statement of what Aiken means by the word *Ushant.* The
fact that the chosen passage deals with the inability of Nietzsche's "Argo-
nauts of the ideal" to accept the man of the present day indicates that Aiken's
apocalyptic vision of the coming of the god-man is present throughout his
book. Like his grandfather Potter, he continued to believe that people choose
to follow a path that will lead the race to achieve a god-like nature at some
future time in history.

Ushant for Aiken is a word suggesting at once the destructive, alluring,
and castrating powers that bar the pilgrim's way to the new age and at the
same time the new age and the new land in which man becomes fully united
with the divine essence at the center of everything. That this concept is central
to the book can be seen by studying its ending. Aiken quotes a "dream-song"
from his young daughter Jean's long poem "The Playlanders" and cites her
"Juhoohooa" as another Ushant—that is, as an image of the archetype that

Aiken himself calls "World's-end." He concludes the book with one of the most poetic passages he ever wrote:

> Floating upwards towards that vast, that outspread, sheet of illuminated music, which is the world; and above which, as we now dimly make out, is—what exactly? the face of the Teacher from the West?—But first, no, it is only a hand that we see; and then, above the hand, a face that is turned away from us, as if it were turned away to sing to someone else, someone behind, and farther off; and towards this as yet unseen face we rise, we rise, ourselves now like notes of music arranging themselves in a divine harmony, a divine unison, which, as it had no beginning, can have no end—(*U*, 365).

The centrality of this passage cannot be overemphasized because it links us to the opening action of the book, to the fear of sinking in a ship off the shoals of Ile d'Ouessant: the small island off Brittany that Aiken once passed on his way to England, an island whose name suggests the word *Ushant*. It also refers to a dream he had at the time he was close to Malcolm Lowry, a dream about a Teacher of the West who is speaking to a group of four, including Aiken and Lowry, about the journey of the soul to the West, or World's End. The teacher is clearly one image of the archetype of the saviour, the Christ-figure often seen in dreams and visions at critical moments in one's life. This figure, who is divine in nature, turns in Aiken's final passage to speak to the hidden God, that "hidden face" to which all pilgrims rise.

The dream of the teacher of the West was for Aiken the central dream of *Ushant*, stating the fact of his pilgrimage just as *Ushant* itself is the central document in his life's work about that pilgrimage. The dream shows a group of four people working on a text in German with the help of the teacher; thus they seek answers to how they should proceed on their pilgrimage. Translation for Aiken becomes essentially the reading of significant symbols in one's own life and in the lives of others close to him. As he says, "Every symbol was rooted in the sensory phenomena of experience, phenomena thus become noumenal" (*U*, 30). Significant figures in one's life can thus be transformed into images representing basic archetypes. Thus the poet's father is at once an image of the castrating power that says in effect you shan't go forward and become fully mature and separate from my control and also an image of the archetype of the initiatory wise old man who shows the youth the way to the path leading to full maturity. Similarly, the mother is the negative anima that draws the child to her bewitching and relentless embrace and the true anima who gives a love and guidance necessary for the pilgrim to find his mature existence. Men and women with whom one closely associates after childhood, Aiken suggests, take on semblances of both the creative and destructive aspects of anima and animus first encountered in childhood experience.

In *Ushant* Aiken precisely uses Jungian terms like *anima* and *persona*, and one might simply assume he was a Jungian in his viewpoint. Yet he preferred Freud as his modern psychological leader because, as he puts it, Freud had picked up the "magic words" Aiken most admired—know thyself—from "where Socrates, the prototype of highest man, had let them fall" (*U*, 220). Actually Aiken was, as his friend Charmenz S. Lenhart has noted, more of a practical Jungian in many ways than he was a Freudian. In an article called "Conrad Aiken's Fusion of Freud and Jung," I have attempted to show how he made use of both in constructing a psychological and a philosophical view of mankind.[10] Freud seemed to him more scientific than Jung and more of a prophet of what he would call in *Ushant* "the only religion that was any longer tenable or viable, a poetic comprehension of man's position in the universe, and of his potentialities as a poetic shaper of his own destiny, through self-knowledge and love" (*U*, 220). The result of this freely chosen destiny was a path leading to "ever more inclusive consciousness" (*U*, 220). For Aiken, Freud was the chief modern figure to point writers toward developing the consciousness.

According to Hoffman, consciousness for Aiken is "very much akin to what Santayana calls the 'realm of spirit,' or sensations, passions, the pressure of the mind upon matter, with the object of 'elevating' and shaping it."[11] Santayana more than any other philosopher influenced Aiken's understanding of what the evolutionary development of man meant. For both men, a developed consciousness meant the harmonious working together of both the intellect and the emotions, and in Aiken's conjectures concerning the word *consciousness,* we find some of his deepest thoughts about the uniting of science and art. To be able to develop one's consciousness means moving on a pilgrimage that involves one of Aiken's key concepts: Great Circle. One aspect of the circular journey, as Hoffman and other Freudian critics have related, is the return to the early life with all its traumas in order to face one last time the parental tragedy every human is subject to, given the nature of humanity. As Rountree puts it, "He [Aiken] must work out 'the cause of life'

---

[10]Ted R. Spivey, "Conrad Aiken's Fusion of Freud and Jung," *Studies in the Literary Imagination* 13:2 (Fall 1980): 99-113.

[11]Hoffman, *Conrad Aiken*, 21.

(*U*, 361) around the tragedy of his childhood in order to forgive and finally to love the father and mother responsible for that tragedy.''[12]

The concept of Great Circle must also be seen in its Jungian context. At the end of *Ushant* Aiken views his own child's vision of World's End and echoes Wordsworth: ''The child had been father to the man. And wasn't it all too ridiculously like the vision, somewhere described in the notes for that book, the final vision for its beginningless and endless end'' (*U*, 364). Man, as he grows up, moves into ever greater involvement with time and its ambiguities and uncertainties, not to mention its griefs and pains. If, however, he is drawn by love to take the path of pilgrimage, he finds himself going in a circle: dying to the wounds of time to continually discover the images of archetypal paradise, which the archetypal child, who is man's father, has all along possessed. The great thing, Aiken shows throughout *Ushant,* is to have the key to open doors leading to the next stage of one's development in expanded consciousness: ''The key was charity: *caritas,* the love of loves!'' (*U*, 211).

There is a remarkable similarity between Eliot's *Quartets* and *Ushant.* For both poets these works are the culminating poems of pilgrimage of their entire careers. Eliot's ''East Coker'' with its opening reference to returning to one's beginning and its ending picture of dying to the past in order to move ''Into another intensity / For a further union, a deeper communion'' contains the essential idea of Great Circle found in Aiken's work.[13] The *Quartets* contain great lines of poetry, but nowhere in them do we find that sense of celebration and of comradeship that *Ushant* continually reveals. By the time he came to write his autobiography, Aiken felt the need to express the joy he had often experienced both alone and with others as well as the sense of both solitary thought and reading. Communal literary endeavors and the closeness and love of family life are always strong in the book. In one of its most beautiful passages Aiken writes:

> How often had the shadow of Eros passed by unrecognized, unhonored, the ethereal wingbeat unheard, or, if heard, mistaken for something else! Once — the poet — Rimbaud? — had said — ''If I remember rightly, my life was a feast where all the hearts opened, and joy flowed like wine'' (*U*, 211).

Throughout the book we see remembrances of moments with Eliot and Lowry

---

[12]Rountree, ''Aiken's Heroes,'' 83.
[13]T. S. Eliot, *The Complete Poems and Plays* (New York: Harcourt, Brace and World, 1952) 129.

or Fletcher or any number of others in which the shadow of Eros was remembered and in which individual consciousnesses were expanded together, for Aiken's pilgrimage must always be made with others.

Steven Olson reminds us that "Aiken, like Hawthorne and James, adhered to the moral position that the artist was obligated to combat, rather than perpetuate, the propensities of so-called American 'individualism'."[14] Olson goes on to show some of the connections between the ethical vision he inherited from his maternal grandfather and that of Henry James, Sr., who passed many of his thoughts on to his sons Henry and William. For Aiken the chief sign that one's pilgrimage was progressing properly was the ability to communicate with others and finally to think less about oneself in moments of love than about the beloved. Through the love of both individuals and of nature, consciousness is expanded so that, momentarily at least, one can sense the presence of the divine essence, which dwells everywhere. The awareness of this essence makes possible the banquet of life and all its joys. Aiken's idea of pilgrimage then is not that of the lonely traveler with stern face and eyes directed skyward. Instead, he would agree with a great American poet he helped to discover: Emily Dickinson, who in "Some Keep the Sabbath Going to Church" wrote, "So instead of getting to heaven at last, / I'm going all along!"

Although a dominant impression of *Ushant* is one of the celebration of moments of expanded consciousness, the sense Aiken always had of modern pain and ambiguity is present throughout. He could never be a transcendentalist like Emerson or even Dickinson because he was too much aware, even in his happiest moments, of life's continuing chaos. This is why, no doubt, the last epigraph for *Ushant* is a passage from Melville's *Moby-Dick* that begins with Ahab saying, "By heaven, man, we are turned round and round in this world, like yonder windlass, and Fate is the handspike." Although *Ushant* is about a man who shapes his own destiny by following the path of love and self-knowledge, it is also about a man being driven by forces he cannot comprehend, by powers of dissolution that seem to defy all the insights of human wisdom. Aiken took the optimism of his transcendentalist forebears and subjected it to the doubts and questionings he found in both Melville and writers like him who shout "No" to much of experience. The result is a life-view

---

[14]Steven E. Olson, "The House of Man: Ethical Symbolism in Conrad Aiken's *The Clerk's Journal*," *Essays in Arts and Sciences* 10:2 (May 1981): 84.

that includes both joy and sorrow, a continuing love and a continuing joy and, above all else, an awareness that the pilgrimage is never ending.

Ushant is surely Aiken's greatest single work, and certainly it deserves Malcolm Cowley's encomium that it is one of the great American autobiographies. It was not, however, his summing up; he reserved that for a volume that appeared three years later in 1955. *A Letter from Li Po and Other Poems* is, as E. P. Bollier suggests, "a valedictory, a final statement in many ways."[15] Bollier shows how the title poem of this volume and several other later poems are connected with *Ushant* and how they deal primarily with the author's own ancestors, both actual and philosophical. In these works Aiken comes to grips with the problem of poetry and science as well as with the problem of the past, his own and the nation's. In one final work, *Thee* (1967), he confronts once more his own religious feelings and states his vision of God. In old age Aiken as both poet and philosopher came at last fully to grips with his long sought insights into the ways man can once again reintegrate himself so that reason and imagination, mind and heart, can work together harmoniously.

III

Walker Percy with *The Second Coming* (1980) would show more clearly than in any previous novel the fruits of pilgrimage; yet, unlike *Ushant, The Second Coming* is not about the continuing pilgrimage of one man. As a literary artist Percy has very skillfully disguised certain obvious autobiographical elements of his book with the kind of plot and characterization that would make it not only a critical but also a popular success soon after its publication. Yet *The Second Coming,* taken as a continuation of the story of Will Barrett begun in *The Last Gentleman,* is very much the story of the pilgrimage of Walker Percy, even though the details of the two books often do not coincide exactly with the facts of Percy's own life. The essential themes of the books are nevertheless very much the themes of Percy's own personal pilgrimage.

The similarity between the basic themes of *Ushant* and *The Second Coming* is remarkable. At the core of both books is the problem of parental suicide and the necessity to love and forgive destructive parents so that one can get on with one's life. Above all, there is the problem of coming old age as well as the problem of one's ancestors. There is the problem of society becoming

---

[15]E. P. Bollier, "Conrad Aiken's Ancestral Voices: A Reading of Four Poems," *Studies in the Literary Imagination* 13:2 (Fall 1980): 72.

ever more violent, more chaotic, with the individual being tossed about by unknown powers. Yet there are in both books an awareness of the fruits of pilgrimage and a resulting celebration of life. Both authors through religious commitment and the application of concepts from the work of Freud and Jung come to grips with the powers that threaten the pilgrim, and both manage to present a worldview that contains love and understanding as central components. In short, they show the possibility of discovering joy at an age when modernity has pronounced human life to be drawing to a distinct conclusion. Both manage to present old age as a new beginning leading to the best time of life. They do not sing of old age as Robert Browning does in "Rabbi Ben Ezra," as if it were an unmixed blessing. Instead they show the pilgrim, though surrounded by chaos, continually discovering a depth of life that the young never see.

Percy from the beginning of his career as a novelist sought to show some of the fruits of pilgrimage. Binx Bolling in *The Moviegoer* is given a small grace that enables him by the novel's end to reach out meaningfully to another person and by so doing to save both her life and his own. In *The Last Gentleman* and *Love in the Ruins,* the fruits of the pilgrimage are more obvious. By the end of the former, Will Barrett has given up his withdrawal from life to accept an ordinary job in a car agency and at the same time engage in helping, through grace given him, not one but several people. Tom More in *Love in the Ruins* is shown fully engaged in the heroic life of the Christian who performs the ordinary duties of his job, accepts with love his wife and those around him, and follows a religious discipline. *Lancelot,* the fourth novel, is primarily about the failure of an ordinary American hero to find grace and the resulting shadow possession of his life. Yet Percival, the psychiatrist-priest who listens to Lance's story, is himself an embodiment of those virtues that come by grace to those who continue to seek God. He is able to listen to all the blasphemy of his friend while continuing to forgive him. He cannot speak the good news of Christ's gift of grace because Lancelot is not ready to hear it. In fact, he utters only thirteen words in the novel; but, as William J. Dowie points out, "The priest's way quietly becomes the true thematic center of the novel in its final pages."[16] Yet only in his fifth novel, *The Second Coming,* does Percy show the quester seriously enjoying for a period of time the fruits of the quest. This book, like the first three, is about a man finding the path of

---

[16]William J. Dowie, "Lancelot and the Search for Sin," *The Art of Walker Percy,* ed. Panthea R. Broughton (Baton Rouge: Louisiana State University Press, 1979) 257.

pilgrimage after seeing that without it life eventually becomes meaningless, but it goes on to present some of Percy's understanding of a modern shaman's discovery of love and joy in contemporary society.

To write about a person successfully entering old age, like Barrett in *The Second Coming,* it was seemingly necessary to write *Lancelot* as a preparation for the vision of grace that the best pages of *The Second Coming* contain. By the time Percy wrote *Lancelot,* he had entered upon a prolonged study of the work of C. G. Jung; and insights thus gained would play a definite part in it and in his succeeding book, giving both books a depth they might not otherwise have had. Concerning my article "Walker Percy and the Archetypes," Percy wrote to me in a letter in 1979:

> Your Jungian reading is very close and very interesting to me, because for one thing I was not interested in Jung at the time of the writings you speak of, and so it is all the more gratifying to be seen by to [*sic*] as onto something of value, even when it involved more archetype-possession than encounter. The exception is Lancelot, which you diagnosed quite correctly as successive anima and shadow possession, and which I was more or less aware of doing.[17]

Percy in writing *Lancelot* was obviously aware of the possibility that one can be seized and psychically destroyed by those powers Jung calls archetypes. But he was equally aware that it was possible and even necessary for psychic development to encounter creatively the major archetypes. In the same letter Percy described his own awareness of this creative encounter with archetypes by writing thus of *The Second Coming,* which he had just completed: "It takes up, as I may have mentioned, Will Barrett's later adventures, perhaps 15 or 20 years after the Close of The Last Gent—and deals rather more explicitly with Jungian individuation—but not too much, I hope, since as you suggest in the article a fellow could get himself in all sorts of trouble by being too much influenced by this or that theory of the psyche."[18] Will Barrett in *The Second Coming* creatively encounters both the anima and the shadow powers within himself and within the world around him, whereas Lance Lamar is possessed and overcome by both these forces. One should, of course, ask why. Will moves forward with a faith in God that gives him the grace, or free gift of divine energy, that makes it possible to overcome shadow powers and to interact fruitfully with those powers of the feminine in both oneself and oth-

---

[17]Letter to Ted R. Spivey dated 29 October 1979. The article referred to is "Walker Percy and the Archetypes" in *The Art of Walker Percy.*
[18]Ibid.

ers. Lance, being without such faith, is gradually possessed first by his mother's image, then by the hero image, and finally by the destructive powers of the shadow. By speaking in his letter of Will's movement toward individuation in *The Second Coming,* Percy shows that he accepts the validity of Jung's concept of pilgrimage. For Jung the master archetype was the mandala, and an acceptance of its center as a symbol of the divine power available to all who sought it was necessary for the pilgrim to continue making spiritual progress. Percy, however, is also writing about the Christian pilgrimage, which for him was only partially described by Jung's concepts concerning the archetypes. Yet Jung too goes beyond the archetypes into myth and religion. It was in *Symbols of Transformation*—"this pivotal work of his career," as Joseph Campbell calls it—that he began to wonder about myth in relationship to his own life at a particular moment in history, that moment when man began to think he could live without myth. As Joseph Campbell goes on to show in his introduction to *The Portable Jung,* he began to question himself upon completing *Symbols of Transformation:*

> "Hardly had I finished the manuscript," he states, "when it struck me what it means to live with a myth, and what it means to live without one. Myth, says a Church Father, is 'what is believed always, everywhere, by everybody': hence the man who thinks he can live without myth, or outside it, is an exception. He is like one uprooted, having no true link either with the past, or with the ancestral life which continues within him, or yet with contemporary human society. This plaything of his reason never grips his vitals."[19]

What Jung sought to find in existential terms for his own life was the essence of myth and religion by living out his own myth as a twentieth-century scientist with roots in both the Judeo-Christian and the ancient gnostic traditions. Aiken and Percy sought much the same thing. They differ from each other and from Jung in many ways because of personal differences and an adherence to different branches of Christianity. Yet all three seek to work out mythic solutions to the problems of twentieth-century humanity in terms of their own lives, and all three eventually recorded their experiences in various literary works. Unlike most of their contemporaries, they saw that modern people seldom grip their vitals, as Jung puts it, meaning that they ignore those inner psychic powers he called the archetypes. The result is that they may project their shadow archetypes onto others, always seeing evil in various scapegoats

---

[19]Joseph Campbell, Introduction, *The Portable Jung* (New York: The Viking Press, 1971) xxi.

instead of in themselves, and ignore their own destructiveness; they become possessed by their animas (or animuses in the case of women) and end by attempting to possess and destroy members of the opposite sex. Another possibility is that they will either hate themselves for not being heroes, falling victim to Adler's inferiority complex, or else they will be seized by the hero image and imagine that they are saviors of the world. Jung saw all these flaws in the German people as a whole after World War I and tried ineffectively to warn them of the inevitable triumph of an evil like Nazism. In the aftermath of World War II he saw the psychic disease caused by ignoring the archetypal powers becoming prevalent everywhere; and in one of his last books, *The Undiscovered Self,* he tried to warn the world. Aiken and Percy saw the world in a similar way, and some of their best writing is at once a record of their own analysis of the modern failure to confront the archetypes and of their own pilgrimages, which to be meaningful had to involve archetypal confrontation.

I am not attempting to brand Aiken and Percy as Jungians, though their obvious debts to Jung as well as the similar ways in which all three approach modern psychic and spiritual problems must be taken into account for an understanding of myth and pilgrimage in our time. What I will suggest in the next chapter is that all three are part of a search for a new psychology and anthropology for Western man like those described in Ira Progoff's *The Death and Rebirth of Psychology.* But it is also necessary to take Jung into account when discussing *The Second Coming* because Percy, for one thing, is dealing with that area of life where Jungian psychology is most valid for gaining an understanding of the development of the psyche. Jung has said that Freud's discoveries were extremely important for understanding man before the age of thirty-five because the sex drive and procreation are the strongest elements in the human makeup at this stage. He felt that his own psychology explained better than anyone else's what the life of the human was in middle and old age, a time when man increasingly searches for the meaning of his life and for its renewal. This in essence is what Will Barrett seeks and finds in *The Second Coming:* meaning and life renewal. His method is that of the mythic pilgrimage. In finding meaning in old age, Will Barrett, like Jung, asks what is the essence of the reward one receives as a result of pilgrimage. The answer is that meaning comes in the form of an existential experience engaging the head, the heart, and the will. Above all, grasping this meaning involves experiencing love and joy. In his earlier books Percy has dealt very sparingly with these emotions, but in *The Second Coming* he celebrates them. At the same time, he attacks various forms that Christianity takes in the modern world.

As the book ends, Will Barrett sounds as if he were at odds with the Catholicism he had embraced as a young man in *The Last Gentleman*. He tells an old Episcopal priest, "That is to say, I am not a believer but I believe I am on the track of something." Then he begins to sound like a Unitarian as he tells the priest about his desire to become a church member:

> You can't turn down a penitent, can you? We are also willing to take instructions, as long as you recognize I cannot and will not accept all of your dogmas. Unless of course you have the authority to tell me something I don't know. Do you? (*SC,* 358)

For one in the Unitarian tradition of the nineteenth century like Aiken, religion was not primarily a set of dogmas, as it was for many in traditional faiths; rather, it was a fire of the spirit, or grace, passed from one generation to the next—a fire that made possible the two great virtues, love and joy.

In Barrett's questioning of the old priest concerning his authority to speak about God's grace, Percy is echoing concepts stated in his essay "The Message in the Bottle." There he speaks of one who "receives the commission to bring news across the seas to the castaways and does so in perfect sobriety and with good faith and perseverance to the point of martyrdom."[20] What Barrett seeks is a true apostle, in the sense Kierkegaard means in his essay "The Genius and the Apostle." Father Curl, the rector of the church, is not one, Barrett tells the old priest, who is Curl's assistant. "No, you're my man," he says. "I perceive you seem to know something—and that by the same token Jack Curl does not" (*SC,* 358). The old priest, who was a missionary in the Philippines and was finally sent home to be an assistant to a rector, reacts to Will's statement by speaking in a Kierkegaardian vein:

> How can we be the best dearest most generous people on earth, and at the same time so unhappy? How harsh everyone is here! How restless! How impatient! How worried! How sarcastic! How unhappy! How hateful! How pleasure-loving! How lascivious! Above all, how selfish! Why is it that we have more than any other people, are more generous with what we have, and yet are so selfish and unhappy? Why do we think of nothing but our own pleasure? I cannot believe my eyes at what I see on television. It makes me blush with shame. Did you know that pleasure-seeking leads to cruelty? That is why more and more people beat their children. Children interfere with pleasure.

---

[20]Walker Percy, *The Message in the Bottle: How Queer Man Is, How Queer Language Is, and What One Has to Do with the Other* (New York: Farrar, Straus & Giroux, 1979) 149.

Do you hate children? Why can't we be grateful for our great blessings and thank God? (*SC*, 359)

Kierkegaard influenced Percy more than any other thinker, yet in his essays and novels we seldom hear directly the full accents of that philosopher's essential message: the people of Western Christendom are no longer really Christian because they are not pilgrims who express that faith in love, thankfulness, joy, and praise. This was not a welcome message to Kierkegaard's fellow citizens of Copenhagen in 1850, nor is it one today. Realizing this, Percy has sought to be far less harsh than the Danish theologian; nevertheless, he has tried to be true to his mentor's vision while at the same time actually portraying the fruits of faith, which Kierkegaard in his brilliant writing seldom did.

The book closes with Barrett asking the old priest if he thinks that "in fact there are certain unmistakable signs of his [Christ's] coming in these very times." The old man is too stunned to answer, but nevertheless his faith has helped Will to believe more strongly than ever in continuing his quest through the medium of the church. Yet his chief thoughts at this crucial point in his life are about God and his gifts of love and joy in the form of his newfound love.

> Will Barrett thought about Allie in her greenhouse, her wide gray eyes, her lean muscled boy's arms, her strong quick hands. His heart leapt with a secret joy. What is it I want from her and him, he wondered, not only want but must have? Is she a gift and therefore a sign of a giver? Could it be that the Lord is here, masquerading behind this simple silly holy face? Am I crazy to want both, her and Him? No, not want, must have. And will have (*SC*, 360).

Thus Percy ends his fifth novel. Critics have found certain flaws in *The Second Coming,* but its value will no doubt take some years to assess. This book clearly demonstrates the direction that Percy's philosophy was taking as he moved into old age. Above all, it reiterates his theme that the quester can choose to continue his mythic pilgrimage, can in fact *will* that continuation, as the name of his protagonist and the book's last sentence ("And will have.") so clearly indicate. The continuing fruits of this pilgrimage are a growing love and joy, and for Percy the gift of love is the sign of the giver ("Is she a gift and therefore a sign of a giver?"). The pilgrim then through his choice can find God and love because the divine essence is at the center of humans, waiting to be sought and found by the pilgrim. At this point Percy's view is almost identical with Aiken's formulation of the divine-human relationship.

The chief difference between the visions of Aiken and Percy concerning the pilgrim entering old age is that Aiken in *Ushant* is recalling his entire life, whereas in *The Second Coming* Percy is presenting in a novelistic form certain basic problems of the pilgrim entering old age. Some of these problems are Percy's own, and some are everybody's problems, but the events of the novel are not strictly autobiographical. The story of Will Barrett's love for the young woman Allie is based in a very general way on the marriage of a cousin. In fact, in an article on the Spalding family of Atlanta, the *Atlanta Constitution* reports: "At the party, Percy jokes that his newest novel, *The Second Coming*, 'is dedicated to Hughes and his new wife.' "[21] The description of the relationship between Barrett and Allie is fiction, but in showing the relationship between a man entering old age and a young woman, Percy seeks to explore the relationship of the pilgrim to his own anima. This relationship becomes possible because the pilgrim has faced certain destructive, or shadow, forces both within himself and in the world he inhabits. The essential theme of the book, as Percy makes clear in his letter to me concerning it, is "Jungian individuation," which is another way of saying that the book is about the development of the soul of an individual who is on a pilgrimage. The formula for this development is essentially that given by Mircea Eliade for myth: "suffering, death, and resurrection (= rebirth)."[22] The hero encounters pain and dies a ritual death through encounter with shadow forces and is reborn and receives the fruit of rebirth in his union with the creative side of his soul, symbolized by the anima image. The bounty in Barrett's own life is then given to others in a movement dedicated to creating fruitful communal relations.

In the letter discussing his concept of individuation, Percy goes on to say that "when I wished to bring WB [Will Barrett] into an encounter with his shadow, something else took over and what comes to pass is a rather queer-marginal-Jung encounter (I had in mind something like Ivan Karamazov's encounter with his devilshadow, a rather seedy Mephistopheles, but it didn't happen this way.)"[23] The "queer-marginal-Jung encounter" is much deeper than the author thinks, I believe. In a limited sense he is no doubt referring to a descent into a literal cave that Barrett makes in order to find if God really exists. Instead of overcoming some great darkness, followed by a vision of

---

[21]Emma Edmunds, "Spaldings: On the Inside," *Atlanta Constitution,* 31 August 1981, B: 6.

[22]Mircea Eliade, *The Sacred and the Profane,* trans. Willard R. Trask (New York: Harper and Brothers, 1959) 196.

[23]Letter to Ted R. Spivey dated 29 October 1979.

divine radiance, the protagonist rather absurdly emerges from the cave to find Allie, the young woman that he has befriended. This action in effect states Percy's philosophy, found throughout his work, that a sincere attempt to find God is eventually rewarded by the gift of love. Will's descent into the cave, however, is not his chief encounter with the world of darkness. Instead, it is Will's struggle with the shadow power of his own father that is the heart of the book and its strongest fictional element. In *The Last Gentleman* Will had confronted the problem of his father's suicide. In *The Second Coming* Percy deals with Will's confrontation with the residue of self-destruction left in his soul by the shattering experience of the father's suicide and his attempt to kill his own son in what would look like a hunting accident but would be a murder-suicide. The details of Barrett's life are fictional, but the situation described is that of one who has suffered parental suicide. Like Aiken, Percy uses his literary art to describe the death wish one experiences as a result of this trauma. Further, he describes the process of encountering this shadow power and of overcoming it through a continual facing of its latent but dangerous ability to drive one to repeat the self-destruction of one's parents. As a result of overcoming the shadow in the form of the ogre parent who seeks to destroy his offspring, he experiences the renewing power of spiritual rebirth with one's ability to love others greatly enhanced as a result. Thus he can perform for others, as Barrett does, the modern shaman's act of healing and restoring communication between people.

When Will has at last come to grips with the shadow pursuing him in the form of his father's and his own suicidal impulses, he understands that it is death he has always been struggling with and that to stand up against this power with faith in God is to overcome it and to experience a release from the pervading sadness of ordinary life. With the release comes the joy of life itself. The center of the entire book is probably the second chapter of Part 2, where Will at last sees the shadow for what it is and denounces it.

> Old father of lies, that's what you are, the devil himself, for only the devil could have thought up all the deceits and guises under which death masquerades. But I know all your names. Here are the names of death, which shall not prevail over me because I know the names (*SC*, 272).

Will at last sees what "death-in-life" is. This term is basic to *The Second Coming*, but it also needs to be applied to all of the novels because it describes what Percy finds most horrible in ordinary existence. Before, he has only skirted the issue, but in *The Second Coming* he faces it squarely. Will's father is clearly a composite figure, embodying many people Percy knew in the older generation of Southern stoics: people who molded his youthful thinking and who ultimately sought to tie him to a death-oriented existence in which the very idea of pilgrimage is meaningless. Will's father was happy only when contemplating war and death, and we are reminded of the question Percy asked in "The Delta Factor" about his Uncle Will: "Why is it that the only time I ever saw my uncle happy during his entire life was the afternoon of December 7, 1941, when the Japanese bombed Pearl Harbor?" (*SC*, 4).

The failure of Uncle Will and all of Percy's other initiatory figures to know happiness except in the contemplation of destruction brands them as people who never discovered the path of pilgrimage. Not to move forward into new spiritual realms is to be stuck in death-in-life. Will Barrett at last sees that he must continue his pilgrimage to escape death in all the guises in which he has found it—in, for instance, "the guise of old Christendom in Carolina" as well as in "the new Christendom in Carolina." There is also "Death in the guise of God and America and the happy life of home and family and friends, Death in the guise of belief" and "Death in the guise of unbelief, Death in the guise of the new life in California." Finally Will says,

> Death in the form of isms and asms shall not prevail over me, orgasm, enthusiasm, liberalism, conservatism, Communism, over Buddhism, Americanism, for an ism is only another way of despairing of the truth (*SC*, 273).

Then Will defines the pilgrim as the truth seeker, the one who challenges all the hidden sadness of those who cling to the death-in-life: "What is this sadness here? Why do folks put up with it? The truth seeker does not" (*SC*, 273).

By the term "seeking the truth," Percy, as the context of the novel reveals, does not mean a search for a particular truth about nature or man. Instead he means first identifying and rebelling against the death-in-life condition and then seeking and finding God: " '*Why this sadness here? Don't stand for it! Get up! Leave!*' And then Will thinks: '*What is missing? God? Find him!*' " (*SC*, 273). The truth then is a condition that is sought spiritually and that when encountered brings with it happiness. Thus Percy uses the term in its traditional theological sense. The truth is not knowledge to be possessed but rather a condition one gradually achieves in which the total outlook is changed so that a new life emerges.

Will Barrett at the beginning of *The Second Coming* had given up his earlier pilgrimage described in *The Last Gentleman*. He had married a rich woman, "one of the good triumphant Yankees who helped out the poor old

South" (*SC,* 157). He went to live on Long Island and practice law, finally retiring in Western North Carolina. The death of his wife finds him at loose ends, but the sudden discovery of how violent the world had become unleashed within his psyche the old hidden shadow figure of his father's self-destructiveness. He must relive the suicide and face again his own self-destructiveness. In the process of facing the shadow, Will encounters Allison, a young woman who though mentally ill is trying to find herself in a schizophrenic world where communication seems impossible. Her own schizophrenia has resulted in confinement in a mental institution. She escapes and encounters Will Barrett; and, as in all of his earlier novels except *Lancelot,* a man and a woman who need each other begin working out together a salvation that involves both love, joy, and communication.

In *The Second Coming* Percy has explored, as in none of his previous novels, the complex relationship between an older man and a young girl who comes to symbolize his own anima, or female inner self. Because he struggles with and overcomes the hidden shadow power within himself, he is able to struggle against the destructive energies in the soul of Allison and thereby help her overcome her fear of life. Although on the literal level of the novel—a level Percy always skillfully maintains in his fiction—the central story is that of an aging man's courtship of a young girl and the winning of her heart, on the deeper symbolic level the book is about encounter with both shadow and anima figures and about the joy that results. For the first time in his work, Percy actually shows in detail what it means to live the ordinary life joyfully. In his earlier fiction he shows a few moments of joy illuminating the dullness of what he has referred to as "ordinariness," but in *The Second Coming* he portrays two characters who by finding the secret of communication through the shared discovery of themselves and of God are able to see ordinary life illuminated by joy. An example of this illumination is seen in Percy's description of Allison's epiphany:

> She clapped her hands for joy. What a discovery! To get a job, do it well, which is a pleasure, please the employer, which is also a pleasure, and get paid, which is yet another pleasure. . . . She had thought (and her mother had expected) that she must do something extraordinary, be somebody extraordinary. Whereas the trick lay in leading the most ordinary life imaginable, get an ordinary job, in itself a joy in its very ordinariness , and *then* be as extraordinary or ordinary as one pleased. That was the secret (*SC,* 247).

The key word in the above passage is, of course, *joy*. The joy of ordinary life comes from encountering love and a true communication growing out of love. Allison discovers that life lived in joy is a continuing celebration. The same is true for Will, who is able to convince other aging men who are whiling their time away watching television that it is possible to find a joy through communal agricultural labors that is nonexistent in the pseudo-life of electronic entertainment. Will's new life after overcoming his own and Allison's shadow images will be one of marriage, the communal religious life of the church, and a shared life with other old people. But above all it will be a life of shared celebration of the "ordinariness" of existence. It is finally in his fifth novel, published when he was sixty-four, that Percy gives his readers a detailed fictional answer to the problems of boredom in ordinary life and of the compulsion to escape ordinariness through the electronic media, both first dealt with so well in *The Moviegoer*.

IV

Ushant is for most critics Aiken's greatest single work, but the same cannot be said for Percy's *The Second Coming*. It is a good book with flaws, but it does contain some of the author's deepest philosophical and lyrical insights and represents a partial resolution of problems posed in his earlier essays and novels. What *The Second Coming* has most in common with *Ushant* is the ripe and joyous wisdom of two authors who have met and overcome legacies of pain and destructiveness that grew in part out of childhood traumas. Books like these are rare in America; we more often expect to find them in the more mature literatures of Europe. They result from long meditation over the deepest problems of the shared life of man, and we expect them at the best to be written by mature men of letters.

Percy will no doubt expand his vision of the celebration of life and of the fruit the pilgrim finds, perhaps in the new novel he is completing as this is being written. But it is possible to say too much of the theme of celebration in Aiken and Percy. I speak of it as strongly as I do because it is hard for many to believe that serious modern writers ever celebrate life. Aiken and Percy are pursuing a vision that will allow them to pause momentarily to speak of pilgrimage's fruit, but even in *Ushant* and *The Second Coming* there are the primary accents of continuing the journey. And to find what? Love and joy, as I have suggested, but also a new vision of life in which science and art are carried on as simultaneous activities by people in a renewed culture. Aiken's most important work following *Ushant* was "A Letter from Li Po" in which the chief problem confronted is the need for a unity of science and art. Percy's return to the essay form after writing *The Second Coming* indicates that he must come again to the problem that has continually haunted him since he first read Kierkegaard. This then is the essential problem of both. Aiken deals with it in terms of one word—consciousness, and Percy in terms of another—communication. What they do with the problem and with those two words we now must examine.

The Metaphysical Ground
of Science and Art

Chapter VII

I

If one looks briefly at the lives and works of Conrad Aiken and Walker
Percy, he will note many surface differences; but when he encounters the
deep currents of their lives and works, he will note deep similarities. Above
all, he will come to see a long, sometimes profound, and often hidden
struggle with one of modern civilization's deepest single problems: the split
between the sciences and the arts, between the objective and critical side
of the mind and the intuitive and imaginative side. Of the basic similarity
between the inner development of their lives and works I have already
written at length, but I will sum up the principal likenesses in this way: (1)
early parental suicide, precipitating a basic life crisis, which—though often

but not always hidden in the unconscious—causes various small physical and mental instabilities; (2) a way of seeing one's life as a pilgrimage to find a lost love and joy; and (3) the gradual overcoming of a deep death wish and the achieving of a psychic growth in which life and death, love and violence, are seen in a perspective that makes possible a full acceptance of life. Yet how did the two men deal with the fundamental split in modern civilization? They grew up in different times and with different life goals, and their solutions to the problem are formulated in somewhat different terms; but underneath it all, their belief that there is an underlying unity that connects the arts and sciences emerges in the same way—through their becoming what Aiken calls a "divine pilgrim."

Aiken and Percy are, philosophically, existentialists in that they came to believe that one must have certain life experiences in order to "know" certain "truths" necessary for living the good life. When one attempts to "live out of his head," the result is, both say along with many existentialists, that one perceives life as a series of irreconcilable opposites. In Western thought this kind of perception is best exemplified by Descartes' philosophy. Allen Tate—who influenced both Aiken and Percy (he was Aiken's good and admired friend)—has written better than any other American essayist about the "Cartesian split": the inability, if one accepts Descartes completely, to see the object and the subject (or body and mind) as anything but totally separated entities. Since Descartes, Western philosophy has tended to fragment into two divergent movements: objectivism and subjectivism. The former claims "reason" and science as its own; the latter claims "soul" and religion and art.

Existentialism as a philosophical movement appeared in the nineteenth century when Kierkegaard, Nietzsche, and Dostoyevski challenged the philosophical claims of Hegelian rationalism to be a system for understanding everything. The human soul, they claimed, had been left unaccounted for in modern rationalism. The existential challenge was picked up by Freud and the depth psychologists who claimed that modern rationalism had left out of its consideration the unconscious mind, which had laws of its own waiting to be discovered. The depth psychologists and the existentialists were only extending the two traditions of science and imagination that had been growing ever sharper in antagonism since the late seventeenth century. The basis of the struggle has to do with what human reason is and with how it functions. Aiken and Percy began their pilgrimages with a strong belief in reason and never abandoned it. But they were also aware of the claims of the soul as well as of art, which grows from the pilgrimage of the soul, and could not abandon either. They were both seeking a new anthropology and a new psychology beyond the clash of Cartesian opposites.

To write as if Aiken and Percy first hit upon the possibility of uniting civilization's warring opposites would make them out to be far more heroic than they are. Actually, they belong to a somewhat obscured school of Romanticism that included figures as diverse as Blake, Wordsworth, and Goethe. This school, which sought to unify the opposites of head and heart, derives in large part from certain Renaissance traditions, particularly those concerned with the concepts of microcosm and macrocosm. For instance, Kierkegaard, whose influence is strong on Percy, is one of those romantic individualists who were desperately trying to preserve their souls from dissolution in a rationalistic machine and at the same time rise above lonely individualism to make contact with the unity of early Christianity. I have no doubt that Percy adopted Kierkegaard as a spiritual mentor with enthusiasm because the Dane wrote with a deep concern for the individual psyche and for religion as inner commitment and because he, Percy, had for years been caught up in a rigid medical and scientific training that seemed to ignore the demands of both art and religion. Yet when Percy began writing essays, he did not adopt a style and method of argument like Kierkegaard's but instead took up the methods of American philosophy and science for most of them.

The figure in Aiken's life who most parallels Kierkegaard's place in Percy's life is Herman Melville, a writer who for Aiken was one of the first to rediscover for modern man the depths and complexities of the soul. I have already indicated that both Aiken and Percy felt a need to go back to the nineteenth century to find guides for their pilgrimage. Kierkegaard was always Percy's chief guide, and Aiken tells us his grandfather Potter was his guide *par excellence*. Yet the close study of Melville and Aiken done by Douglas Robillard indicates that Melville inspired Aiken not only as a sounder of the soul but also as a pilgrim who had finally come home and could, because of his return, celebrate life. Aiken, Robillard tells us, "designates Melville as a 'Much-loving hero' and applauds his homeward journey after a long life of pilgrimage and deep sounding."[1] Yet Aiken

---

[1] Douglas Robillard, "Conrad Aiken and Herman Melville," *Studies in the Literary Imagination* 13:2 (Fall 1980): 97.

would also turn to another mentor, George Santayana, to define for him the life of reason. Because of his Harvard education and his continuing study of Santayana, Aiken early in his life became connected with the mainstream of both Western and Greek humanistic education.

Aiken, I believe, is more deeply learned in the Western philosophical tradition than Percy or, for that matter, other members of his generation whose formal education, coming after World War I, was increasingly centered on the natural and social sciences. What Aiken got from Santayana was an awareness of human reason as a faculty of the total being of man that must pervade all basic human activities—science, religion, art, politics—if they are to be fruitful and not destructive. Aiken also was close to the spirit of the German philosopher and scientist Alexander von Humboldt, whom his grandfather studied and actually visited in Germany. Humboldt represents a tradition of rationalism that comes down directly from the Greeks, is contained in the Christian theology of Augustine and Aquinas, and is carried forward by scientists and philosophers (with notable exceptions) from Renaissance thinkers to such modern figures as Planck, Einstein, and Whitehead. In this tradition reason is the means whereby the basic harmony of both microcosm and macrocosm (the great harmony of the universe) is perceived. Planck himself tells us that the scientist must have "a prophetic faith in the deeper harmony."[2] Einstein speaks of Leibniz's idea of a "pre-established harmony" and goes on to say of Planck in a speech honoring the physicist that "the longing to behold this pre-established harmony is the source of the inexhaustible patience and endurance with which Planck has devoted himself, as we see, to the most general problems of our science."[3]

Like his grandfather and like Santayana, Aiken desired to hold in tension in his own consciousness the most profound elements in both the arts and the sciences. As an artist, he still believed that the medical researches of his father and of friends who were psychiatrists were valid human activities that could also be part of the continuing evolution of human consciousness along with the intuitions of the artist. He was a close follower from his college days onward of scientific advances in, among others, three

---

[2]Max Planck, *The Philosophy of Physics,* trans. W. H. Johnson (New York: W. W. Norton and Co., 1963) 124.

[3]Albert Einstein, *Essays in Science,* trans. Alan Harris (New York: Covici-Friede, 1934) 4.

important fields: medicine, psychology, and archaeology. But also as an artist, he believed that the poet must think as well as feel and intuit. Steven Olson reminds us that even as a Harvard student Aiken had with "T. S. Eliot, his friend and classmate . . . sought 'a new poetic voice, one in which one could think.' "[4] At the time, Aiken was caught up in the fashionable philosophy of deterministic naturalism; but as he grew both artistically and philosophically, he accepted the concepts of reason and harmony. His continued reading of Santayana and Potter, along with his study of the Greeks, led him toward the idea of the good life as a quest involving both free will and the encounter with harmony. Aiken most deeply touches the perception of harmony (reason's ultimate goal) in the areas of symbolic language and music. Like Emerson, Baudelaire, and other nineteenth-century thinkers and poets, he believed that symbolic language is based on an underlying unity between mind and matter as well as between all aspects of both the individual and the universe. From this viewpoint we can understand the many mandala images that are to be found in much of his best prose and poetry. But the chief way in which Aiken approaches the concept of harmony is in his continuing concern with music. It is this more than anything else, Helen Hagenbuechle tells us in a lengthy article, that makes Aiken a philosophical poet: "His preoccupation with musical structure in poetry is at the same time an epistemological concern. His search for a style is also, and above all, a quest for truth."[5] There we have it: quest, truth, and harmony. These terms are for Aiken and Percy basic to their views of both the philosophical and the religious life.

In showing how Aiken and Percy arrive at similar positions, I also must indicate certain basic differences. The most important is their attitude toward certain scientists. Aiken never calls into question the scientific enterprise. Percy as quasi-prophet attacks certain aspects of this enterprise. His attack derives generally from the existentialist position toward science and specifically from Allen Tate's views on positivism and abstraction as enemies of literature. The existentialists, as William Barrett suggests, see a split between existence and thought. "If existence cannot be thought, but only lived, then reason has no other recourse than to leave existence out of

---

[4]Steven E. Olson, "The House of Man: Ethical Symbolism in Conrad Aiken's *The Clerk's Journal,*" *Essays in Arts and Sciences* 10:2 (May 1981): 80.

[5]Helen Hagenbuechle, "Epistemology and Musical Form in Conrad Aiken's Poetry," *Studies in the Literary Imagination* 13:2 (Fall 1980): 25.

its picture of reality. As the French scientist and philosopher Emile Meyerson says, 'Reason has only one means of accounting for what does not come from itself, and that is to reduce it to nothingness.' '"[6] Barrett records the existentialist vision of a split between those who believe in reason and as scientists pursue its work and those who cling to an existence that lies outside rationality. Here again is the old Cartesian split: soul against matter, feelings against thought, reason against existence. Percy in his essays often seems caught up in the split himself, but in his novels we find visions of wholeness. Ultimately, the struggle between the two camps is based on the much older struggle between those who put a primary emphasis on being and those whose emphasis is on meaning. The last great metaphysician in Western philosophy, Martin Heidegger, saw that the two ways of looking at the universe both had behind them the voices of the gods, who make communication possible. Heidegger's influence on Percy is greater than many of his critics realize; he, more than the other existentialists, taught Percy to seek the mystery of an underlying unity in the metaphysical principle that makes all communication possible. And in Heidegger also he found confirmation for his belief that communication begins with an act of the will, which sets in motion a continuing search for an encounter with essence, or Being, as Heidegger prefers to call the ultimate metaphysical principle.

Although Percy often seems unaware of the significance of reason for the ancient world, he is never against science as such; but, in his role as quasi-prophet, he is an attacker, particularly in *Lost in the Cosmos,* of the modern gnostic who hopes to use what he calls "reason" to order the universe to suit himself. The "reason" he uses is not, however, reason in the traditional sense but rather what Kant called the understanding: the aspect of the mind that organizes knowledge as opposed to pure reason, which is basic to the entire human makeup. The modern gnostic—as Percy, following in the steps of Tate, shows—believes that humanity is alone in a spiritually empty, totally material universe and that he has only his conscious mind and will to order the world around him. The gnostic thinks he must create, in the words of Jacob Bronowski describing the function of science, "concepts which give unity and meaning to nature."[7] But if it is man alone who bestows unity upon the universe, then man must think of him-

---

[6]William Barrett, *Irrational Man* (Garden City NY: Doubleday, 1958) 142.
[7]Jacob Bronowski, *A Sense of the Future* (Cambridge: MIT Press, 1977) 261.

self as a kind of god, or angel, circling above a world he created. Percy in his novels shows that such pride can be felt only by a few, who are finally driven mad with lust and rage because of their loneliness. And the others on the ground watching them feel worthless and bitter because they cannot assume the role of angel. Nietzsche summed up this modern problem when he said that if God is dead, then man must become God.

Aiken never explored deeply the problem of angelism, except in his novel *King Coffin,* because in most of his writing he held to the traditional concept of reason that he had inherited from Humboldt by way of his grandfather and from Santayana—one of the few modern philosophers who knew thoroughly the Greeks, from whom our traditional concept of reason derives. For Aiken reason cannot be separated from imagination and vision; thus he resembles a Renaissance figure like da Vinci, who moved with comparative ease from his role as scientist and engineer to his role as artist. The Renaissance understood the Greek concept of reason as a human power for perceiving underlying unity in man and the universe. But reason has been central to the activities of Western man in a continuing tradition from the Greeks to the present, though its function has been dimmed from time to time—for instance, in the late Middle Ages as well as in the later modern period, that is, the twentieth century. Conrad Aiken upheld, along with thinkers and scientists like Planck, Einstein, and Whitehead, the concept of a faculty that could perceive both individual and universal harmony in a century when a kind of scientism called by some Evolutionism came to dominate the thinking of most people. The economist and philosopher E. F. Schumacher calls Evolutionism "The Faith" for modern man, and says that it "as currently presented has no basis in science." In essence, what "The Faith" does is to present the "whole of nature, which obviously includes mankind . . . as the product of chance and necessity *and nothing else;* there is neither meaning nor purpose nor intelligence in it—'a tale told by an idiot, signifying nothing.' "[8] Although as a young man he was a Darwinist, Aiken would in his maturity attack the effect of Darwinism, as Evolutionism is called, on the arts. In 1965 he would write the following:

---

[8]E. F. Schumacher, *A Guide for the Perplexed* (New York: Harper Colophon Books, 1978) 114. See also Alexander Wilf's *Origin and Destiny of the Moral Species* for a discussion of the use of computers in showing how Darwinism suggests certain problems for modern science.

And, of course, the vision was the thing, as it was and always will be: without that, no amount of observation, or cataloguing, or mere naming, or immersion in the thingness of the thing—that insidious destructive bequest of William Carlos Williams—can ever add up to any sort of totality of response to the universe with which we are faced, outer and inner.[9]

In attacking the immersion in "things," Aiken is in effect denouncing the reductionism of Darwinians and other naturalists who proclaim that the universe consists only of what the naked eye seems to perceive—a collection of unrelated things moving about in an emptiness called space. The antidote to this poverty-stricken reductionist insight, Aiken tells us, is "vision," which sees things as part of a totality, or harmony, in the universe. For Aiken vision grows out of the imagination and the unconscious mind as well as from the conscious perceiving mind. These two, though in some ways separate, are also unified. Aiken's distrust of Jung was that in constructing a view of man he put too much emphasis on the myth-making and unconscious side of man. For that reason, though not strictly speaking a Freudian as he is sometimes presented, Aiken more readily accepted Freud's insights because he thought they left room for a view of conscious and unconscious working together in a process that could be seen as rational in the oldest meaning of the term.

Aiken and Percy as artist-philosophers most resemble each other when they speak in their works of the reductionist attitudes taken toward humanity by followers of various forms of scientism and of the need for a comprehensive view of man. Percy has never retreated from the knowledge he gained about man in his medical studies as well as in other fields of science that he has studied. He has remained stubbornly "scientific," so much so that one of his close friends has called him a "scientific Catholic."[10] But in his essays, particularly in *Lost in the Cosmos,* he steadfastly refuses to accept the reductionist concept of man as an organism who must "adapt to his environment." Man, for Percy, must be seen primarily as an individual capable of loving. Kierkegaard inspired Percy to begin his serious study of man as individual instead of only the normative creature posited by the natural and social sciences. Yet his mature view of humanity owes more to Catholic theologians than to any other source. Before dis-

---

[9]Conrad Aiken, "Author's Preface," *3 Novels* (New York: McGraw-Hill, 1965) 3.

[10]See Patricia Bowden, "The 'It and the Doing': Sacramental Word and Deed in the Writings of Walker Percy" (Master's thesis, Georgia State University, 1980) 26.

cussing how Aiken and Percy each approach the definition of man in terms of their own key words: consciousness and communication, let me indicate how the two men are also inheritors of the Greek tradition of reason through their involvement in philosophical studies.

Needless to say, the Catholic Church got a bad name among modernists for opposing the new science of Galileo in the seventeenth century, but this fact obscures the deeper meanings inherent in Christian theology from Augustine through Aquinas. In Catholic theology, reason is seen as the faculty that distinguishes man from the animals and that, as Augustine tells us, is necesary for perceiving God. "Let us therefore walk while we have the day, i.e., while we can use reason. Let us turn to God so that we may deserve to be illumined by his word, the true light, and that darkness may not take possession of us."[11] Augustine often refers to "number," or harmony, a sign that his work embodies both the insights of Greek rationalism as well as of early Christian thinking. Aiken read little Catholic theology, but his own elevation of Jesus and Socrates as the two great examples of the good life indicates that he also fully accepted the continuing Western tradition that blended elements of Greek, Judaic, and Christian thought and experience. In the seventeenth century this tradition began its long decline as something called "reason," later to be defined by Kant as understanding, was deified. Augustine is clear concerning the function of reason: "All rational life obeys the voice of unchangeable truth speaking silently within the soul. If it does not so obey it is vicious. Rational life therefore does not owe its excellence to itself, but to the truth which it willingly obeys."[12] By truth Augustine clearly means not knowledge as such but rather the power of God, the spark within the soul that unites man to cosmos. It is this kind of truth that W. B. Yeats refers to in his last letter: "When I try to put it all into a phrase I say 'Man can embody truth but he cannot know it.' "[13] The artist, according to E. F. Schumacher, strives "to communicate truth, the power of truth, by appealing to man's higher intellectual faculties."[14] He might have added that science too, when it appeals to the "higher intellectual faculties," or what was once called reason, commu-

---

[11]St. Augustine, *Of True Religion*, trans. J. H. S. Burleigh (Chicago: Henry Regnery, 1959) 76.

[12]Ibid., 103.

[13]Quoted by Richard Ellmann, *Yeats: The Man and the Masks* (New York: W. W. Norton, 1978) 289.

[14]Schumacher, *A Guide for the Perplexed,* 128

nicates truth by showing us a vision of cosmic harmony. The loss of the good of intellect was for Dante, for instance, the great tragedy that could happen to one who became separated from God.

The problem of the meaning of consciousness and of art is central to the viewpoints of Aiken and Percy. The basis of this problem is the concept of harmony. The faculty called reason apprehends harmony in various ways, through the quests and rituals of both science and art; but the faculty of reason used to apprehend the wholeness underlying diversity cannot function properly unless it obeys the essence to which it is linked—the essence through which everything lives, moves, and has its being. Aiken and Percy are thus thoroughly metaphysical in an age that has largely renounced metaphysics, or the study of Being. The ways of approaching the problem of Being in this century have seemingly all collapsed. The discipline of epistemology has swallowed up metaphysics in general and ontology in particular. Thus most modern educated individuals have, knowingly or unknowingly, rejected the possibility of Being's intimate relationship with man for the simple reason that they cannot answer the great epistemological question: how do we know man is intimately related to Being? In their best work, Aiken and Percy continually answer this question by the pragmatic method employed by various members of the Romantic movement from 1750 to the present. In doing so they show their basic affinity with America's most influential philosopher, William James, though their probing of the realm of Being is far deeper than James's. The answer, simply given, is that where love and joy are to be found, there we find Being. Love and joy appear when harmony is apprehended. Thus Wordsworth writes in "Tintern Abbey": "While with an eye made quiet by the power / Of harmony and the deep power of joy / We see into the life of things." Thus reason apprehends harmony, and this apprehension makes the individual aware of the love that permeates the universe.

Alfred North Whitehead in his seminal book *Science and the Modern World* demonstrates the ways in which Romantic poets like Wordsworth and Shelley helped to prepare the way for a *Zeitgeist* that would in time make possible the new physics of the twentieth century. Both poets renewed in English the Greek vision of cosmos and reason, and their work made it possible for many to look beyond the static vision of eighteenth-century neoclassicism to discover a universe of energies and of underlying harmony. Aiken and Percy both were open to the new physics without being themselves scientists, but as thinkers and artists who accepted new scientific discoveries they felt the need to apply the new awareness of universal energies and universal design to the subject of their concern: the human himself. Jung, I believe, helped them more than any other of the new depth psychologists who were concerned with man not as a static unit but as one who, like the universe, is a grid of energies. With his concept of the archetypes in general and the mandala in particular, Jung reintroduced into psychology the concept of man as a little cosmos connected with the great cosmos. Where Aiken and Percy differ from the depth psychologists is in their determination to put the concept of pilgrimage at the center of their concern. Each writer, however, deals with particular problems—Aiken with consciousness and Percy with communication. How they approached these problems tells us much about their particular visions of the unity of science and art.

II

When Aiken was studying at Harvard, the concept of consciousness was central to the latest philosophical speculation and to the new science of psychology. William James—philosopher and psychologist—even coined the term "stream of a consciousness" to show how man's mind actually worked under ordinary circumstances. Aware as he was of James's work, Aiken also knew of Henry Adams, as he tells us in *Ushant*. Adams had proclaimed that "the early years of the twentieth century would witness the flowering of an ultimate phase . . . in man's thinking, a final brilliance of consciousness."[15] What was this brilliance and what did it portend, Aiken asks throughout his life. These are the key questions of his wisest book, *Ushant*. For one thing, the brilliance of modern consciousness did not for Aiken rest on the conscious, cogitating mind that Descartes had so carefully observed. It did not exclude this side of the mind, but it welcomed all forms of awareness, and it accepted as important to humanity all the new acquisitions of twentieth-century knowledge and art—particularly the insights and intuitions of the new writers and other artists.

Yet Aiken, like Adams, knew that the brilliant new consciousness would be fragmenting as the century grew older. In *Ushant* Aiken, discussing Adams, goes on to speak of the "final brilliance of consciousness" that is "the world itself coming to self-knowledge, even to the point

---

[15]Conrad Aiken, *Ushant* (Cleveland: The World Publishing Company, 1962) 219.

of then coming apart, dissolved, dispersed in its own sense of series—the series, like relativity, beginning in man's own mind to show at last its wonderful and profoundly disturbing themes'' (*U*, 219). The great task for Aiken on his pilgrimage, which began not long after the death of his parents, was to develop his own consciousness and to encounter others who shared in the "final brilliance of consciousness." Then as he grew older and began to experience the disintegration of the modern consciousness, the poet's great task came to be that of surviving and of stating a formula for survival.

Helen Hagenbuechle rightly says that for Aiken "the problem of consciousness is basically a problem of language.''[16] For that reason *Ushant* is about the author as a man of language. It is also about the author's intersubjective relationship with other important people of language: notably Pound, Eliot, Lowry, Fletcher, and Williams, among others. Aiken finds himself in the London of the twenties amidst one of the richest literary movements of the century; and yet, after describing a meeting with Katherine Mansfield and Virginia Woolf, he notes: "Envy and hatred, alas; yes one might as well admit it" and "a jungle scene, simply this literary forest" (*U*, 293). Some poison, he sees, is subtly destroying the evolving consciousness of modern humanity; and Aiken knows that he cannot live at the center of a literary movement, as his friend Eliot could do. But how can one avoid collapse, the sort of disintegration that finally overtook Malcolm Lowry? For Aiken, Lowry was the sunniest genius of all his literary friends: a man for whom "life itself was a picnic of genius in which everyone could share alike," (*U*, 292) but his disintegration was total—as was John Gould Fletcher's. Why did Lowry sink into alcoholism and Fletcher go insane? What happened to make Pound fall into crackpot schemes and Eliot seek the refuge of the Middle Ages? Eliot's work, Aiken says, was "a miracle, a transformation" but "was it not to have been, also, a surrender, and perhaps the saddest known to D. in his life" (*U*, 216). The answer, Aiken discovered slowly and painfully, was that they all either stopped or slowed down the development of their own consciousnesses.

The central idea of *Ushant,* as the title suggests, is that certain forces threaten the pilgrim; these forces either lure him back to what he perceives to be a pleasurable past or they frighten him with what might happen to him if he goes forward or else they promise him some great reward in ego

---

[16]Hagenbuechle, "Conrad Aiken's Poetry," 7.

satisfaction or social satisfaction if only he will stand still. Narcissism and fear of castration are present from birth, and the pilgrim finds even in middle age they have not been overcome. To give in to them is to inhibit consciousness and to stop its development, and to do this is to lose the ability to use language effectively. The pilgrim who hopes to survive and continue his journey must see that journey as central to his existence and the search for inner and outer harmony as the meaning of pilgrimage. The pilgrim must also see that total pleasure or total ego satisfaction is an impossibly seductive goal that must be continually denied. But there is an inner and outer harmony, or essence, that will occasionally manifest itself to the pilgrim in a moment of brilliant apprehension. A clairvoyant whom Aiken meets early in his life tells him about his own pilgrimage and all its visionary qualities, its mistakes, and its triumphs. It was

> the most wonderful of experiences, the blessed experience of coming suddenly upon a veritable gold-mine of consciousness, seemingly inexhaustible, too, and with the words already hermetically stamped on the gold: perhaps out of some such experience you will even achieve one of those "controlled" masterpieces that are both controlled and uncontrolled, and these are the best, the true artesian water of life, moments of abundance and joy, and the memory of power (*U*, 131).

What the clairvoyant sees as a failure in Aiken—and the author agrees with him—is the lack of "disciplined knowledge that will enable you to perfect, at will, and repeatedly, true works of art" (*U*, 131). Yet Aiken always sought knowledge as well as the intuitive vision of the artist. Where the failure lay was in his occasional lack of discipline.

In looking back over his creative life, Aiken sees *Blue Voyage* as a turning point in his career—one that helped to set his literary course, leading in time to his other novels, to *Ushant,* and to his best poetry. In his preface to *3 Novels* he describes his method of seeing himself in *Blue Voyage* as artist-hero-servant: one who "could understand his neurosis, and then proceed to create with it, on the one hand, while he analyzed both the neurosis and himself away with the other." Aiken's literary method would nearly always be the one described here, one involving the "creative" or intuitive side of man as well as his analytical, conscious side. And when in *Great Circle* he is less autobiographical, he tells us, he is equally as "psychological," meaning that he probes with knowledge and with the analytical "left side of the brain" the problems of man in a disintegrating modern culture. In continuing his discussion in his preface to *3 Novels,*

Aiken proudly points to the fact that *King Coffin* is "almost a case study, and has been used as such in college classes in psychology."[17] He ends the preface by telling his readers that *Ushant* is the summing up, "the statement of the writer at the *end* of his career, and, if anything, a deeper probing into the problem, or predicament, or *obligation,* of the artist in society." Finally, he speaks of *Ushant* as containing "an analysis of my aims" and being "on the one hand, a contribution to the increase of consciousness—the evolution of consciousness—and, on the other, toward the perfecting of the statement, or artifact in which it is made" (*3 N,* 4). Thus the author states as his goal the increasing of consciousness and the perfecting of the work of art that serves this high purpose. Obviously, the two aspects of mind—the analytical and the intuitive—are for Aiken both involved in what he calls the development of consciousness.

Aiken's greatest problem is breaking through to the unity that lies behind the two aspects of the mind; but, as the clairvoyant mentioned in *Ushant* told him he would, he does achieve moments of rich conscious awareness springing from a rational perception of harmony. It is not in the accumulating of knowledge or even in the depth of his analysis that Aiken so often fails, but rather it is in what the clairvoyant called discipline, which ultimately is related for the artist-philosopher to a continuing rational insight. Yet let it be said immediately that the primary concern of Aiken as artist is never analysis and knowledge on one hand or intuition and imaginative insight on the other but the integrative power that unifies all human endeavor. His great symbol of this power is music. As Martin suggests, "For Aiken the poet uses music—derived from number by Pythagoras—in order to define reality correctly, to say the things which prose cannot."[18] Martin is referring in particular to Aiken's last great poem, "A Letter from Li Po," which Bollier rightly calls "a valedictory, a final statement in many ways."[19] In this work Aiken deals with the harmony of the universe in terms of the philosophy of Pythagoras, who sought among other things, to demonstrate the underlying unity of music and mathematics. For Aiken music is the most basic of the arts, and mathematics is the foundation stone of modern science. In "A Letter from Li Po" he traces

---

[17]Aiken, "Author's Preface," *3 Novels,* 4.

[18]Jay Martin, *Conrad Aiken: A Life of His Art* (Princeton: Princeton University Press, 1962) 245.

[19]E. P. Bollier, "Conrad Aiken's Ancestral Voices: A Reading of Four Poems," *Studies in the Literary Imagination* 13:2 (Fall 1980): 72.

both to their source in the cosmos. In no previous effort was Aiken so concerned with writing about the concept of unity, though in one sense it and the other works in the volume called *A Letter from Li Po and Other Poems* (1955) represent a continuation of his greatest poetic effort, the Preludes. As in the Preludes, he seeks in his last important book to reveal his own evolving consciousness by demonstrating that *all* of that consciousness— the analysis, the dreams, the prophecies, the questionings, the essential quest—is ultimately related to the individual microcosm at the center of the soul as well as to the macrocosm that is the universe. Therefore, Aiken tells us, the "alchemy by which we grow" is

> *the self becoming word, the word*
> *becoming world. And with each part we play*
> *we add to cosmic Sum and cosmic sum.*
> *Who knows but one day we shall find,*
> *hidden in the prism at the rainbow's foot,*
> *the square root of the eccentric absolute,*
> *and the concentric absolute to come.*[20]

Aiken, like Jung, uses the term *self* here and in the Preludes to refer to the center of the psyche: the essence, god, or truth that holds all parts of the design together in unity, whose worldwide symbol, Jung tells us, is the mandala. Out of the self spring words that create both ourselves and add to the cosmos. But these words must be sought diligently with the faith that out of the chaos in which man is forced to live will emerge those images of cosmic unity that are the poetry and mythology of every human who chooses the path of pilgrimage—the only road to psychic growth and an evolving consciousness.

In no other poem does Aiken so clearly identify the search of the mathematician (and by extension the scientist) with the search of the poet. Both seek to view the same reality, which is the essential unity, Martin clearly tells us, that allowed Aiken to relate himself to Pythagoras the mathematician. Both, he tells us, have chosen to search for the one universal harmony. "He and Pythagoras agree that both the heart and the mind must be satisfied by the choice. That is, the one thing which would best symbolize a whole life must combine the concrete or actual (the heart) with the ideal

---

[20]Conrad Aiken, *A Letter from Li Po and Other Poems* (New York: Oxford University Press, 1955) 18.

(the mind).''[21] That Aiken fully understood the intellectual implications of the above statement is seen in the fact that he worked closely with Martin in the writing of his book. Aiken, as he told me in conversation, was not fully satisfied with Martin's exploration of his ideas, but he believed generally that Martin was on the right track as opposed to those critics like Frederick J. Hoffman who believed that Aiken is the poet of "the self peering through . . . a glass into the universe, in which he sees himself as part of the chaos he is observing.''[22] Aiken was convinced that before an individual could begin his pilgrimage he had to accept the chaotic aspect of the human condition, but he believed the traditional teaching of all religions and philosophies on the subject of pilgrimage. This teaching centers on the concept of an underlying harmony that must be sought. On the road of pilgrimage the seeker receives those moments of love and joy that are ultimately the only "proof" we need of God and that make possible, as Aiken puts it at the end of *Ushant*, our rising "like notes of music arranging themselves in a divine harmony, a divine unison, which as it had no beginning, can have no end—.'' In the last lines of the Preludes Aiken clearly adds his belief that the true scientist also searches for and often finds harmony and by doing so creates himself, thereby overcoming in his own life the sea of chaos all must swim in.

And what of Li Po, the Chinese poet of the work's title? In him Aiken makes an important statement about unity: all people are ultimately one, but to know this each must seek his true self, which is apprehended as a microcosm. In dealing with the Greeks as he does, Aiken reveals the centrality of his position in the Western tradition of reason and of self-knowledge, which for Socrates meant not only self-examination but encounter with one's divine essence, or true self. But in turning to China, Aiken shows us that any honest human who seeks essence is ultimately rewarded by the gift of love and the vision of harmony. Li Po in the poem is paired with Aiken's Quaker ancestor Abiel, a farmer who was as much a pilgrim as Li Po or Aiken himself. Through pilgrimage all three are united. At the same time, Aiken acknowledges that both are spiritual ancestors: one learning his knowledge of God from the Bible and the other from the *I Ching*, or Book of Changes, as Aiken refers to this Chinese Bible. But to prove the truth of what they studied, both make a pilgrimage of their lives and dis-

---

[21]Martin, *Conrad Aiken*, 243-44.
[22]Frederick J. Hoffman, *Conrad Aiken* (New York: Twayne Publishers, 1962) 290.

cover firsthand the promised spiritual riches. Both men become for Aiken spiritual guides, and in acknowledging them he announces his awareness of the pilgrim's need for figures from the past who are both helpers and initiators into the life of harmony hidden behind chaos. Thus Aiken realizes, writing at the end of his life, that he too will fulfill the role of "wise old man," as Jung calls the initiatory archetype. But this is a subject that will be taken up in the final chapter on the artist as culture hero. Now let us consider how Percy deals with the problem of communication in his search for ways of writing about the arts and sciences.

III

Walker Percy is the rare example of a literary artist who began the practice of his art after having for years devoted himself first to science and then to philosophy. From the time he entered the University of North Carolina as a freshman until he contracted tuberculosis as a medical intern at Bellevue Hospital in New York City, Percy devoted himself almost exclusively to the study of science. He majored in chemistry and minored in mathematics and German at North Carolina, and at Columbia University's College of Physicians and Surgeons he was totally absorbed in the study of medicine. While he was in a sanitorium recovering from tuberculosis, he turned to Kierkegaard and Dostoyevski, among others, who set him on the path of pilgrimage. His first published works were a series of essays appearing in philosophical journals. His novelistic career began in 1961 with *The Moviegoer*. By 1980 he was both a popular and a critical success as a literary artist, but he never ceased to be concerned with science and philosophy as he continued to write novels. Indeed, his novels are about the healing of the modern individual. For this healing to take place, Percy is continually telling us, there must be a profound change in modern man's conception of communication.

Percy would in fact approach the problem of communication in his first published essay, "Symbol as Need," both from the scientific as well as the humanistic viewpoint. The very first sentence uses the term semiotic, and this usage is prophetic of Percy's later interest in semiotics: the science of signs. This first essay incorporates many of his basic philosophical views, which were largely existential in nature. From Kierkegaard he had learned that the subjective life should once again be put at the center of the philosophical endeavor. Percy, however, would go beyond the subjective individualism of Kierkegaard to accept Marcel's concept of intersubjectivity, which emphasized subjective relationships between people. Nevertheless, in discussing the philosophy of Susanne Langer in his "Symbol as Need," he does not take as his ultimate authority either an empirical semiotics or a subjective existentialism but rather Thomas Aquinas. "It is apparently Saint Thomas and not Mrs. Langer or Cassirer who had the first inkling of the mysterious analogy between the form of beauty and the pattern of the inner life."[23] Percy here fails to place Aquinas in the tradition of harmony and reason that begins with the Greeks and extends down through Augustine to Aquinas, the Renaissance Platonists, and finally to Langer's mentor, Alfred North Whitehead. Yet this statement sums up Percy's own pilgrimage from this first published essay on through the rest of his essays, including *Lost in the Cosmos,* which emphasizes the relationship between love and cosmic harmony. Love is the basis of the communication that will enable the human being to achieve a healing of mind, body, and spirit.

To understand Percy's approach to the three areas of mind, body, and spirit, one must take into account the term "scientist-philosopher-artist," which he used in "The Message in the Bottle" to suggest that the categories of specialization must be set aside if the individual is to accept all three sides of himself. The scientist puts his primary emphasis on "left-side" thinking, which involves calculation. The artist, certainly since 1750, has put his primary emphasis on the "right side" of the brain, which involves intuitive, subjective, and imaginative ways of looking at life. Presumably, it is the philosopher, placed in the middle in Percy's term as well as in Percy's career, who will reconcile the two ways of looking at the world. Yet another figure must emerge for the "scientist-philosopher-artist" to find a true communication, the individual that Percy calls the apostle.

In "The Message in the Bottle" Percy suggests, following Kierkegaard's essay on the genius and the apostle, that two categories of communication exist: that of the "genius," whose sphere is immanence and that of the apostle, who relates primarily to transcendence. Many theologians will object that Kierkegaard and Percy are denying any connection between transcendence and immanence and therefore that God for them

---

[23]Walker Percy, *The Message in the Bottle: How Queer Man Is, How Queer Language Is, and What One Has to Do with the Other* (New York: Farrar, Straus & Giroux, 1979) 290.

can rarely, if ever, touch the life of man. Yet immanence is everywhere to be found in Percy's fiction, as Patricia Bowden demonstrates in her study of the sacramental word and deed in his novels. Nevertheless, in his image of the apostle, Percy says he is making a statement about "news as a category of communication," and about "a unique Person-Event-Thing in time."[24] What then is Percy saying with his image of the apostle? I think he is following Kierkegaard in saying that Christianity will not be renewed until a specific form of communication called news delivered by an apostle comes into the world. For Percy this is the highest form of communication, based as it is on faith. The emergence of the apostle is necessary for both true religious renewal as well as cultural renewal. Percy shows an awareness of the need for the apostle but admits that he has little real knowledge of what one is. What he does have knowledge of is the relationship between the two sides of man—one side best represented in our time by science and the other by art.

Percy in effect is saying that the role of the scientist-philosopher-artist in our time is to prepare for the coming of the apostle. This preparation is best accomplished by an opening up of all the avenues of communication. In learning this opening up process for himself, Percy in the long run was greatly aided by thinkers in the tradition of theologians like Tertullian who believed because of the very absurdity of his belief. This tradition made important contributions to Percy's thought: Kierkegaard more than anyone else taught him about modern despair and how this despair is proof that man is a castaway who must never try to feel at home in a society of his own creation, lest he forget his role as pilgrim. Pilgrims in all traditions suffer from feelings of despair and homelessness. For Aiken chaos is the category that corresponds to despair in Percy. The fictional characters of both men react to the psychic pain of chaos and despair by responding either with open violence or, more often, with depression. It might be said that both authors take as their primary subject the manic-depressive nature of man. Yet both are equally aware of an invasion by that destructive force Jung calls the shadow, which always happens when man falls into one-sidedness. Kierkegaard often seems to be saying man must leave the civilized world altogether because it has ceased to be grounded in true religion. Percy and Aiken—one following in this matter Marcel, the other Santayana— tell us to work with the tools of modern civilization while at the same time

---

[24]Ibid., 140-41.

continuing the pilgrimage through a world that is dying to make way for a new world. The chief tools for both are science, philosophy, and art. But in using them, both authors tell us, the individual must encounter a harmony, or grace, that makes true communication possible. This harmony, for both men, is apprehended by the pilgrim, and this apprehension is related to the pilgrim's ability to heal others.

In his essays and in his fiction Percy says that art can awaken man to a sense of cosmic harmony and to his need to begin a pilgrimage in order to discover his individuality. The novelist at his best in our time, Percy believes, must—like Joyce's Stephen Dedalus—call "on every ounce of cunning, craft, and guile he can muster from the dark regions of his soul."[25] In his essay "Notes for a Novel about the End of the World," Percy defines our time as "the passing of one age and the beginning of another."[26] The novelist who writes with this in mind is not a prophet (they are as rare as apostles because they communicate directly with God) but is instead a quasi-prophet. The difference between him and the scientist is clear in Percy's mind: "If the scientist's vocation is to clarify and simplify, it would seem that the novelist's is to muddy and complicate."[27] And he quickly adds one of his most oft-repeated ideas, first learned from Kierkegaard: "What will be left out of even the most rigorous scientific formulation is nothing else than the individual himself." No better statement is to be found in Percy's work concerning the two sides of the mind: the analytical, clear working of the left side and the darker, intuitive side that is the right hemisphere.

When we ask how the two aspects of the mind are united, we must turn again to the novels, where the central concern is not really quasi-prophecy, as Percy has indicated in various interviews and essays, but rather the healing of broken relationships. Like some of his critics, Percy has suggested that as a novelist he is very much like a diagnostic physician. He puts his finger on the basic disease of human culture as being the inability of people to relate to each other, a problem that at its deepest is one of communication. The failure of relationship and communication, Percy tells us both in his novels and essays, is one-sidedness based on a withdrawal into one's "knowledge," one's skill or profession. We are not, as Percy has said many

---

[25]Ibid., 118.
[26]Ibid., 114.
[27]Ibid., 115.

times, simply organisms that must adapt to an environment through the use of knowledge. Instead we are beings connected with what he calls in one essay "a metascientific, metacultural reality, an order of being apart from the scientific and cultural symbols with which it is grasped and expressed."[28] In the same essay he calls on social scientists—and by implication all scientists—to "take seriously the chief article upon which their method is based," that article being the belief in an underlying harmony most prophets, artists, and scientists have accepted from the time of Greece until the modern period when so-called scientific naturalism, growing out of Darwinism, proclaimed the emptiness of the universe and the unrelatedness of all entities in it. This failure of most people to recover the metacultural reality has led to an understandable withdrawal into specialized knowledge and a one-sided view of existence.

Since some general belief is needed to overcome the loneliness of modern existence, civilized individuals in this century have turned to a particular kind of gnosticism that has led to the inability to communicate at deeper levels. Percy defines this gnosticism as an "absorption by the layman not of the scientific method but rather of the magical aura of science, whose credentials he accepts for all sorts of reality." Percy then goes on to show how this absorption not in science or the scientific method but in scientism, that is, the worship of knowledge, leads to a splitting of the consciousness.

> Thus in the lay culture of a scientific society nothing is easier than to fall prey to a kind of seduction which sunders one's very self from itself into an all-transcending "objective" consciousness and a consumer-self with a list of "needs" to be satisfied. It is this monstrous bifurcation of man into angelic and bestial components against which old theologies must be weighed before new theologies are erected. Such a man could not take account of God, the devil, and the angels if they were standing before him, because he has already peopled the universe with his own hierarchies.[29]

The bifurcation of man must inevitably lead to sickness. "When the novelist writes of a man 'coming to himself' through some such catalyst as catastrophe or ordeal, he may be offering testimony to a gross disorder of consciousness and to the need of recovering oneself as neither angel nor

---

[28]Ibid., 242.
[29]Ibid., 113.

organism but as a wayfaring creature somewhere between."[30] The novels all illustrate this philosophic statement by showing central characters who awaken to their own sickness due to modern "bifurcation" and who seek a true communication with other sick individuals. Gradually the central characters awaken to a sense of harmony within themselves and in the universe. Thus they become able to heal others. They by no means reject knowledge, medical or otherwise, as a necessary component in healing others, but their deepest efforts at healing are based on their growing ability to communicate with others. The fact that they have made contact with harmony, or God if one will, is shown in their recovery from some form of psychic illness that threatens to annihilate all depth of consciousness. This recovery is paralled by a discovery of moments of love and joy.

In Percy's fictional viewpoint those who discover their real humanity become a kind of doctor for others who lack that awareness of harmony necessary to communicate at a level deeper than the kind of "objective" expression taken by many to be the only form of communication possible. The communication of the wayfaring healer uses objective knowledge but also addresses others from the subjective levels of consciousness, from in fact that intuitive, imaginative side of the mind that is denied by many in the modern world.

In Percy's novels all the protagonists are involved with knowledge, but all seek a deeper communication. However, in *The Second Coming* he makes explicit what was often implicit in the other novels: the person who accepts his own wound is the one who can best heal another, or rather who can, by choosing the path of pilgrimage himself, invoke the essential harmony that makes the healing process possible. Knowledge plays a role in healing, but the deliverer of healing services is the chief agent in the process. Sickness, in Percy's view, is due to a withdrawal from cosmic unity. The result is the inability and even the lack of desire to communicate with others. When one accepts the wounded self within and begins a search for a restoration with Being, then he finds certain tasks to fulfill, among them the beginning of a true communication with others who have turned away from Being. In *The Second Coming* Will Barrett, living tranquilly on the surface of life, rediscovers through a violent incident that he has hidden from himself the pain of his father's attempt to kill his own son and subsequent suicide. But when he chooses to seek release from this hidden pain,

---

[30]Ibid.

he finds the grace to help others, like Allison, who have also suffered and have withdrawn into a mental cocoon. The result is the beginning of the restoration of true communication in which neither the analytical mind nor the imagination is rejected. Through this communication Percy sees hope for the eventual restoration of harmony within men that would make possible an awareness of the unity underlying those two basic activities of man: the arts and the sciences.

IV

Literary investigations into the problems of the dissociation of the consciousness, or bifurcation as Percy calls it, reveal that several important literary artists put this matter at the center of their considerations. In her book *Virginia Woolf and the Androgynous Vision,* Nancy Bazin shows how Woolf with the help of music revealed in a masterwork like *To the Lighthouse* how every mind is essentially bisexual, being able to operate both on analytic and poetic levels. Like Woolf, Aiken and Percy held out hope to modern people that they could once again be both scientific and artistic at the same time. In fact, they tell us that man, to move forward into full human development, must be both at the same time. Percy, in particular, points to what happens when a civilization tries to live out of knowledge alone, that is, solely out of the working of the analytical side of the mind. Even the light entertainments and the cookery of such a gnostic society become inane because they are cut off from the imaginative side of life. The result is a boredom that drives people to live on drugs that destroy essential humanity and create a violence hitherto unseen. Both Aiken and Percy also show what happens when the artistic personality turns from the analytic mind, refusing to think hard and long about essential issues. The result can be personal chaos of the sort that occurred in the lives of several of Aiken's closest friends—John Gould Fletcher and Malcolm Lowry, among others. Aiken and Percy both knew that all humans in a time of cultural collapse must turn to the analytical mind for all the help it can give. Science for them represented one of the highest attainments of that analytical mind. Percy's essays and some of his best fiction are filled with insights that spring from science. One of the most recent studies of Aiken—Steven Olson's dissertation, "The Vascular Mind: Conrad Aiken's Early Poetry, 1910-1918" (Stanford University, 1981)—tells us that his poetry reveals a considerable knowledge of such fields as biology, botany, medicine, physiology, and psychology. Both authors diligently pursued the development of the natural and behavioral sciences of their time, but both also plunged deeply into philosophy and art. Yet it is not their diligent work in both areas that makes them important in the solution of the problem of the unity of the arts and sciences. Instead, it is their rediscovery of certain basic knowledge about man and their application of that knowledge to their own lives.

Both Aiken and Percy create in their work an anthropology and a psychology that describe in detail how certain people are able to move toward a fulfillment of human destiny, which is that of an ever growing development of consciousness moving, as Percy tells us, toward the level of angels. In Aiken's terms, true pilgrims move toward the fulfillment of man's inherent godlike nature. Both tell us that man contains at his center a unifying essence, or self, that is discovered gradually as one accepts the path of pilgrimage. Northrop Frye points out that the quest myth is the basis of all literary genres. Aiken and Percy write of the human quest for the essence that unifies all the activities of human existence. In *Time in the Rock* (1936) Aiken revealed that he had discovered that unifying Self, as he calls it; and in *The Last Gentleman* (1966) Percy made it clear that he too had put his finger on the essential unifying element. By making contact with this element and by dramatizing their encounter with essential harmony, the two authors point to a psychology that shows two forms of human behavior. One form springs from the quest and enables man in time to develop his powers in a harmonious manner and to communicate effectively with his fellow man. Failure to pursue the quest leads to the fragmentation of man, to a wasting of his powers or to a seizure by archetypes that drives him to become godlike but leaves him isolated and destructive, unable to communicate effectively with other humans.

For both Aiken and Percy the development of the full consciousness is necessary for communication. The highest form of communication is poetry, which every developed human is capable of in one form or another. Aiken thus tells us in the *Paris Review* that ''as poetry is the highest speech of man, it can not only accept and contain, but in the end express best everything in the world, or in himself, that he discovers. It will absorb and transmute, as it always has done, and glorify, all that we can know.''[31] Aiken is in complete agreement then with Allen Tate's definition of poetry as the complete knowledge of man's experience or with Lewis P. Simp-

---

[31]''Conrad Aiken: An Introduction,'' *Paris Review* (Winter/Spring 1968): 117

son's statement that poetry is a way of being fully human. Without poetry
and the other arts, Aiken continually tells us, man cannot fulfill his role as
man but must sink to a one-sided, barbarian level. Aiken seems fully aware
of the meaning of the Chinese saying that one-sidedness might lend mo-
mentum but turns a person into a dangerous barbarian.

Walker Percy's theory of literature is not as highly developed as Aiken's, but then he has never been a critic or theorist of literature. In an interview Percy has said that "a novelist these days has to be an ex-suicide.
A good novel . . . is possible only after one has given up and let go."[32]
He is, of course, speaking about his kind of religious novel dealing with
the end of an age. His books are, without his ever saying so, much more
than the works of an ex-suicide who "lets go," though they are that too.
They are also more than simply novels of ideas—as some critics, observing Percy's brilliant exercise of intellect, have maintained. I believe the
mainstream of critical opinion that speaks of the artistic validity of *The
Moviegoer* and of *The Last Gentleman* is correct and that *Lancelot,* a generally misunderstood novel as this is being written, will in time be seen as
a masterpiece. *The Last Gentleman* and *The Second Coming,* though weak
in places, also contain sections of great imaginative power as well as novelistic statements of ideas that are as valuable as those made by earlier novelists of ideas like H. G. Wells and Aldous Huxley.

The novelist has often been thought of as little more than a recorder of
emotions, ideas, and social scenes. When a novelist uses his intellect, it is
often assumed that he has no emotions and is writing fiction to fit a thesis.
Percy's novels are something new because he has chosen to write from his
head as well as from his heart and his instincts. At his best he is, like Aiken, a poet who uses his poetry as a way of writing best about everything
we know. Like Aiken, he also writes about the greatest of all traditional
subjects, the pilgrim seeking God. Seen in this light, Percy—a man deeply
influenced by Aquinas—must be placed in the tradition of Dante. In fact,
as E. F. Schumacher has written, "All great works of art are 'about God'
in the sense that they show the perplexed human being the path, the way
up the mountain." Schumacher goes on to illustrate this statement by
quoting Dante on the subject of why he wrote *The Divine Comedy:* " 'The
whole work . . . was undertaken not for a speculative but a practical end

---

[32]Walker Percy, "Questions They Never Asked Me: A Self-Interview," *Esquire* 88
(December 1977): 193.

. . . the purpose of the whole is to remove those living in this life from a state of misery, and lead them into a state of felicity.' ''[33] Although Percy did not write a great Christian epic like Dante, his work follows in this tradition by portraying a hero in his novels who realizes he can no longer rely on his culture alone but must, to know lasting happiness, transform his inner life.

Man in the twentieth century cannot speak confidently of God, as could Aquinas and Dante; but, as cultures disintegrate, individuals are faced with futility in watching disintegration without belief in a reintegrating principle. Aiken and Percy have, like earlier shamans, sought such a principle and have found it in a harmony that undergirds the entire universe. In their encounters with harmony their own futility was overcome again and again. Because of these encounters they could envision the possibility of cultural renewal.

---

[33]Schumacher, *A Guide for the Perplexed*, 129.

The Man of Letters
as Culture Hero

Chapter VIII

Conrad Aiken and Walker Percy began their literary careers solidly entrenched in the American liberal tradition. When they became established as important men of letters at a time of advanced age when most other American writers are usually either dead or burned out, they were in large part still liberals. But they had also advanced far beyond what is known today as the twin poles of liberalism and conservatism. Lionel Trilling said not long before his death that one of his tasks as a liberal intellectual was to fight the slide of liberalism into Marxism—a philosophy that denied a fundamental tenet of all liberal philosophies, which is a responsible individualism. Aiken and Percy tackled the very problem that underlay the disappearance of individualism itself, which was in essence the crisis of cultures collapsing all over the world.

Aiken and Percy both began their personal quests equipped with the inherited liberalism of their times. Percy rightly dedicates his first novel

to William Alexander Percy with the words "In Gratitude to W.A.P."
More than anyone else, W. A. Percy made possible the beginning of his
adopted son's whole artistic and intellectual development. The elder Percy
was one of the great Southern liberals who opened himself to the intellectual, artistic, and political advances made possible by the prevailing liberal
atmosphere of the American intelligentsia in the first half of the century.
In many ways he was a Southern Stoic and a paternalist, as his *Lanterns
on the Levee* indicates; but his involvement in the arts and sciences, particularly psychology, had its deep effect on Walker Percy. Walker revolted against the Stoicism and paternalism but accepted the liberalism and
the involvement in the arts and sciences.

Conrad Aiken began his own personal development under even more
auspicious cultural circumstances. In *Ushant* he records both the cultural
influence of a father who was a doctor, poet, and inventor and the possibly
greater cultural influence of his "Beloved Uncle," Alfred Claghorn Potter, Librarian of Harvard's Widener Library. Growing up in Cambridge
and then attending Harvard, Aiken was deeply aware of the richness of a
liberal tradition based on a new intellectual outlook pioneered by William
James in both his psychology and his philosophy. Harvard itself would become, along with Columbia University and New York City, the center of
this developing American liberalism. Yet the new flowering of American
intellectual life was spoiled for both men by the fact of violence: not only
the violence of parental suicide but a psychic violence experienced in many
American activities by two highly sensitive individuals who had early
glimpsed the underlying tragedy of the twentieth century.

World War I and its aftermath produced a growing awareness by most
people of cultural decline. For some, the American dream was at its bright-
est in the twenties, but the Great Depression brought to America in strength
what many thought was the antidote to the nation's cultural decline: Marxism. Yet Marxism in practice meant the snuffing out of liberal individualism and with it the suppressing of those cultural activities that the liberal
prized. Aiken had already in the twenties foreseen that the last great cultural flowering of Western civilization was taking place. When the dis-
tress—both personal and social—of the thirties came to him, Aiken met it
with a vision of the renewal of humanity in works like the Preludes and
The Coming Forth by Day of Osiris Jones. Marxism and other forms of
modern gnosticism were based on an attempt to arrange humans in cultural
patterns by dictatorial orders as if they were objects. Based on the tenden-

cies to objectify and to quantify exhibited by modern scientism, Marxism as it developed in practice under Stalin denied individual integrity and at last put its total emphasis on social order at all cost. But in the meantime many schools of the old liberalism began to degenerate into an emphasis on individualism to the exclusion of order. The search for individual expression to the extent that it denied responsibility and the rights of others often turned into its opposite, a gnosticism demanding an order that denied individual initiative and often led to violence and more cultural disintegration.

Aiken early knew that violence develops first in the individual due to some failure of individual culture. He saw in modern society a split developing that would tend to put science and scientism on one side and the arts, the imagination, and the expression of individual thoughts and emotions on the other. He also saw that this development was due in part to the failure of individuals to find a harmony within themselves. As one who was early devoted to science, art, and philosophy, Aiken could not let any one of these necessary human activities go in order to cultivate one at the expense of the other. His maternal grandfather had taught that religion, science, and art could all work hand in hand; and his paternal grandfather, who had taught science and mathematics in New York City, believed that civilization demanded interaction between the different branches of learning. Therefore, it was not only a psychic trauma that put Aiken on the road of pilgrimage but the need to achieve a harmonious inner development that would allow him to use both hemispheres of the mind as an artist and philosopher who was called to take into full account the modern advances of both the sciences and the arts.

Aiken's discovery of Freud reinforced his belief that the inner life of man could be developed. Freud was a scientist who was not afraid to use the arts in his quest for the development of man. Percy too as a young man became an intense believer in Freud, yet both Aiken and Percy would go beyond Freud in working out their own concepts concerning the inner life. By the time Aiken was writing *Blue Voyage,* he had realized that it was necessary to make choices about courses of action in order to develop his psyche. He saw that Freud's concept of making conscious the unconscious, that is, of understanding one's psychic trauma, would not of itself lead to the healing of a wounded soul. Thus he and his hero in *Blue Voyage* came to see that psychic change meant following a path based on a series of choices that would set in motion the healing powers at work both in the psyche and in the world around it. In writing *The Moviegoer* Percy reveals, as does the book's hero, a similar understanding that choices involving certain symbolic actions lead to encounters with divine energy, or grace— finally the only agent of psychic healing.

Years before Aiken and Percy wrote their pivotal first novels, *Blue Voyage* and *The Moviegoer,* they had begun to discover concepts that led to the recording of their own pilgrimages in their best creative works. They both found those masters who would lead them to an understanding of pilgrimage. This discovery was made in an intense and prolonged manner because, like pilgrims before them, they had fully encountered the facts of human disease and death. Suffering psychically and physically from early traumas, they encountered at several levels the thinking of initiatory figures like Santayana and Kierkegaard, who provided them with a deeper wisdom than they received from their own father figures. Aiken and Percy would always recognize the important cultural influences of men like Alfred Claghorn Potter and W. A. Percy. But these early influences, based as they were on liberal views and on a cultivation of both the arts and the sciences, did not provide for them an understanding of the act of pilgrimage. Without ever surrendering liberalism or the cultivation of the arts and sciences, Aiken and Percy went back to what was for them the basis of the development of both individual and social culture: the pilgrimage.

Where then did pilgrimage lead Aiken and Percy? First, it led them backward in time to a recovery of their own religious traditions. Percy's paternal ancestors had been both Catholic and Episcopalian, and his own conversion at the age of thirty was the beginning of his search for the meaning and experience of traditional sacramental Christianity. Aiken's background was primarily Unitarian and Quaker, and in his life's pilgrimage he sought not only to understand but to live out the radical Protestant Christianity that was his heritage. Yet the path of pilgrimage leads backward only to gather the wisdom of the past necessary to guide one on his spiritual journey. What the future holds for the pilgrim is never predictable because of the mysterious nature of human and divine creativity. For instance, though Aiken maintained his radical Protestant outlook, he nevertheless developed a strongly ritualistic view of religion and life; and although Percy has remained a Catholic, the influence of the radical Protestantism of Kierkegaard is strong in his work, especially in *The Second Coming.* Above all, pilgrimage leads the two authors into certain places in time and into certain basic human experiences. The experiences, recorded in their works, are those of a deepening psychic growth and awareness of the possibilities of new cultural life. The places are also important. In England, Massachusetts, New York, and Savannah, Aiken faced various aspects of himself as well as of his cultural background. In Birmingham and Greenville, Mississippi; in New Orleans and New York, Percy made those individual journeys necessary to confront not only his own traumas but also those places where he could find environments that would aid him in his pilgrimage.

In contemplating the experiences and the places sought and found by the two authors, one must inevitably ask what they accomplished. Most obviously, they have given us a body of literary works that have already had an effect on many serious readers. Aiken has so far missed popular success; but Percy, having attained a contemporary following, has gone on to speak directly, as Aiken did, to many who think deeply about the death of the world's cultures and the possibility of their rebirth. Therefore, while it is necessary to examine critically their best works, as I have attempted to do, it is also necessary to understand the visions they have given us as both writers and men of letters if we are to see how truly unusual they are for our times. Steven Olson is correct in saying that Aiken "was one of the few artists of his generation to face the exigencies of the modern age without rejecting the previous century's mandate that human existence can be understood in terms of conscious ethical purpose."[1] Olson also might have added ethical purpose combined with the use of the conscious and unconscious minds in all of their activities, including the natural and social sciences. The same is true of Percy. Both authors are almost unique in modern American literature in their concern with developing an artistic vision that held in tension the imagination and the intellect in its philosophic and its scientific functions. They were well versed in both science and art; yet that fact alone does not set them apart from other writers. Aiken's friend William Carlos Williams was both doctor and poet while Percy's friend Shelby Foote is both historian and an imaginative writer of fiction. What truly sets them apart is their personal pilgrimages, which led them deeply into both their own psyches and into the lives of others. Their pilgrimages resulted in a living encounter with both microcosm and macrocosm, with that har-

---

[1]Steven E. Olson, "The Vascular Mind: Conrad Aiken's Early Poetry, 1910-1918" (Ph.D. diss., Stanford University, 1981) 1.

mony or unity that sages once taught was everywhere but had to be sought to be fully experienced.

One naturally must ask if Aiken and Percy in time became sages themselves. Jay Martin says in his last chapter, "—and Culture: The Poet as Sage," that Aiken should be thought of as such. I cannot agree because Aiken himself points to the coming of the true sage. I do agree that Aiken, as Martin suggests, should be thought of—along with Percy—as being in the tradition of writers like Goethe and Emerson. But these men, contrary to what John Holloway tells us in his influential *The Victorian Sage,* did not achieve the unity of consciousness and the charisma that accompany the activities of the traditional shaman in his different social roles as shown in the work of Mircea Eliade. Yet Aiken and Percy and certain figures like Goethe and Emerson before them have helped to prepare the way for the sages who must come to restore that cultural life necessary for the renewal of human existence.

What one really needs to ask in studying Aiken and Percy is just what it is they have that the sage has in a much greater quantity. I think it is the ability to establish a true and deep communication with others, one that comes out of the growing unification of the personality. Kierkegaard showed us that essentially religion is not a doctrine but a way of communicating. In his most influential essay, "The Message in the Bottle," Percy points to our present need of that man he calls the apostle. It is this man who speaks to all of us castaways, people bereft of a supporting culture, "in perfect sobriety and with good faith and perseverance to the point of martyrdom."[2] Neither Aiken nor Percy ever pretended to be such a one, but in their works they foreshadow the coming of this figure.

Aiken and Percy nourished that "life of significant soil," to use T. S. Eliot's term for it in "The Dry Salvages," necessary for the emergence of apostles and saints by going more deeply into all aspects of themselves than any two similar American writers. Their pilgrimage in fact provides a good example of the pattern Eliade gives us of the shaman's development. One may conclude, as Aiken did in writing "Cosmos Mariner—Destination Unknown" as his epitaph, that their pilgrimage is still continuing as they move into what Eliot in "East Coker" calls "another intensity." The im-

---

[2]Walker Percy, *The Message in the Bottle: How Queer Man Is, How Queer Language Is, and What One Has to Do with the Other* (New York: Farrar, Straus & Giroux, 1979) 149.

portant point to observe is that they began their pilgrimage in the classic
shamanistic sense by acknowledging their own and others' sickness and by
searching for the hidden unity necessary both to heal that sickness and to
communicate with love to others. Thus Eliade defines the pattern of shamanistic development: "The primitive magician, the medicine man or
shaman, is not only a sick man, he is, above all, a sick man who has been
cured, who has succeeded in curing himself."[3]

Anthropologists use the term culture hero to denominate the shaman
who withdraws from his society to encounter cosmic energy and then returns to renew his people's rituals. Aiken and Percy are not full-blown shamanistic figures; yet by withdrawing for a time and finding an inner healing
for early trauma and then by making their central concern the living language of humanity, they have followed the shamanistic path. Possibly what
makes them fall short of the status of culture hero is their lack of the psychic
energy necessary to actuate a major change in the ritual language of their
societies. What in effect they have done is to help prepare for the coming
of such a hero or heroes who might accomplish major cultural changes in
Western civilization. Like Aiken and Percy, many important writers of this
century have suffered in their own psyches the death of culture and have
through that suffering achieved a personal rebirth. Thus they have partic-
ipated in what Eliade calls the "initiatory schema" that is found "in all
mysteries; no less in puberty rites than in the rites for entrance into a secret
society." This formula is simply "suffering, death, and resurrection
(= rebirth)."[4] Many modern artists began pilgrimages but did not complete them because they were overcome by death or bitterness or, possibly
worse, commercial success based on a flight from essential issues and
agonies. The achievements of Aiken and Percy stand as works in the field
of cultural heroism, pointing as they do to the fact that all culture heroes,
no matter what their individual callings, give new life to those ritual com-
munications that undergird all cultural activity. Percy and Aiken both seek
and find the underlying unity of the human mind that makes possible the
practice of both art and science. In doing so they are true to the deepest
philosophy of both Greek and Western civilization, which is based on the

---

[3]Mircea Eliade, *Shamanism, Archaic Techniques of Ecstasy,* trans. Willard R. Trask
(New York: Pantheon Books, 1964) 27.

[4]Mircea Eliade, *The Sacred and the Profane,* trans. Willard R. Trask (New York: Harper and Brothers, 1959) 196.

concept of an underlying reason that when put to use lends order, harmony, and joy to creative effort. Whether that creativity expresses itself in a Greek temple, a Gothic cathedral, a da Vinci painting, a Leibniz theory, a Bach fugue, a Tolstoy novel, or an Einstein formula, it is still the essential rational genius of humanity that speaks. More than most modern artists, Aiken and Percy affirm this genius.

Both Aiken and Percy prepare us for a time of renewal when the still present cultural values are remolded in new patterns by rational activity. They are members of a small band of pioneers who push on into the new age. Above all, they do not confuse reason with the conscious working of the analytical, left-hand side of the brain. For them the right side with its image-making qualities, which scientists are now showing us can lower blood pressure or raise the number of white corpuscles when put to proper use, is equally important. Reason underlies both and unites both. Thus Aiken and Percy in their work do not advocate a return to the purely right-hand approach to life or any intensification of our already overworked left-hand activities. They would never declare with a man who influenced both of them—Allen Tate—that they would use "mind against itself," a dubious concept in that it suggests prolonging the schism that already rends the modern mind. And yet Lewis P. Simpson tells us that this is "the central motive of Western letters: a paradoxical and aggressive movement of mind against itself."[5] I would agree with him and would add to "letters" most of the other arts, major and minor, as well as modern philosophy. Simpson is a follower of Tate's but has gone beyond him in seeing that mind itself is not at fault, that what is wrong is the use of the analytical side of the brain to manipulate the world. Simpson, following Eric Voegelin, writes brilliantly of this misuse of mind by modern gnostics, putting his finger squarely on why gnosticism can never bring to birth culture: he tells us that Mark Twain and others wrote works that move "toward the revelation that society as created by mind is intrinsically a slave society. In the total sense, for it enslaves everybody."[6] Attempts to impose a culture with all its values on declining societies by the action of the conscious mind have always failed, just as the attempt of the will to control the in-

[5]Lewis P. Simpson, "The Southern Republic of Letters and *I'll Take My Stand*" in *A Band of Prophets: The Nashville Agrarians Fifty Years Later* (Baton Rouge: Louisiana State University Press, 1982) 71.

[6]Ibid., 83.

stincts always ends with an eruption of those suppressed instincts. The Victorian attempt to severely repress human sexuality is but one example of what happens when a particular knowledge pattern is forced on individual behavior.

Aiken and Percy in their best work define the relationship of man to culture and show how the perception and cultivation of love, of harmony, of grace—to use various terms for the manifestation of transcendence in human affairs—are necessary for a balanced social existence that allows for both human freedom and responsibility and for both individual and a creative social order. They reveal what happens when cultural unity collapses in a time of extreme tension like the twentieth century, but they also reveal the nature of the quest of individuals for the necessary grace and reason that will make new cultural patterns possible. They understand that a purely mental order imposed from on high leads to extremes of constricting social conformity and irresponsible, unloving individualism. While rejecting modern gnosticism, their work points to the development of an inner harmony and grace that will make possible communication at all levels of the psyche. For them most of the inherited abstractions about God and man have become useless. It is enough for men, they tell us, that God is revealed as the power of love in human affairs and as a grace manifesting itself momentarily to the pilgrim, a grace that lies behind and makes possible the harmony that reason perceives. Those shamans, saints, and apostles yet to appear must, if culture is to be restored, manifest this grace in order to renew the deepest language of man: the ritual communication that is the essence of effective religion. Thus culture has always come into existence with the renewal of language.

Besides presenting their visions of the possibility of cultural renewal, Aiken and Percy provide practical insights into ways in which the artistic imagination, the ethical will, and the scientific intelligence can work together harmoniously. The growth of new cultural patterns is always mysterious, and different cultures develop along markedly different lines. Yet Aiken and Percy are together in realizing the values still inherent in Western science and the need to preserve those values to undergird the technology necessary to sustain ever larger populations. But they also see clearly a fact ignored by most gnostics and others who believe technology alone can support a civilization: our old cultures are disintegrating because of ethical and imaginative failures. Humans cannot be forced to do good. Carrot-and-whip techniques alone cannot sustain society forever. Only cultural values that call forth a deep desire in individuals to be both ethical and imaginative can support social life. And for modern man to experience cultural renewal, ethics and aesthetics must be integrated with science and technology in new social patterns.

Aiken and Percy did not fully achieve this goal. However, by understanding the problem and by continuing their individual quests into old age, they have helped to show how the problem can eventually be outgrown. The great human problems are never solved so much as they are outgrown through individual and social renewal. Like certain other artists and philosophers, Aiken and Percy point the way to this renewal.

Aiken in particular must, with more study, be seen as one who is helping us to enter a new age based on what probably is to become a meeting of Western and Chinese values. His poem "A Letter from Li Po," showing as it does the basic similarity of the Greek and Chinese visions of essential harmony, is possibly one of the pivotal poems of the century. In this poem Aiken takes us back to the mathematical vision of Pythagoras and shows how it is similar to the Chinese view of cosmos. Aiken, through his study of Pythagoras and the *I Ching,* reveals in the language of our own day the meaning of the essential unity that Cartesian thinking with its mechanical view of the universe has denied to Western man since the seventeenth century. Amaury de Riencourt in his *The Soul of China* states thus the Chinese view of the unity between objective and subjective knowledge: "Already strongly pragmatic, the Chinese assumed that synchronism, implying parallelism rather than causal succession, must be meaningful: the *objective* phenomenon is somehow related to the *subjective* state of the observer."[7] Aiken never rejects the principle of causality, basic as it is to Western science; but he also accepts the Chinese idea of synchronism, or synchronicity as Jung calls this important principle for understanding objective-subjective relationships. Just as modern China has accepted Western science without rejecting its own vision of the universe, there is the possibility, as Aiken suggests in "A Letter from Li Po," that the West can retain its own science while discovering those principles of objective-subjective unity that once formed the basis of both Greek and Chinese philosophy. The leaders of Western science in this century have already taken us far in this direction. For instance, de Riencourt tells us that the sciences "are beginning to see a cosmic order that resembles Chi-

---

[7]Amaury de Riencourt, *The Soul of China* (New York: Harper and Row, 1965) 18.

na's traditional picture to an amazing extent."[8] He goes on to compare Niels Bohr's concept of complementarity to the Chinese concept of interdependence and to insist that Leibniz, the first European philosopher heavily influenced by the Chinese, prepares us for a cosmic view that puts prime emphasis not on absolutes but on relationships.

Pragmatism and relationship are basic to both Chinese thinking and to much of the thought of Aiken and Percy. For them the power traditionally called God is expressed in terms of an energy that makes all relationships—objective and subjective—possible and fruitful. Like the Chinese, Aiken and Percy begin and end their philosophies in the world around them. Although they do not fear abstract thinking, they nevertheless examine human problems in terms of the human environment. First they ask, as the Chinese traditionally do, how we can have good relations with other humans as well as with our environment. This is a question that Aiken and Percy, like the Chinese, consider from three viewpoints: the ethical, the aesthetic, and the metaphysical. From the answers they get they mold a philosophical view that makes man's knowledge—his science, that is—a part of his human and natural environments.

Thus in closing this discussion of the efforts of two American men of letters to relate to the harmony of the universe and grasp the underlying unity of the arts and sciences, it is fitting to recollect their intense concern with their surroundings. Both authors are always recalling in their art those two cities—Savannah and Birmingham—where the most important unity for the child, the family, was first shattered. Like the Chinese, they would in their lives and works emphasize the importance of the family as a basis for the pilgrim's search for unity on many levels. And like the Chinese, they would emphasize also the need to return both actually and imaginatively to the first scenes of one's life. It was the continual returning, primarily in the imagination, to these cities that helped to release them from the effects of early trauma. Yet there was another even more important return that in one sense began when as boys of eleven and thirteen they were taken to environments where the act of learning was the central fact of life. This return is the search into the wisdom of the ancestors, one that is necessary in order to begin a true pilgrimage and one generally ignored by modern questers. Aiken went to Cambridge, Massachusetts, seat of Harvard University. Percy went to the university city of Athens, Georgia, and

---

[8]Ibid., 87.

then after two years, to W. A. Percy's plantation near Greenville, Mississippi, where possibly his deepest education in the arts and sciences began under the influence of a miniature university consisting of "Uncle Will" Percy and his brilliant circle of friends. For both writers, there would then be the great cities: Boston, New York, and London for Aiken; New York as well as European visits for Percy. There would even be a similarity in the way both men approached the cities they selected for a time as their own. Aiken would at first live and work in London and then would withdraw to the town of Rye. Percy would live for a time in New Orleans and then withdraw for a long stay in the exurban town of Covington, twenty-five miles from the inner city New Orleans. After World War II Aiken would invoke his New England ancestors by living on Cape Cod in Brewster, and then after 1960 he would live half the year in Brewster and half in Savannah, writing his last book-length work there in 1967 under the title of *Thee*. Percy's fifth novel, *The Second Coming,* reflects his own part-time living in Highlands, North Carolina and shows an imaginative concern for his mother's native state of Georgia.

For Aiken and Percy the quest for individual spiritual development and for cultural renewal is very much an American concern. As several critics have shown in detail, Percy records the decline and fall of the American dream; and, as I have sought to show, he presents us with a vision of the possibility of that dream's renewal. Aiken in his later poetry is also concerned with an American vision. Yet what both men sought first and above all else was that unity in the individual, in the family, in the nation, as well as in the cosmos that makes new life possible on many levels. Their success as both artists and pilgrims is now being discovered at ever deeper levels. This discovery—the task of every serious reader of their works—will in time reveal fully the great gifts they have for those who seek to be fully civilized.

INDEX